# THE
# EVERYTHING®
## GUIDE TO 2012

Dear Reader,

You may have heard about the significance of 2012 from any one of a number of sources: books, films, friends, or websites. The closer we get to this year, the more intense the speculation about what may—or may not—happen becomes. You may have heard about prophecies that foretell doom. Alternately, you may have heard that this date signifies a fundamental change in human consciousness and a planetary shift into a new age.

I am happy to share with you the research I have gathered over the last decade. The search for the meaning behind 2012 has been an incredible adventure that has taken me from conversations with indigenous elders at sacred sites to discussions with researchers on the cutting edge of new science. I will leave you to make your own conclusions from the evidence presented here, but my personal belief is that 2012 represents an extraordinary opportunity for positive change for both humanity and our planet.

The road to 2012 may not be the best paved or straightest route, and there may well be a few large bumps along the way, but it certainly is heading somewhere interesting. I hope you enjoy this book and find in it the same inspiration I did in writing it.

*Mark Heley*

# Welcome to the EVERYTHING® Series!

These handy, accessible books give you all you need to tackle a difficult project, gain a new hobby, comprehend a fascinating topic, prepare for an exam, or even brush up on something you learned back in school but have since forgotten.

You can choose to read an *Everything*® book from cover to cover or just pick out the information you want from our four useful boxes: e-questions, e-facts, e-alerts, and e-ssentials.

We give you everything you need to know on the subject, but throw in a lot of fun stuff along the way, too.

We now have more than 400 *Everything*® books in print, spanning such wide-ranging categories as weddings, pregnancy, cooking, music instruction, foreign language, crafts, pets, New Age, and so much more. When you're done reading them all, you can finally say you know *Everything*®!

## QUESTION
Answers to common questions

## FACT
Important snippets of information

## ALERT
Urgent warnings

## ESSENTIAL
Quick handy tips

**PUBLISHER** Karen Cooper

**DIRECTOR OF ACQUISITIONS AND INNOVATION** Paula Munier

**MANAGING EDITOR, EVERYTHING® SERIES** Lisa Laing

**COPY CHIEF** Casey Ebert

**ACQUISITIONS EDITOR** Lisa Laing

**ASSOCIATE DEVELOPMENT EDITOR** Elizabeth Kassab

**EDITORIAL ASSISTANT** Hillary Thompson

**EVERYTHING® SERIES COVER DESIGNER** Erin Alexander

**LAYOUT DESIGNERS** Colleen Cunningham, Elisabeth Lariviere, Ashley Vierra, Denise Wallace

Visit the entire Everything® series at *www.everything.com*

# THE
# EVERYTHING®
# GUIDE TO
# 2012

All you need to know about the
theories, beliefs, and history surrounding
the ancient Mayan prophecies

Mark Heley

Avon, Massachusetts

*I would like to dedicate this book to the memory of Oliver L. Reiser, the cosmic synergist who saw all of this coming.*

An Everything® Series Book.
Everything® and everything.com® are registered trademarks of F+W Media, Inc.

Published by Adams Media, a division of F+W Media, Inc.
57 Littlefield Street, Avon, MA 02322 U.S.A.
*www.adamsmedia.com*

ISBN 10: 1-60550-161-1
ISBN 13: 978-1-60550-161-1

Printed in the United States of America.

J   I   H   G   F   E   D   C   B   A

**Library of Congress Cataloging-in-Publication Data**
is available from the publisher.

This publication is designed to provide accurate and authoritative information with regard to the subject matter covered. It is sold with the understanding that the publisher is not engaged in rendering legal, accounting, or other professional advice. If legal advice or other expert assistance is required, the services of a competent professional person should be sought.

—From a *Declaration of Principles* jointly adopted by a Committee of the American Bar Association and a Committee of Publishers and Associations

Many of the designations used by manufacturers and sellers to distinguish their products are claimed as trademarks. Where those designations appear in this book and Adams Media was aware of a trademark claim, the designations have been printed with initial capital letters.

*This book is available at quantity discounts for bulk purchases.*
*For information, please call 1-800-289-0963.*

# Contents

# Praise for *The Everything® Guide to 2012*:

# Acknowledgments

I would like to thank all of the amazing and inspiring teachers and sharers of knowledge I have met on the road to 2012. I have been lucky enough to spend time with many of the people whose ideas are written about in this book and I am deeply grateful to all of them. Special thanks go to Jose Argüellés, John Major Jenkins, Terence McKenna, Daniel Pinchbeck, and Hunbatz Men. An extra-big thank you to Geoff Stray for the generous loan of rare books, frequent conversations, and selfless sharing of knowledge. You are definitely the most cosmic bus driver.

I would also like to thank Daphne Lorian, Tammy Newcomer, Chris Mitchell, Louis Standen, Finn O'Brien, and all my friends and family for their love, support, and encouragement. I would also like to thank Lisa Laing and Adams Media for their trust and patience.

# The Top Ten Interesting Ideas
# about What Might Happen in 2012

1. December 21, 2012, is the end of a 5,125-year cycle in the Mayan calendar. This is the very last day this ancient calendar counts up to.

2. In 2012, the winter solstice sun will rise in conjunction with the center of the galaxy. This alignment only happens once every 26,000 years.

3. A prediction based on the ancient Chinese oracle of the I Ching claims that time itself may end in 2012.

4. 2012 is the peak of the next sunspot cycle, when the sun's magnetic poles are due to reverse. NASA scientists are predicting the possibility of a large solar flare that could affect worldwide communication.

5. The magnetic field of our planet is weakening and the magnetic poles are shifting at an accelerating pace. Some researchers think that this means a pole shift is possible in 2012.

6. The amount of cosmic radiation entering our solar system has doubled in the last decade. By 2012, these changes may be producing significant effects on our climate, increasing extreme weather events and even the development of human ESP and telepathy.

7. By 2012, there may be proof our sun is part of a binary star system. Our companion star may have played a role in a cycle of catastrophes that caused the extinction of the dinosaurs.

8. Crop circle formations found in the English countryside seem to encode a series of astronomical messages relating to 2012.

9. Global oil production will be going into decline by 2012 and more than half of the world's oil reserves will have been used up.

10. Some analysts are predicting that in 2012, society will reach a global tipping point where stark choices will have to be made about the future of human civilization.

# Introduction

ON DECEMBER 21, 2012, one of the most important cycles in the Mayan calendar ends. This is the 5,125-year cycle that is also known as the thirteen baktuns. What is striking about this date is that it is the last date the Maya counted up to. Why is this important? The Maya were sophisticated astronomers and mathematicians. Their calculations of the cycles of eclipses and the motions of Venus are very nearly as accurate as those made by modern astronomy, even though they were made with the naked eye many hundreds of years ago. Their calendar system is one of the most refined and ingenious ever known, far surpassing even the modern-day Gregorian calendar in many ways.

Did the Maya know that something was going to happen around December 21, 2012? They certainly believed that the world had been destroyed several times previously. In each case humanity was remade in some way so that life could once again continue. Some of the few remaining authentic Mayan prophecies also speak about the destruction of this world at the end of this cycle. The first part of this book is dedicated to an overview of the Maya and their calendar system. There will be an explanation of how the calendar works, what it is used for, and how to use it.

The author, John Major Jenkins, has put forward a theory that the end of the Mayan calendar marks a thirty-year period that only happens once every 26,000 years, when the winter solstice sun rises in conjunction with the center of the galaxy. Jenkins believes this galactic alignment tells us the Maya understood an important astronomical cycle called the precession of the equinoxes. This describes the way the stellar background relates to the rising sun on a fixed day of the year changes over time. Every 26,000 years, that background will move through every sign of the zodiac and come back to where it started. Does the mythology of the zodiac warn us that this cycle marks the rise and fall of human civilizations?

On the great celestial clock of the zodiac, the galactic alignment of 2012 seems to mark the midnight hour. This is the point at which the old cycle ends and a new world age begins. According to the astrophysicist Dr. Paul LaViolette, the zodiac and the cycle of precession may also encode the key to understanding a cycle of huge outbursts of energy that seem to emanate from the center of our galaxy. LaViolette has named these galactic superwaves, massive ripples in gravity that are powerful enough to ignite supernovas in their paths. LaViolette believes we may be due for a superwave event in the near future, and the ending of the Mayan calendar in 2012 may even mark this.

These ideas and many others will be covered in depth in the following chapters. Different theories suggest that the precession of the equinoxes could affect climate change, cycles of catastrophe on Earth, and even the process of evolution itself.

That our world is currently going through a significant crisis is no longer a controversial opinion. Financial instability, depletion of resources, the extinction of species, and booming population growth are all forcing us to review humanity's relationship to the planet. Many of these factors seem to be coming to a point of convergence in the near future. At this critical juncture, the fundamental values of our global culture may have to change in order for humanity to survive. A number of writers, including Professor Ervin Laszlo, the author of *The Chaos Point*, are suggesting that this could coincide with 2012.

Is it possible that despite all the technology, transport systems, and communication networks of our global industrial society we are subject to the same influences that caused the collapse of the great Mayan culture? To answer that, first we must meet the Maya.

# CHAPTER 1

# Who Are the Maya?

The Maya are a group of tribal peoples who live in an area of Central America stretching from the Chiapas region of Mexico down through Guatemala and modern day Honduras. The indigenous Maya still follow the traditions of their ancestors, and though they have been subjected to severe persecution over the centuries that has not abated fully even today, they have kept their traditions and culture alive.

# The Rise of a Civilization

The Mayan people gave rise to a remarkable civilization that flourished for about 600 years, from around A.D. 300 to A.D. 900. This period is usually called the classic period. The period leading up to it is referred to as the preclassic or formative. The period after the classic period is the postclassic or Mexican. The beginning date of the classic period roughly corresponds to the first date that an inscription of the Mayan calendar appears and the ending date to the last point at which distinctively Mayan architecture was being built.

This was a rich period for culture in Central America, and the Maya were surrounded by several other strong civilizations, including the Zapotec, centered around Monte Alban in Oaxaca; the Teotihuacán near present-day Mexico City; the Olmec of southern Veracruz; and the Totonac of northern Veracruz.

During this period the Maya built a whole series of city-states typified by elaborate ceremonial complexes with remarkable step pyramids, ceremonial ball courts, and other buildings sometimes called monasteries or palaces, though they may have been neither. The centers of the cities were almost exclusively ceremonial structures on a grand scale. The pyramids and other buildings were often very ornately decorated with features such as stylistic heads of jaguar or rain gods; elaborate murals featuring scenes of battle, the taking of prisoners, and human sacrifice; complex date inscriptions rendered in hieroglyphs; and statuary of kings and gods.

## A Ceremonial Elite

The centers were inhabited by the aristocratic and priestly elite who were responsible for the ceremonies and divinations the rest of the Maya relied upon. The majority of the Maya lived in small buildings that clustered around these centers and worked in small fields and gardens that radiated out into the rainforests and mountainsides. They would come into the centers to hear the oracles spoken by the priests and to participate in the frequent ceremonies that made up the round of Mayan life. They understood these practices were necessary to fulfill needs of their gods so the harvests would be good and plagues and famines could be avoided.

This aristocratic class of shamanic intermediaries practiced bloodletting, astrological divination, and sometimes human sacrifice on behalf of the gods. They wore elaborate headdresses and ornamental costumes, made complex pottery, and carved statues in stucco and stone. They also developed one of the most sophisticated calendrical systems ever devised and took every opportunity to record in extraordinary detail every possible cycle of time they could find.

**FACT**

For Mayan priests, bloodletting was related to divinatory practices and ceremonial preparation. In order to cleanse themselves for a ceremony, they would offer a blood sacrifice every day for a specified number of days leading up to an event. Techniques included piercing the ears, passing a cord of thorns through the tongue, and even drawing blood from the penis using a stingray spine!

For the classic-era Mayan civilization, the measurement of different cycles of time was an all-consuming passion at the very center of their culture. It is necessary to understand just how important it was in order to fully comprehend their unique and extremely evolved world view. In fact, the whole development of the Mayan form of writing, a system using symbolic pictures called hieroglyphs, was based on a desire to record different moments in time as accurately as possible.

## The Center of Mayan Life

The way the Maya viewed time is radically different from the way most people living in the industrialized world see it today. Time wasn't something to be spent or whiled away or even passed.

For the Maya, time was the essential center of their culture, an all-important singular focus that pervaded every aspect of their way of life. The question, "What time is it?" was a monumental search for meaning that was conducted daily throughout the civilization. Its answers were given on ornately carved monuments and in beautifully illustrated books filled with long tables of glyphs. By learning to see through the eyes of the Maya, you can begin to explore the refreshingly different perspective the Mayan calendar system offers to present times.

## The Divine Order of Time

For the Maya, each day was conceived not just as a moment in time, but also as a god. The god of the day would carry that time as his burden before passing it on to the next in the succession. Each god would have particular influences, making a particular day good for hunting and another day inauspicious or unlucky. For the Maya, each day would be a unique combination of the influences of the various presiding divine energies. Mayan priests and prophets would try to determine the influence of each god to come up with the most auspicious course of action.

Keeping track of all of the different cycles and the corresponding astronomical observations required huge amounts of time, energy, and dedication. For example, tracking some of the eclipse cycles and the appearances and disappearances of Venus took many generations of meticulous observation and accurate recording. This was a culture that was immersed in time and ruled by it. For the Maya, the changing influences of the gods of time were the NASDAQ and Dow Jones stock indexes of their time. They dictated the popular mood and had to be tracked at all times.

**ESSENTIAL**

The Katun cycles, the most important prophetic cycles, lasted just under twenty years each. Their influence was determined by the energies attributed to the very last day. These were always one of the Ahau signs, the very last in the sacred calendar sequence of twenty days. Most of the existing Mayan prophecies we know of relate to the Katun cycles.

## Using the Past to Predict the Future

The Maya belief in prophecy was based on the idea that if you had enough information about each time cycle, you could successfully use that to see into the future. Certainly, the practice of prophecy was associated with rites and rituals, but at its core was observation of the cycles of nature. In essence, Mayan prophecy was as much a science as a religious or divinatory practice.

A lot of the surviving Mayan prophecies are relentlessly gloomy. Many warn of bad harvests, pestilence, and political turmoil. In the midst of these, there are a few more favorable ones, but they are definitely in the minority. Then again, if you were to take all of the newspaper headlines of one year and use them to predict the events of the next year, it would probably make pretty grim reading, too. This is the point of prophecy. If life were inherently stable, there would be little of value to report as life went on in the villages and ceremonial centers. Good news is not very often big news. It was the big events that the Maya were interested in predicting and these, by their nature, were more inclined to include conflict and disaster.

# Contrasting the Mayan Sense of Time with Our Own

To understand a little more about the Mayan view of time, it's very helpful to understand a little about our own view of time. To illustrate this, it is useful to look at the European view of time at the same point in history as the height of the classic-era Mayan civilization.

## A Cyclical World

The life of a seventh-century European would have been dominated by saints' days and the seasons, and the traditional pagan holidays of the equinoxes and solstices were still very strong. Past and future were, relative to modern times, ill-defined concepts. They were, at best, ideas to be debated by ecclesiastical scholars arguing about the date of the world's creation and its inevitable ending at the revelation of the Apocalypse.

Most people measured periods longer than a year in the length of the reign of the current king. The overwhelming sense of time would have been simply of cycles repeating. It's also important to remember that this was a time when it was also believed that the earth was flat and that the sun and moon revolved around it. The world, and the sense of time in it, was very human centered. It was marked by births and deaths and seasonal return; nothing at all like the accelerating global progress of our own times.

## The Origin of the Past and the Future

At the height of the classic-era Mayan civilization, on the very northern edge of Europe in a Northumbrian monastery, a scholar called the Venerable Bede was reinventing the Roman idea of *Anno Domini*.

First proposed by the Roman scholar Dionysius Exiguus, this dating system creates a linear chronology. It places Year 1 as the year of the birth of Jesus and dates everything in reference to that, either in years after or in years before. Bede popularized this by using it in his much-revered book the *Ecclesiastical History of the English People*, which was published in 731. This convention not only established the "timeline" against which all dates are now measured, it created the sense of a past and future that could be defined against this fixed point in time. This was a defining moment in establishing how we now think of time as having a "before" and "after," rather than as a repeating cycle, like the seasons of the year.

Though they seem to be like laws of nature, our laws of time are essentially theological dictates handed down from the days of the Roman Empire. They shape a remarkable amount of our experience, but, nonetheless, they are just conventions. If we change our conventions, our experience of the past and future also changes. In order to change our ideas about time, there have been many attempts to reform or replace the calendar we use today.

**FACT**

Calendars are important to the way that societies organize themselves. Our current calendar is called the Gregorian calendar, after Pope Gregory XIII, who presided over its last significant reform. Every country in the world uses it for commerce and business, but the Vatican, not the United Nations, makes its rules.

## Changing Our Sense of Time

Some calendar reforms—like the Khmer Rouge's Year Zero policy in Cambodia—were designed specifically to destroy the previous notions of the past and the future. In that case, the change brought about terrifying and terrible results. Pol Pot's regime was able to use the ideology of Year

Zero to "restart civilization." In reality, this meant forced labor in collective farms and a purge of intellectuals and Buddhist monks that resulted in more than 1 million deaths.

A revolutionary calendar was introduced at the time of the French Revolution. It had strange and wonderful new names for each of the months. It was seen as an embodiment of the break with the past, the very essence of the revolutionary spirit. It too resulted in a reign of terror, though not on the scale of the Khmer Rouge. Although it survived for a few years, it never really took hold in rural areas, and as revolutionary fervor faded, so did the calendar. A major objection was the abolition of Sundays, which caused a massive rift between the church and the new revolutionary state. Eventually, on the date 15 Fructidor, Year XIII (September 9, 1805), it was quietly abolished. Our habits of thinking about the past and future are well engrained and take a large amount of energy to change!

**ESSENTIAL**

It may come as a surprise, but science has remarkably little to say about time. Albert Einstein's theory of relativity is based on the formulation that time is the fourth dimension, but Einstein was able to say very little else about the actual nature of time. Past and future are overwhelmingly cultural concepts and the perception of time radically changes as cultures change.

## Cycles Within Cycles

So what was it like for the Maya? The seventh-century Maya lived in a world where every day was effectively a saint's day; many gods acted together in concert.

There were yearly ceremonies like those associated with the solstice, but these slowly drifted through the seasons, repeating over a fifty-two-year period. At these junctures, huge fire ceremonies would sometimes destroy the huts of most of the ordinary Maya (and occasionally the ceremonial centers) so they could be renewed. This was followed with extensive celebrations. There were also much wider horizons. Important prophetic cycles lasted 260 years. Most significantly as we approach 2012, there was one great cycle lasting 5,125 years.

The Maya were embedded in a rich sense of time that had many simultaneous rhythms and interweaving harmonies. They saw themselves at the center of time, from which cycles of time extended out both forward and backward toward infinity, not at time's leading edge, as we do. It was a safe place to be for a culture that believed the world was cyclically destroyed and renewed!

**QUESTION**

**Do any of the Mayan monuments mention anything beyond 2012?**
No. Although there are dates that go further back than the beginning of the great long count cycle in 3114 B.C., there is no unique date that refers to any date further in the future than December 21, 2012. The only known inscriptions that refer to dates beyond 2012 are anniversaries projected into the future from past dates, like the accession of kings. Most scholars consider these to be mythical rather than actual dates.

## The Cult of Time

To the Maya, the search for meaning in time was central to their whole culture. It was a driving force that could be compared to the influence that technology has had over the twentieth and early twenty-first centuries. Huge amounts of the Maya's resources were focused on keeping the necessary observations, both astronomical and ceremonial. The recording of dates on carved monuments called stelae spread like a cult around the different Mayan centers, with each one vying with the others to come up with the grandest, most elaborate recordings of the exact time.

It is widely believed that auspicious dates were so important that the births of rulers were occasionally changed to fit the best possible cycles. Accession to a throne and even the death of a ruler were determined by the best date. This belief in auspicious timing may even have been the original reason for the offering of human sacrifice, which may have started with the self-sacrifice of kings attempting to fulfill their divine roles by dying on the most auspicious days possible. Mayan beliefs about death were quite different from our own and there is a theory that suggests many engravings of kings and rulers depict them at their dying moments. In these cases, death was seen as a glorious climactic moment when the right kind of exit on the right kind of day would propel them successfully into the afterworld and ensure that the rightful order in this world was maintained.

## The Disappearance of the Maya

By around A.D. 900, the Mayan civilization was in steep decline. New building stopped and the pyramids and ball courts were gradually abandoned to the jungle. Around this time the lowland population dropped by around 90 percent. There has been a lot of debate about what caused the collapse of the classic-era Mayan culture. Some suggest the burdens of ritual warfare between city-states became too much or that a great epidemic decimated the population.

The most likely explanation is that the Mayan system of agriculture, which relied upon a system of clearing rain forest and burning the vegetation to enrich the soil, broke down under the weight of their population. As soon as they surpassed a critical mass, the fields couldn't be left fallow long enough for them to return to fertility. This led to a downward spiral; fields were overworked and the carrying capacity of the Mayan system of growing corn simply collapsed.

The lesson of the classic-era Maya's demise could be interpreted as a very stark reminder that civilizations that use vital resources at an unsustainable rate face the same fundamental issues. However great the architecture, learning, or history of a people, if there is no food, everything comes to a grinding halt and the balance of nature returns.

## CHAPTER 2

# The Mayan Calendar

This chapter introduces some of the different cycles of the Mayan calendar system and explains what makes it so special. In order to understand the calendar's beauty and power, it is necessary to begin by looking at how the Maya count so that we can understand the basis of their mathematics and appreciate its differences from the decimal system. This then reveals a quite remarkably elegant way of counting that is very much in tune with the cycles of nature.

## The Mayan System of Numbers

The first striking thing about the Mayan counting system is the fact that the Maya counted in twenties, rather than tens. This number base differs from the Arabic numbers of the decimal system used worldwide today, which uses base ten. A simple way of thinking about this is that instead of using their fingers to count to ten, the Maya used their fingers and toes to count to twenty. This is base twenty or the vigesimal system.

In the decimal system, the more zeros that follow a number the more times it is multiplied by a factor of ten. For example, the base ten or decimal number 786 can also be written like this:

*6 × 1 (6) + 8 × 10 (80) + 7 × 100 (700) = 786*

Here's another example. The decimal number 3,440 can be written:

*0 × 1 (0) + 4 × 10 (40) + 4 × 100 (400) + 3 × 1,000 (3,000) = 3,440*

Each extra column adds a factor of ten: increasing from ones to tens, then hundreds, thousands, tens of thousands, hundreds of thousands, and millions. This is something so familiar that it may come as a surprise that there are other equally valid ways of doing it.

For the Maya, each position in a number raises the number by a factor of twenty, rather than ten. The Maya use columns of glyphs to represent the position of their numbers, rather than numerals. The higher up the column the glyph is placed, the higher the multiple of the number. Representing these vigesimal numbers in Arabic numerals looks something like this:

In base twenty, the vigesimal number 786 looks like this:

*6 × 1 (6) + 8 × 20 (160) + 7 × 400 (2,800) = 2,966 in base ten*

In base twenty, if we were to write the number 3,440, it would look like this:

*0 × 1 (0) + 4 × 20 (80) + 4 × 400 (1,600) + 3 × 8,000 (24,000) = 25,680 in base ten*

Instead of ones, tens, hundreds, thousands, and tens of thousands, the Mayan number system went from ones to twenties, four hundreds, eight thousands, and one hundred and sixty thousands. By the time the fifth position of a number is reached, the factor of that number is sixteen times bigger than it would be in the base ten. Numbers get much bigger much more quickly than in the decimal system. There are some definite advantages to this: This way of counting gave the Maya the ability to be easily able to conceptualize very big numbers and to add and subtract from them very quickly.

## The Concept of Zero

The Maya were sophisticated mathematicians and had a concept and symbol for zero, something the Romans never had. Zero didn't exist in the west until the Arabic numbering system was adopted around A.D. 1000. The Mayan zero is represented as a shell, which means that the position in the number is empty, just like the number 0 in Arabic numerals.

The Mayan symbol for one is a simple dot. For the number two, just add another dot. Add more dots for three and four. The number five is represented as a bar. Six is simply another dot placed above the bar and further dots are added in the same way for seven, eight, and nine. Ten consists of

**Mayan numbers from zero to nineteen**

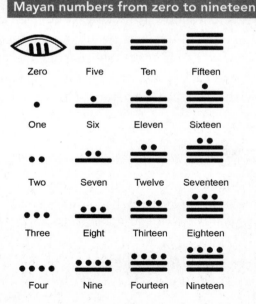

| Zero | Five | Ten | Fifteen |
| One | Six | Eleven | Sixteen |
| Two | Seven | Twelve | Seventeen |
| Three | Eight | Thirteen | Eighteen |
| Four | Nine | Fourteen | Nineteen |

two bars. Eleven adds another dot above those two bars and so on, all the way up to nineteen, which is written as three bars with four dots above it. Nineteen, like nine in Arabic numbers, is the highest number that can occupy any position. Twenty is represented by introducing another position. In the Maya's case, it was by adding another column of glyphs.

This is actually a very elegant number system. Having just three symbols makes it one of the simplest ever devised mathematically. There is the shell symbol for zero. The dot represents one and the bar stands for five. It's capable of representing big numbers very easily and it doesn't require the learning and memorization that the abstract symbols of the Arabic numerals from one to nine do.

## Numbers Make a Difference

In his book *Outliers*, social psychologist and author Malcolm Gladwell suggests that one of the most important factors that makes Asian children generally better at mathematics is the fact that the words for numbers in Asian languages are generally shorter and more logical than those in western languages. This seemingly small advantage translates into quite a large effect over time. What Gladwell shows is that these tiny differences in the speed of computation add up cumulatively to a significant general advantage. It seems that the Mayan vigesimal system may have had even greater advantages because of its inherent simplicity and logic. This idea shows that mathematical ability may be more of a culturally determined trait than it is an inherent talent, so the Maya would have been able to compute larger numbers and dates faster and more easily than we can today. Effectively, what this means is that the Maya were probably better at math than we are.

## The Twenty Day Signs

Having looked at the basic number system, it is now possible to introduce the most important and fundamental cycle of the Mayan calendar. This is a round of twenty days that repeats perpetually. Each day corresponds to one of the numbers from zero to nineteen in the Mayan vigesimal counting system, but it also has a glyph or symbol that corresponds to it. These day signs are the key to the calendar. Each of the other cycles the Maya measured builds upon this twenty-day period. For us, the week, the month, and the year are the most familiar and important divisions of time; for the Maya, it was this repeating cycle of twenty that was paramount. They saw it as much more important than even the year.

**FACT**

This twenty-day cycle of time is found not just in the Mayan calendar, but also in all the Mesoamerican cultures of antiquity, including the Olmec, Zapotec, and Aztec. The earliest recorded inscription of these glyphs goes back to Zapotec sites San Jose Mogote and Monte Alban, which may date from between 800 B.C. and 400 B.C.

Each one of the day signs not only marks a quantity of time, but also a quality of time. Each has its own specific energies and correspondences to plants and animals. Some were auspicious, others inauspicious. They were seen not just as units of measurement, but as living entities or gods. For the Maya, the twenty day signs are, in many ways, the embodiment of gods of time or the twenty faces of the sun.

# The Tzolkin

Each of these twenty day signs also has thirteen different variations, each represented just by an added number, which repeat to make the first bigger cycle of the calendar. This 260-day cycle is called the Tzolkin. This is a combination of the Yucatec Mayan words *tzol*, meaning "to count," and *kin*, meaning "a day." This word was made up by modern academics, as it is not known what the classic-era Maya actually called it. The Quiché Maya, among whom the traditions of keeping the calendar are still very strong, call it the Chol'qij. (For simplicity we will call the 260-day cycle the Tzolkin, except where referring to the traditional Quiché practice of day keeping.) The Tzolkin is the sacred almanac from which predictions and prophecies can be made. Each of the numbers also has its own qualities, so the combination of the numbers and the day signs combine to create 260 distinct possible energies.

Here are the twenty day signs and their names in Yucatec Mayan:

## The twenty day signs of the Mayan Tzolkin

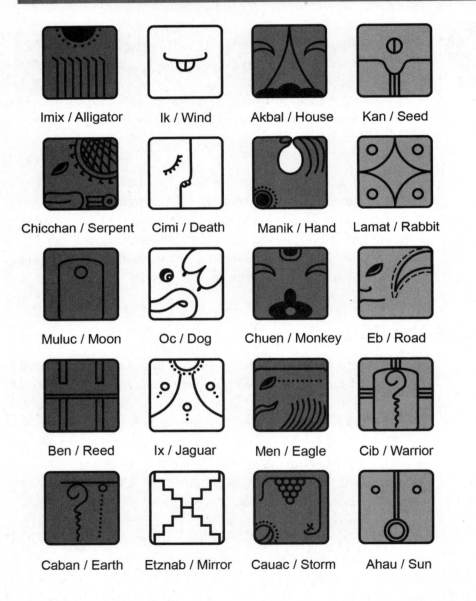

| | | | |
|---|---|---|---|
| Imix / Alligator | Ik / Wind | Akbal / House | Kan / Seed |
| Chicchan / Serpent | Cimi / Death | Manik / Hand | Lamat / Rabbit |
| Muluc / Moon | Oc / Dog | Chuen / Monkey | Eb / Road |
| Ben / Reed | Ix / Jaguar | Men / Eagle | Cib / Warrior |
| Caban / Earth | Etznab / Mirror | Cauac / Storm | Ahau / Sun |

There has been a lot of scholarly discussion about what day the Tzolkin calendar begins and ends on. One point of view is that, because it is a repeating cycle, it is possible to start and end anywhere. The most common convention, however, is to start on the day One Imix or Alligator and to finish on the day Thirteen Ahau or Sun.

**ALERT**

The traditional Quiché day keepers of Guatemala begin their count on Eight Batz or Thread. This is the day corresponding to Eight Chuen or Monkey in the Yucatec. On this day the Mayan day keepers hold one of their most important ceremonies, the Wajshikib Batz, to mark the re-creation of the sacred 260-day cycle and to initiate new day keepers. Other tribes use different days.

## A Biological Calendar

The significance of the numbers of the Tzolkin cycle is directly related to our physical bodies. The 260-day cycle is roughly equivalent to the cycle of human pregnancy. The twenty day signs are equivalent to our twenty extremities: ten fingers and ten toes. The thirteen numbers correspond to the thirteen major articulations of the body: our ankles, knees, hips, wrists, elbows, shoulders, and neck.

The harmonic of Tzolkin's 260-day cycle is also found elsewhere in the cycles of nature and can also be observed in the movements of the planets. The period of the growth of corn from planting to harvest is around 260 days. Also, at the latitude of the Maya, 260 days is the period between the zeniths of the sun, a very significant event for the Maya.

The period for which Venus is visible (261 days) is also very close to one Tzolkin, and this fact was used to good effect in tracking the cycles of this planet. The synodic period of Mars, which is the amount of time the planet takes to return to the same place in the sky, is equivalent to just a fraction under three Tzolkin cycles at 780 days (779.94 days). The Maya's ability to record these cycles of time is so accurate that study of Mayan calendar inscriptions has led to the discovery of astronomical cycles unknown to modern science.

## The Mayan Oracle

The Tzolkin was much more than just a way of counting; it was part of the fabric of Mayan identity. Up until the time of the European invasion, the classic-era Maya took the glyphs of their day of birth as their given names. Though this practice has died out, there is still a traditional ceremony that happens when a child is 260 days old to mark the completion of its first Tzolkin round. The day sign of your birth is still believed to be responsible for shaping the whole of your life path and much divination and astrological reading is still done to determine what days are most lucky or prosperous on the basis of the sign of your birth. In traditional Mayan communities, it is common to consult a day keeper in matters of love to make sure that the two day signs are compatible for a good relationship. Among its many facets, the Tzolkin can be seen as a combination of a biological counting system, an astrological and divinatory oracle, and one of the most elegant astronomical calendars ever devised.

**QUESTION**

**Where did the calendar come from?**
No one really knows. The Maya say that Itzamna, a creator god and an initiator of civilization, gave the sacred calendar to them. The calendar predates the Maya and was widely used by other contemporary Mesoamerican cultures. It definitely wasn't something they invented, but they surpassed all other cultures in their development and use of it.

## Cycles Within Cycles

Within the Tzolkin are significant smaller cycles. Every set of numbers from one to thirteen is called a trecena and is governed by the glyph that starts the series. The energy of that glyph is taken into account when doing astrological readings or divination relating to any particular day. Traditional day keepers like to hold ceremonies on the middle three days of these thirteen-day periods. This is when the energies appropriate to this work are said to be most balanced. The energies at the beginning of the trecena are considered too weak and those at the end are too strong.

The sacred almanac can be divided by four, each of these quarters corresponding to a direction and called a season. It can also be divided by five, each fifth sometimes being attributed to one of each of the five worlds of creation.

## The Haab

The Haab is the cycle of the calendar the Maya use for recording the year. From a contemporary point of view, it has some very unusual properties. Instead of dividing the months into twelve sections, it divides the year into eighteen sections of twenty days each. Each of these periods is called a *uinal* and has a special glyph and name. The days of the uinal are numbered from zero to nineteen. For example, the uinal of Pop starts on the day 0 Pop, also known as the seating of Pop, and finishes on the day 19 Pop.

This gives a total of 360 days, which is a nice round divisible number but somewhat short of the true length of the year, which lasts 365.2422 days. The Maya compensated for this by adding five extra days at the end of the year called the Uayeb. These were considered unlucky days, when the gods rested and the normal barriers between the underworld and the waking world were open because the days fell outside the round of the year. Rites of purification, fasting, and prayer marked the time. The beginning of the next year was waited for expectantly.

**FACT**

The division of the year into 360 days plus an additional five is not unusual. The ancient Egyptian calendar did the same thing and also had a period at the end of the year when the gods rested. There are Jewish, Chinese, and Indian calendars that also use 360-day cycles. It seems that the desire to make the year into an orderly and exact cycle has been a long and persistent tradition.

The Maya did not make any provision for the remaining quarter day of the year and they recorded no leap year. As a consequence of this, the beginning of the year drifted through the conventional year over time. At the time of the European invasion, the beginning of the Haab, on the day

0 Pop, was equivalent to the date July 26 in the Julian calendar. Over the passing centuries, this has drifted backward, to the end of February.

This kind of arrangement would be pretty unthinkable to most of us. Certainly it made the Haab somewhat ineffective as an agricultural calendar. For a while, archaeologists thought that the Maya just weren't able to work out the length of the year. This isn't the case though, as it has been shown that some inscriptions actually record corrections for this backward drift. The reality is that they didn't really care too much about it. Instead, they were interested in making sure that a bigger cycle called the calendar round tied up accurately; by leaving the intercalary day of leap year out, they were able to achieve this.

# The Calendar Round

The harmonization of the 260-day Tzolkin cycle and the 365-day Haab cycle was done by meshing them together to create the bigger calendar round cycle. The common factor between the two calendars is 18,980 days, which equals exactly seventy-three Tzolkins and fifty-two Haabs. Each day in a calendar round has a unique combination of the Tzolkin and Haab signs. Only after 18,980 days will the same Tzolkin and Haab combination be repeated. This cycle, of very close to fifty-two years, equates psychologically to the equivalent of our century.

## Calculating Dates

The calendar round was longer than the average life span and was considered to be sufficient for day and date calculation for most civil purposes. If a person knew both the Tzolkin and Haab dates for a day, they would be pretty sure of their place in time. The synchronization of these two calendars was of extreme significance to the Maya, and much more important than having a fixed-year calendar. The reason for this is that many of the functions of the fixed-year calendar like accurately dating the equinoxes, the zenith passages of the sun, and eclipse cycles were already being performed by following the 260-day cycle. This meant they just didn't need it. Agricultural cycles were measured from these reference points and also in divisions of twenty-day periods from the first rain of the year, so the calendar round was sufficient for most purposes.

## Significance of the Calendar Round

What the Maya liked in the calendar round was that everything came very exactly to a perfect moment of synchronization once every fifty-two years, creating a mathematical perfection that was very appealing to the Mayan mind. It was a predictable and useful way of measuring time for them and they celebrated the end of a calendar round by holding massive festivities. Entire new layers were often added to pyramids to remake them anew for the next fifty-two-year cycle. Great fires were set alight and sometimes all of the huts and wooden buildings the Maya lived in were burned as well. It was a time of great anticipation as they waited to see if the gods would grant them the grace of another fifty-two years.

On a personal level, the fifty-second birthday of a Maya was the point at which an individual was recognized as a true elder, having completed what was seen as an entire lifetime. They were then effectively reborn into a second life, though during the classic period, few would have been lucky enough to live this long. The calendar would be pretty remarkable if this was its totality, but for the Maya, this was just the beginning. In the next chapter we will explore their greatest achievement: the Long Count, the calendar that is famously scheduled to end on December 21, 2012.

## CHAPTER 3

# Prophecies of the Maya

When people refer to the Mayan calendar, in most cases they mean a calendar called the Long Count, also sometimes known as the thirteen baktuns. This is a cycle of approximately 5,125 years that is ending, by most accounts, on December 21, 2012. This unique calendar is the subject of several very interesting theories about what may be about to happen in 2012. In the next few chapters, we will explore these and what they are predicting.

## The Origins of the Long Count

The beginning date of the Long Count corresponds to the equivalent of August 11, 3114 B.C. in our calendar. However, the first recorded inscriptions of the Long Count actually appear around 35 B.C. at the pre-Maya sites of Chiapa de Corzo and Tres Zapotes. This was some 300 years before the Maya emerged as a fully fledged culture, so the Long Count wasn't their invention. One of the great mysteries of these early Mesoamerican cultures is how the calendar reached such a remarkable state of development right at the beginning of their recorded history. The Maya inherited this knowledge, but they took its application to spectacular new heights.

Over time, the Long Count calendar spread from city-state to city-state across the Maya lands. Its influence eventually reached from Chiapas in the west to Guatemala in the east and the Yucatán peninsula in the north. The propagation and development of the Long Count was to become one of the greatest cultural achievements of the Maya. It became a defining characteristic of what it meant to be Mayan. City-states and their rulers competed to create the most ornate monuments and statues, incorporating significant and auspicious dates of accessions and conquests.

**FACT**

There has been some confusion about the exact beginning date of the Long Count. This is because of an anomaly with the Christian one: in the *Anno Domini* system there is no year zero. The year 1 B.C. was immediately followed by A.D. 1. This means the Long Count is occasionally mistakenly said to start in 3113 B.C., a year later than it actually did, or that the calendar will end in December 2011. Neither is correct.

Some of these intricately carved statues are huge, up to 25 feet in height, and contain many elaborate inscriptions on all four sides. The artistry of Maya carving, for example at Copan and Quirigua, is surpassed in technique and scale only by the monumental works of the ancient Egyptians.

The Long Count effectively became the unifying symbol of a remarkable civilization that flourished between A.D. 300 and A.D. 900. This was the classic era of the Maya, when they built their most spectacular pyramids and ceremonial centers. At this time, Mayan culture was equal to or surpassed the accomplishments of any other contemporary civilization, including those in Europe.

Around A.D. 900, for reasons still debated, the Maya started to abandon their cities. The most popular explanation of what happened is that their form of slash-and-burn agriculture used for the cultivation of corn and other crops led to an ecological collapse. As a result, they could no longer feed their population.

After the classic-era Mayan decline, the surviving Mayan cities were more open to attack and invasion. The coming of the Mexica and Itzá to the Yucatán peninsula marked the end of this pure form of Mayan civilization. Widespread usage of the Long Count calendar probably only survived for 100 years after this point. After this, under cultural pressure from their invaders, the Maya began to radically shorten the time periods they were interested in recording. Sometime before the European invasion, knowledge of the Long Count was completely lost.

**ESSENTIAL**

The origin point of the Long Count may have been a mythical date, rather than a historical one. The starting date probably corresponds to the creation date for this world age. The Maya believed the world was destroyed and recreated on a regular cycle, and that this had occurred previously a number of times.

The structure of the calendar is very unusual and there are no known parallels to it in the calendars of any other cultures. The Long Count is made up of a total of five different units, but it is really just a count of days. Each of the increasingly bigger units represents a multiple of the number of days. It does have a unit called the *tun* that is 360 days long—a rough approximation to a year's length—but the Long Count doesn't have a New Years day and it isn't tied to a particular starting day of the solar year.

Each tun consists of eighteen uinals of twenty days each. This is exactly the same structure as the Haab calendar we looked at in the last chapter, where eighteen twenty-day uinals make up the main lucky 360-day part of the year. Twenty of these 360-day tuns make a bigger unit called a *katun* that lasts approximately 19.71 years. The katun cycle was given a great deal of importance for the Maya in making prophetic predictions and each katun had its own qualities and characteristics. Twenty of these katuns make up one baktun. Each baktun was a period of close to 400 years—394.25 years, to be more exact. The whole cycle consists of exactly thirteen baktuns in total. This can be further subdivided into 260 katuns. These, in turn, contain a total 5,200 tuns, the equivalent of 5,125.37 years.

The different units of the Long Count are:

- **Kin:** 1 day
- **Uinal:** 20 days
- **Tun:** $18 \times 20$ days $= 360$ days
- **Katun:** $20 \times 360$ days $= 7,200$ days
- **Baktun:** $20 \times 7,200$ days $= 14,4000$ days
- **Thirteen Baktuns:** $13 \times 14,4000 = 1,872,000$ days

A particular day in the Long Count is written as a series of all of these units, starting with the biggest number first (baktuns) and working downward to the number of days that have passed in the uinal. The first day of the thirteen baktuns was written 0.0.0.0.0 in this form of notation. The last day will be 13.0.0.0.0. It is widely agreed that the thirteen baktuns began on August 11, 3114 B.C. and that they will end on December 21, 2012. To make the dates complete, the Tzolkin and Haab dates are added to the end of the Long Count.

The beginning of the Long Count:

*August 11, 3114 B.C. = 0.0.0.0.0 4 Ahau, 8 Cumku*

The end of the Long Count:

*December 21, A.D. 2012 = 13.0.0.0.0. 4 Ahau, 3 Kankin*

One of the earliest known inscriptions on a dated monument of the classic Mayan period was found at Tikal. It records the date of July 6, A.D. 292, or 8.12.14.8.15 in the notation of the Long Count. That's equivalent to eight baktuns, twelve katuns, fourteen tuns, eight uinals, and fifteen kin from the start of the Long Count—1,243,615 days.

One of the last recorded dates of the classic period was carved on a stele at the site of San Lorenzo. This was inscribed with the date of 10.5.0.0.0., or October 5, A.D. 928. That's ten baktuns, five katuns, and no tun, uinals, or kin—a date exactly 1,476,000 days after the beginning of the count. This was a particularly important day in the calendar, as it marked the ending of a twenty-year katun. At that time, the statue of the god of the old katun would have been replaced in the Mayan calendar temple with a statue of the new one, signifying the changeover from one period to another.

**FACT**

The cycles of time found in the Long Count also have some relationship to ones found in nature. The 400-year baktun cycle is equivalent to the time it takes Earth's core to rotate relative to a fixed point on the surface. The twenty-year katun cycle corresponds to the time Earth's magnetic field takes to make one rotation relative to a fixed point on the surface of the Earth.

# The Venus Round

The calendar system based on the cycle of 260 days in combination with the day count has many remarkable properties, none more so than the fact that it allowed the Maya to very accurately record the cycles of other planets. Venus was particularly important to them and was regarded as the celestial equivalent of the god Quetzalcoatl/ Kulkulkan. A whole table of calculations regarding the cycles of Venus can be found in one of the three surviving Mayan books, the Dresden Codex.

The Maya were able to work out that it was possible to follow multiple cycles of time simultaneously by using the 260-day cycle as the common factor. With Venus, which has a 584-day synodic period, they were able to calculate that 146 Tzolkin rounds would be exactly equivalent to sixty-five Venus revolutions. This meant that 37,960 days elapsed between incidences of Venus rising as the morning star. This took place on 1 Ahau, its sacred Tzolkin day. This was also exactly 104 years of their 365-day Haab calendar, or two calendar rounds.

These calculations are remarkable and would have taken many generations of observation to establish. For naked-eye astronomers, subject to the vagaries of weather, to record these events so accurately was a singular achievement. Without the elegance of the vigesimal calendar, especially in the form of the Long Count, none of this would have been possible. At the peak of their culture, the astronomy of the Maya was at least as developed as that of the Spanish invaders, and they did not have the advantage of the invention of the telescope; it is thought that the Maya tracked the stars by watching their motions reflected in specially built pools in their ceremonial centers. Their extraordinary calendar system made this remarkable knowledge possible.

**FACT**

The Maya generally considered Venus's first appearance in the morning sky an evil omen but a good day for warfare. There is evidence that they planned "star wars" to coincide with these specific astronomical events and would conduct raids on neighboring cities.

The fact that so many planetary cycles can be harmonized by using a combination of the Tzolkin and the Long Count strongly suggests that the Mayan vigesimal counting system is tapping into a more fundamental resonance with the laws of nature than the decimal one. It has long been established in astronomy that the orbits of the planets closely correspond to whole-number harmonics. This principle is called Bode's Law. It can be used to predict where a planet's orbits is likely to fall and also what the mass of a planet is likely to be. The Mayan calendar seems to articulate a similar principle. The fact that so many planetary cycles have ratios that fit so well into the calendar system far exceeds the bounds of probability.

## The Mayan Zodiac

Another example of these magical number ratios is found in cycles the Maya were unable to track because they are not visible to the naked eye. For every twenty Venus rounds, there are twelve conjunctions of Uranus and Neptune. This cycle also equals exactly 2,080 Haab years or forty calendar rounds. It also makes one zodiacal age in the Mayan thirteen sign zodiac. In the *Paris Codex,* one of the surviving Mayan books, researcher Linda Schele has identified a Mayan zodiac dividing the sky into thirteen signs, rather than twelve as used in western astrology.

## Other Cycles of the Calendar

Within the Long Count inscriptions even more cycles were recorded. A special glyph was used to record the phase of the moon. There was a nine-day cycle that corresponded to the nine lords of the night and a seven-day cycle that probably corresponded to gods of the earth. There was also an 819-day count that was added at Palenque around A.D. 670 that seems to relate to the cycles of Jupiter and Saturn. The Long Count brought all of these different cycles together in one big picture that could be used to take a "snapshot" of a significant calendrical moment. This could then be recorded forever in stone.

# The Short Count and the *Books of Chilam Balam*

When the Itzá and Mexica influences became dominant in the Yucatán around A.D. 1000, the keeping of the Long Count, which had already started to fall out of usage, went into serious decline. This was largely because the Itzá only used the fifty-two-year–based calendar round. In a compromise between the different cultures of the two calendars, it was the distinctively Mayan Long Count that lost out. What replaced it was the Short Count. This abbreviated version is often illustrated as a wheel of thirteen katuns that make a circle of 260 years. The Mayan priests just shifted their focus from the Long Count cycle of the thirteen baktuns to the smaller scale of the Short Count of thirteen katuns and continued their ceremonies and divination as normal.

## Adapting to the Short Count

Both the Short Count and Long Count cycles end on the sacred day of Ahau, which is critical to the prophetic tradition of the Maya. The records of these Ahau katun prophecies were recorded in the *Books of Chilam Balam.* The Chilam Balam were the hierarchy of jaguar priests that made divination and prophecy, sometimes by standing by the side of a sacrificial victim as their life was taken. The *Books of Chilam Balam* has several different versions. Each is named after the town their manuscript was found in, like Chumayel, Tizimin, and Mani. They are the only actual written record of Mayan prophecy that still exists.

The *Books of Chilam Balam* contains some glaring errors, and the influence of the Spanish is in evidence in some parts, but they are, in large part, authentically Mayan. The prophecies range from the near apocalyptic to the reasonably positive, but tend toward the subject matter of daily life, such as famines, war, harvests, and political stability.

The Chilam Balam were responsible for making the particularly important prophecy that accompanied each twenty-year katun period. These predictions were based upon what had happened in similar cycles and the results of their ritual divination. Each katun would be named after the number of the Ahau day on which it ended. For example, we are currently living in the katun 4 Ahau, the very last and 260th katun of the whole Long Count. Some writers have argued that we can extrapolate from these katun prophecies of the Maya and apply them to our own times. The results are often unconvincing and discrimination is required to make any such equivalence. The evidence that the Chilam Balam still knew much about the 5,125-year cycle is debatable, but there are at least a couple of instances that seem to reference 2012 and the times we are now living in.

## The Coming Religion of Hunab Ku

One of the most important and most quoted prophecies of the Chilam Balam talks about the coming religion of Hunab Ku. This prophecy is predicted for the katun 13 Ahau, which is the last in the Short Count cycle of 260 years. This prophecy was given for the period A.D. 1544 to A.D. 1564, but seems to speak about the future in general.

> *"At the conclusion of the katun 13 Ahau, the Itzá will see . . . the sign of Hunab Ku, the erect tree which will be shown so that the world will be enlightened . . . confusion will be finished when the bearer of the cross comes to us."*—The Book of Chilam Balam of Mani *(Craine/Reidorp)*

This is widely interpreted to refer to the coming of Christianity. The prophecy then asks the Itzá to receive the "bearded ones" as the messengers of a new god whose "commandments . . . will be good and (whose) new truth will be substituted for the old one. The Itzá will accept and worship the one True God who comes from heaven." A parallel between the god of the Spanish and the Mayan creator god Itzamna is drawn, and it appears to be a sincere plea to the Itzá to adopt the faith of the invaders. A different version from Chumayel, however, adds the following paragraph:

*". . . they twist their necks, they wink their eyes, they slaver at the mouth, at the rulers of the land, lord. Behold, when they come, there is no truth in the words of the foreigners to the land."*—The book of Chilam Balam of Chumayel *(Roys)*

So the Chilam Balam seem to be saying something like, "Accept the religion of the Spanish, even though they are completely untrustworthy." What can be confusing is that the Itzá and Spanish are fairly interchangeable in the prophecies. The same insults that had been used to describe the Itzá in older prophecies are even used to describe the Spanish, including the phrase "two day ruler," a term used to denote the inexperience and lack of wisdom demonstrated by both sets of invaders.

**QUESTION**

**What does Hunab Ku mean?**
Hunab Ku is often translated as meaning "One God," but can also be interpreted as "One Sun" or "One Ahau." One Ahau is also the sacred day of Venus. Yucatec Mayan elder Hunbatz Men translates Hunab Ku as meaning the "giver of movement and measure."

The prophecies of the Chilam Balam contain multiple levels of meaning, and reading them too literally can make them seem contradictory. In general, the prophecies are disdainful of both the Itzá and Spanish, even though the later ones are frequently addressed to the Itzá. The Chilam Balam themselves were largely drawn from the Tutul clan of the Xiu tribe, which may explain the snobbery toward the less calendar-literate Itzá. Though the times they record are often gloomy, the prospects of the future appear even worse. As one Chilam Balam, Natzin Yabin Chan, puts it: "Itzá, hate your gods, forget them because they will be destroyed by the foreign god you are going to worship."

There have been a lot of attempts to interpret the prophecies, but the language of the Chilam Balam is filled with subtlety, double meanings, and metaphors. As it says in *The Book of Chilam Balam of Chumayel*, "Who will be the prophet, who will be the priest who shall interpret truly the word of the book?" That is still open to question, but anyone who wants to explore real Mayan prophecy further should start with these books.

## The End of the World?

There is a prophecy in one of the books of Chilam Balam that some commentators think may well relate to the end of the thirteen-baktun count in 2012. The clue for this comes from the text of the prophecy. It talks about "tying up the bundle" of thirteen katuns, but gives the date for this happening as 4 Ahau. The thirteen katuns actually end on a 13 Ahau day; it is the thirteen-baktun calendar that ends on 4 Ahau. This is the date equivalent to December 21, 2012. The prophecy effectively predicts an end to the world.

*"In the final days of misfortune, in the final days of tying up the bundle of the thirteen (baktuns) on 4 Ahau, then the end of the world shall come and the katun of our fathers will ascend on high."*—The Book of Chilam Balam of Tizimin *(Makemson)*

This is as close to a written prophecy about 2012 that can be found in the books of Chilam Balam, or indeed any of the other surviving books of the Maya. It begins in the Makemson translation:

*"Presently the Baktun thirteen shall come sailing . . . bringing the ornaments of which I have spoken from your ancestors. Then the god will come to visit his little ones. Perhaps 'after death' will be the subject of his discourse."*

This does suggest that the Maya thought the world would be destroyed in 2012, but they also believed that when the world was destroyed, it was remade and created anew. This could be interpreted as a worldwide disaster, rather than an apocalypse. The prophecy finishes:

*"These valleys of the earth shall come to an end. For those katuns there shall be no priests, and no one who believes in his government without having doubts."*—The Book of Chilam Balam of Tizimin

What makes this convincing is that after 2012, we will be entering into a new time, uncharted by the Maya, for which "there shall be no priests." But this is not always interpreted as an age without religion. It is also, of course, very true that faith in government is at a historic all-time low. This example of the Chilam Balam's art seems to be the one that has the most relevance to the coming end of the Long Count in 2012.

# The Fall of Mayapan

The prophetic tradition of the Chilam Balam went into decline after the fall of the last great Mayan capital, Mayapan. Mayapan's rule over the Yucatán ended after an army, thought to be that of Aztec king Montezuma, laid siege to the capital. The invaders announced that the Maya were to abandon their calendar and that it was now the katun of the spider. The Maya were also forced to worship a serpent called a sucking snake, considered an evil spirit. This effectively ended the succession of katuns and threw the priests of the Chilam Balam into disorder.

The end to the keeping of the prophecies came soon after the European invasion, but this was largely foreseen in the prophecies themselves. In fact, the Chilam Balam's predictions of what was about to happen seem to be very accurate. The European invaders' religion of Christianity did overtake the ways of the old gods. The Maya were hit with fasting and privation, interrupted only by famine and plague. It ended with the Chilam Balam predicting the Maya would go to war with the Spanish, but that eventually the Maya will wear their clothes, their hats, and speak their language.

## Adaptation to the Spanish Conquest

The Maya managed to continue to make prophecy despite all these changes, even when the new religion of Christianity and its Gregorian calendar was imposed on them. The Maya were not unused to invasion, and adapted to the new system just as they had when the Itzá had invaded. The priests instead made prophecies for the Christian year, basing their divination on which day of the week that New Year's Day fell on.

The content of these prophecies is very similar to the kind of predictions that were previously made for the old Mayan calendar cycles. This was the same tactic that the Maya had used to deal with invaders before—appearing to integrate on the surface level but doing so while keeping their traditions alive. Hence, it was possible to continue the old ways in a different guise. Eventually, as knowledge of the calendar was lost, the art of prophecy also fell into decline amongst the Maya. The traditions and stories of the old gods became blended with the saints and rituals of Christianity.

## The Tortuguero Prophecy

There is one more known Mayan prophecy that definitely relates to the calendar end date of December 21, 2012. This is to be found in an inscription carved on a stele monument at the site of Tortuguero. Mayan scholars have previously mentioned the existence of this stele in passing, but it is only recently that independent researcher Geoff Stray, the author of *Beyond 2012*, has brought its real significance to attention.

The inscription on the monument is quite badly eroded and difficult to read, but the legible part reads:

*The thirteenth baktun will be finished*

*Four Ahau, the third of K'ank'in*

*[Unreadable] will occur*

*[It will be] the descent of the nine support gods to the [unreadable]*

This frustratingly incomplete inscription is the only one known that contains any information about what the Maya of the classic era thought might happen on December 21, 2012. It clearly gives the exact date of the calendar's end point. The nine gods may well refer to the nine lords of the night who ruled the Mayan underworld. These were creator gods who, along with the thirteen lords of the day, were responsible for making the world. It is possible that the descent of the nine refers to an event happening at the ending of one cycle of creation and the beginning of another.

The discovery of the Tortuguero monument does provide a rebuttal to the oft-repeated opinion of some Mayan scholars that the Maya did not think anything special at all was likely to occur at the end of the calendar. Stray points out that there has been a tendency amongst the academics studying the Maya to downplay the significance of 2012. This, he suggests, is because most scholars do not want to associate themselves with the large amount of unreliable information and catastrophic theories about what may happen.

Little more survives from the ancient Mayan sources about 2012 than what we have covered so far. More may be discovered or revealed, but much of what is being written with regard to the Mayan calendar is very modern speculation. In the next chapter we will examine what some of the contemporary Maya are saying about their culture and the ending of the calendar.

# CHAPTER 4

# The Maya Today

Most of what has been discussed so far with regard to the Maya has come from the reconstructions of archaeologists and Mayanists. The ongoing collection of this body of knowledge has involved many different academic disciplines and the dedication of many gifted minds over many decades of painstaking work. Yet, the indigenous Maya of today have a living tradition that is just as important to learn from.

## It Takes a Village

The Maya who live in the traditional way are a rural people who live mainly in the villages and smallholdings of the Guatemalan mountains and rainforest. Their way of life has been largely unchanged since the European invasion. Catholic saints have been adopted in place of many of the old gods, but the feast days and qualities of their deities are often the same. The Catholic Church tried to win over the indigenous people to their form of worship by assimilating rather than destroying the local deities, so a blending of the two cultures has occurred over the last 300 years.

The Maya are also by nature adaptive. During previous invasions, such as that by the Itzá and Toltec peoples in the Yucatán around A.D. 1000, they made considerable efforts to harmonize the new cultures into the fabric of their own. Similarly, the Maya have attempted to bring the calendar and culture of Christianity into the Mayan way of life. The result is a syncretism, where the old traditions remain underneath a slightly different surface appearance.

**FACT**

More than fifteen separate Mayan languages are still spoken today. Each tribe has its own dialect and often its own tongue. The highland languages spoken in Guatemala are very different from the ones spoken in the lowlands to the north, but both are very distinct from any other languages spoken in Central America.

These traditions of the indigenous Maya are of great significance to those interested in learning about the essence of Mayan culture. It is an incredible feat that the tradition of the calendar has been kept unbroken in the highlands of Guatemala for countless centuries, through war, famine, conquest, and persecution. This has been possible because the calendar is woven through the tapestry of life, just as it was for the Maya of the classic era.

## Keeping the Count of Days

The Mayan elders who are responsible for the keeping of the calendar are called day keepers. They keep the count of days by lighting candles and burning incense at the shrines set up to the specific gods of the day. These shrines are usually a short walk away from the village. On the appropriate day, the day keepers will make the pilgrimage to these places to make offerings of corn and to burn the sacred incense copal, which is made from the resin of the ceiba tree.

By making these offerings, the day keepers not only honor the gods, but they keep them alive through the practice of remembering them. For the Maya, the calendar is a way of life, and only by being lived has the calendar survived. If it were just an abstract idea, kept on some precious ancient manuscript, it would almost certainly have disappeared into the mists of time by now. In some of the Mayan areas like the Yucatán, which bore the direct brunt of the conquests, the traditions survived only as fragments and memories rather than as living practices.

## A Living Tradition

In the remote villages around Lake Atitlán in Guatemala, tribal life has remained the least changed and the ancient traditions remain strongest. There is a variety of opinion amongst the traditional Maya about the sharing of their cultural heritage. For some of the day keepers, the calendar is considered knowledge that should be kept for the Maya and the Maya alone.

**ESSENTIAL**

The Maya believe that you cannot use the calendar or benefit from its wisdom if you approach it in a profane way. The day keepers share their wisdom and others listen and learn. This sharing takes place at a pace the day keepers feel is appropriate, and few westerners have been fully accepted into their traditions.

They also see the keeping of the count of days as a practice appropriate for the traditional elders alone. Only the initiated are allowed to speak the names of the day gods. To speak the names of the days is to invoke the gods themselves, and this must be done with full reverence and never lightly or in jest. For the Maya, these gods are real and should at all times be respected. For other Mayan elders, there is a recognition that the time has come to share their wisdom with the wider world. Yet, in order to appreciate this wisdom, outsiders first have to appreciate how fundamentally sacred the calendar is to the Maya.

# Honoring the Directions

The honoring of the directions is not just a staple of Mayan spirituality; it is a fundamental of ceremony throughout the Americas. Almost all indigenous nations and tribes have their version of this universal tradition. All ceremonies, large or small, usually begin with an acknowledgment of the directions and an honoring of the ancestors. The elder conducting the ceremony begins by facing each of the directions in turn and speaking a salutation or prayer to the spirits that reside there. This is usually accompanied by offerings of incense.

Words of gratitude and acknowledgment are then spoken to the spirits of the ancestors and the grandmothers and grandfathers that have gone before. The purpose of the honoring of the directions is to locate the ceremonialists in a sense of sacred place and to connect them to rest of the world. It opens the space for further ceremonial work and establishes a sense of sacredness to the proceedings.

## The Colors of the Directions

The association of a particular color with each of the directions is very important to the Maya. Red is the color of the east, white the color of the north, black the color of the west, and yellow the color of the south. Each direction has further associations with specific birds, animals, and plants. These colors and their corresponding directions also apply to the twenty day signs of the calendar. The first sign, Imix or Alligator, corresponds to the east and is therefore red. The second, Ik or Wind, belongs to the north and is therefore white. Akbal or Night, the third sign, is black, the color of the west. Kan or Seed is yellow and belongs to the south. The succession then repeats four more times for the rest of the glyphs. All the correspondences for the glyphs are given in full in a later chapter on using the calendar in everyday life.

## The Gods of the Directions

Like the days, the directions are seen as gods. They are called the Bacabs, and in the classic period temples there are many inscriptions of them holding up the world in an Atlas-like fashion in each of their respective quarters. The red, eastern Bacab is called Likin; the white, northern Bacab is called Xaman; the black, western Bacab is called Chik'in; and the southern, yellow Bacab is called Nohol. There is also a sacred ceiba tree for each of the directions of a corresponding color. Knowing and respecting the different energies of the directions is fundamental to the Mayan cosmos and everything in the Mayan world is governed by their influences.

## Sacred Corn

One of the most important elements of the Mayan worldview is the sacredness of corn, their principal crop. Corns of different colors correspond to the colors of the directions and are often incorporated into altars to represent them. Ceremonies are always made in the cornfields before clearing the land and before sowing. The traditional ceremony of the Okotbatam, the plea or supplication, is one of the most significant and elaborate of the year. It is a dance performed as a ceremonial offering by the entire village in the fields at the height of the corn's growth in August or September. The purpose of the dance is to ensure a good harvest and to bind the community together for the work ahead.

It has been suggested that a principal cause of the downfall of the classic Mayan civilization was its attachment to corn as a crop. The deification of corn was deeply institutionalized into the very fabric of Mayan society, with the king taking his authority from being the idealized farmer. There are depictions of Mayan rulers that show them working in the fields, and "growing corn" was a key metaphor for good governance.

When the Maya's slash-and-burn agricultural practices led to the exhaustion of all the available land, the worship of corn seems to have blinded them to the possibility of alternate crops. The Maya knew of and used crops such as manioc that do not deplete the soil in the same way as corn, but they never chose to grow them on the same scale.

In his book *The Long Descent*, author John Michael Greer, writing about the cycles of growth and collapse that affect all civilizations, has named this scenario "Peak Corn." Greer draws a parallel with our own culture's current "Peak Oil" crisis, where modern society is just as dependent on the finite resource of oil as the Maya were dependent on corn. He concludes it was ultimately the political difficulties of abandoning corn as their principal crop that led to the demise of the Maya, rather than the decimation of fertile agricultural land alone.

## The Fifth and Sixth Worlds of Creation

A recurrent mythology in Central America is that the world has been created and destroyed a number of times. The most complete version of this myth in Aztec mythology is found in the Codex Vaticanus, where it is recounted that the world has previously been destroyed four times. Jaguars destroyed the first world, storms destroyed the second world, volcanoes caused the end of the third world, and a great flood wiped out the fourth world.

**QUESTION**

**Are we coming to the end of the fourth or fifth world?**
Mayan sources are not conclusive. Some accounts mention that the world has been destroyed twice, others that this is the fourth world. Some scholars consider that the Maya thought the same as the Aztecs in this matter, as there are many parallels between the mythologies of the two.

A common idea is that we are now, in the approach to 2012, in the transition between worlds and that this world will in some way be destroyed. In the Mayan mythology, each time the world was destroyed humanity was somehow recreated so that life could continue. Rather than the complete destruction of the planet, the Maya seem to be talking about a series of cataclysmic events that define the endings and beginnings of the world ages.

For the Maya, each world age was like a great experiment for the creator gods in perfecting the world. At the end of this world age, they hope this perfection will finally be achieved. This means the world will not necessarily literally end in 2012 or at the next ending of the world age; it will simply be recreated anew. There will be a new beginning, although life in the new world may be very different from this one.

## Don Alejandro Cirillo

Don Alejandro Cirillo is the elected leader of the National Mayan Council of Elders of Guatemala and a thirteenth-generation Quiché priest. As such, he is a very important voice for the indigenous Maya. He has been practicing the fire ceremonies and day keeping of his peoples' traditions his entire life. Cirillo, or Wandering Wolf, has been acknowledged by gatherings of indigenous elders from many of the American nations as a healer and medicine elder of considerable prowess.

**ALERT**

Not all the indigenous Mayan elders agree with the calendar end date of December 21, 2012. Cirillo does not have a strong opinion about what will happen on this specific date and does not agree that it is necessarily the correct end date of the Mayan calendar.

Cirillo has spoken of a time that will be coming very soon, for which we should be preparing ourselves. It will be characterized by major earth changes, probably earthquakes and floods, but most significantly by a darkening of the sun. This period will last for several days and nights and people will need to prepare both practically and spiritually for this by staying indoors, having enough supplies of food and water, and praying and purifying in readiness for the beginning of a new time. When the sun returns, this will signify the beginning of the new world age.

## Don't Be Afraid

Cirillo has warned against unnecessary fear mongering and prophecies of doom. His advice on the coming changes is, "Don't be afraid." Dramatic though the changes may be, they will not be an apocalyptic destruction of all life. By having a positive outlook and a willingness to confront our shadow selves, he believes we can directly influence the outcome of these changes.

What will happen during and after this time will depend upon what we do, but we should prepare for it now. It is not wise to wait until December 21, 2012, or any other date in the future for this to happen.

## The Council of the Elders

Cirillo is now very actively involved in international conferences and gatherings where he speaks on behalf of the Quiché Maya about their perspective on the calendar and the current times. The National Mayan Council of Elders of Guatemala has appointed a group of twenty-five elders who have been given the responsibility of sharing knowledge about the calendar and interpreting its significance. This information is expected to be released to the world before 2012.

To bring the message of the Mayan elders and their ceremonies to a wider audience, Cirillo has been working with the Institute for Cultural Awareness (ICA). The ICA has held several vision councils in which indigenous elders of different nations from throughout the Americas have come together to work ceremonially and to share their knowledge. The ICA is a nonprofit organization honoring indigenous tradition and is dedicated to providing a safe and healthy environment for cultural exchange and healing. They can be contacted through their website for information about future events and ceremonies (*www.ica8.org*). There is a also a documentary film in production about the life and message of Don Alejandro Cirillo called *The Shift of the Ages* (*www.shiftingages.com*). It is scheduled for release in 2010.

**FACT**

Cirillo has now been appointed as Guatemala's first ever minister for indigenous affairs, a cabinet-level position, by President Alvaro Colom. The president has been a longtime friend of Cirillo and has been consulting his opinion for more than fifteen years.

# Hunbatz Men

Hunbatz Men is a Mayan elder of Itzá descent who lives in Merida, the largest city in the Yucatán. The Maya of the Yucatán live in quite different conditions from the traditional villages of Guatemala and are much more assimilated into the mainstream of Mexican society. One of the most important roles Men has played is in reopening the ancient ceremonial sites to the indigenous people. Up until the beginning of the 1990s, the Mexican government was very uneasy about ceremonies at sites like Chichén Itzá, Uxmal, and Palenque. Native ceremony was seen as a challenge to the government and to the rule of law. Where traditional forms of worship were allowed, it was strictly controlled and, at many ceremonial sites, it was totally prohibited. Men took the lead in bringing together elders and other interested participants to reactivate these centers.

## Re-Establishing Traditions

The Mexican government resisted the ceremonies at first. Initially, some of the ceremonies were performed surrounded by armed troops. The ceremonialists bravely faced these obstacles to burn copal at the pyramids.

By the spring equinox of 1995, the tide was turning and hundreds of thousands of people gathered in the shadow of the Pyramid of the Sun at Teotihuacán near Mexico City. At the spring equinox in 1997, the Mayan elders were joined by a group of Tibetan lamas in holding a series of solar initiations to join together these two peoples and celebrate their strong histories of ceremony and struggle.

Little by little, the ancient sites have opened up. Today, the spring equinox is celebrated at Chichén Itzá with a major festival with large international sponsors and attracts many tens of thousands of people. Indigenous ceremonialists are at least tolerated at most of the sites, and a general level of awareness of Maya spirituality and its relationship to these great ceremonial sites has increased enormously.

Men still regularly takes groups of pilgrims on tours of the ancient Mayan sites to perform ceremonies, meditations, and healings. Many of the most important sites in the Yucatán and beyond have now been activated in this manner. He is the author of the book *Secrets of Mayan Religion and Science*, which details the importance of the actual sounds used in the Itzá Mayan language and the esoteric meanings behind them. Many of the words can be reversed to reveal related but different meanings. The Mayan language can be seen, Men claims, as a form of mantra, like the ancient Vedic languages of India.

### The Itzá Count

Men has also worked on reconstructing the calendar traditions of the Itzá. The traditions of calendar keeping in the Yucatán didn't survive the European invasion, and Men had to reconstruct this lost knowledge from the fragments that are still known. This enterprise was only partially successful, and eventually, at a meeting of Mayan elders, Men agreed to adopt the traditional or Quiché count, effectively creating a unified count of the indigenous Maya.

# Carlos Barrios

Carlos Barrios is a Guatemalan of Spanish origin living at Huehuetenango who, along with his brother Geraldo, has studied with the local Mam tribe of the Maya for twenty-five years. He has been accepted by them as an Ajq'ij or day keeper of the Eagle Clan of the Mam and speaks and writes on their behalf.

**FACT**

According to Barrios, as we transition between the fourth and fifth worlds, the old economic order will break down and the world banking system will collapse. He also foretells the melting of the polar ice caps and a general rise in sea level, though this has been a mainstay of climate-change prediction for some time.

His principal message has been to speak out about the fact that the Mayan elders wish it to be known they do not believe the world will end on December 21, 2012. Rather, they believe the world will be transformed. This date will herald the beginning of the fifth world of creation, which will be marked by a return of a fifth element: ether. This immaterial, spiritual element will allow for a fusion of polarities that has not been possible within a world that only acknowledges the existence of the four material elements of earth, air, fire, and water. This new element will presage a new way of being for humanity and will be accompanied by significant changes in the material world.

Unlike Cirillo, Barrios accepts the end date of December 21, 2012, and also places great significance on the date of harmonic convergence, August 16, 1987. He considers the twenty-five-year period between these dates to be a period of unprecedented planetary transformation.

In the next chapter we will look more closely at the harmonic convergence, the event that marked the beginning of what could be called the Neo-Mayan movement. This is when western authors began to make their own interpretations of the meaning behind the calendar. These sources have been largely responsible for popularizing the Mayan calendar and inspiring many of the ideas about 2012 in circulation today. However, they are sometimes in disagreement and at variance with both the indigenous Maya and academic Mayanists.

## CHAPTER 5

# Harmonic Convergence and the Mayan Factor

The date of harmonic convergence was created by Tony Shearer, an author of Lakota heritage who was studying the culture and myths of ancient Mexico. His ideas were first published in 1975 in his book *Beneath The Moon and Under The Sun*. He believed that the period between the arrival of the conquistador Cortez, reputedly on Easter Sunday, April 21, 1519, and August 16, 1987, corresponded to a prophecy attributed to the visionary leader known as Ce Acatl Quetzalcoatl.

## The Feathered Serpent

*Quetzalcoatl* is an Aztec word meaning "feathered serpent." The Yucatec Maya equivalent is *Kukulkan*, which translates as exactly the same thing. The Quetzalcoatl was a combination of a prophet, high priest, and king. Mayan legends say Ce Acatl Quetzalcoatl was originally from Tula, just north of present-day Mexico City, and that he came to the Mayan lands of the Yucatán after being driven out by his rival, the god Tezcatlipoca. What we know through Landa's *History* is that a great leader called Cuculcan entered from the west at roughly the same time the Itzá arrived, between A.D. 967 and A.D. 987.

**Quetzalcoatl dressed as the Lord of the Wind, from the Codex Magliabecchiano**

Quetzalcoatl conquered the Yucatecan city of Chichén Itzá and established the beginning of a new culture that was a fusion of Mayan and Mexican/Itzá. He was seen as a great reformer and is also sometimes given credit for the ending of the practice of human sacrifice. At the end of his life, he is said to have floated away to sea on a raft made of serpents. His legend says he will return in a time of need. This is reminiscent of the stories and legends of King Arthur, and should perhaps be taken as a blend of myth and oral history.

The prophecy of Ce Acatl Quetzalcoatl that Shearer recounts is about a cycle of thirteen heavens and nine hells, each of which would last a complete calendar round of fifty-two years, making the whole period last 1,144 years. The cycle of nine is a very significant one in Mayan cosmology and corresponds to the Bolontiku or nine lords of the underworld. These are nine gods that govern the cycle of darkness.

**QUESTION**

**Was there just one Quetzalcoatl or many?**
Quetzalcoatl was a mythic figure, but the name was also the title of the chief high priest and the given name of at least two known historical figures. Sometimes these figures are blended, often making it somewhat confusing. To make things even more complicated, some contemporary authors have also claimed to channel the spirit of Quetzalcoatl and speak on his behalf.

# The Harmonic Convergence

August 16, 1987, or harmonic convergence, marks the ending of this period of descent and oppression and, for many interpreters, the beginning of a rapid period of transformation as we head toward the end of the great cycle that finishes on December 21, 2012. Though Shearer named the harmonic convergence date, he saw it as the end of the fifth world of the Aztec prophecy and the beginning of the sixth world. It was Jose Argüellés, the author of the bestselling book *The Mayan Factor: Path Beyond Technology*, who coined the term *harmonic convergence* and helped turn it into what became a remarkable, globally networked, grassroots event and defining moment in the creation of the New Age movement.

Argüellés had been a founding director of the Whole Earth Festival in the 1970s and understood how to reach out to networks of people and media outlets in a way that captured the popular imagination. Once the initial message spread, others repeated it and joined in. Word spread virally, and people were encouraged to go to a place they considered to be sacred wherever they lived and gather with others to welcome in a new time of global harmony. Many people gathered at locations like Stonehenge, the Golden Gate Bridge, Mount Shasta, Sedona, Glastonbury, and other places they considered to be power spots on Earth.

**FACT**

One belief about harmonic convergence was that if 144,000 people gathered, it would successfully usher in a new age. This number not only refers to the number of the elect that is mentioned in the Bible's Book of Revelation, but is also the exact number of days in one baktun of the Long Count.

Harmonic convergence was a significant success, but not many of the participants knew very much about the origin of the prophecy they were acting out or the end date of the Mayan calendar. It was Shearer's interpretation of the prophecies of Quetzalcoatl, himself a Toltec leader and invader of the Mayan lands, which gave rise to this date, rather than the Maya themselves.

## Calculating the Date

Shearer's calculations of the date have also been shown to have a questionable basis. It has often been claimed that Cortez arrived on the day Ce Acatl or One Reed in the Aztec Calendar. The significance of this is that the day is associated with Quetzalcoatl. This, however, is not substantiated anywhere and corresponds to no known count of any of the calendars. The year 1519 in the Aztec calendar was Ce Acatl, so the idea is broadly correct. There is also a 117-day discrepancy between nine calendar rounds and the number of days between Easter Sunday 1519 and the harmonic convergence of 1987. Shearer attempts to explain this apparent 117-day error by saying that it corresponds to the period between Cortez landing and his confronting Montezuma, the ruler of the Aztec empire. Nonetheless, the numbers don't seem to work out. The date of the harmonic convergence appears to have been decided upon intuitively, rather than mathematically. It certainly doesn't have the same kind of scholarly foundation as the December 21, 2102 end date of the Mayan calendar.

Despite these details, Shearer had the insight to appreciate the essence of the prophecy and turn it into something that people could relate to. To link Quetzalcoatl's prophecy of thirteen heavens and nine hells to this general time period does seem broadly credible, even if the date is not exact.

## The Return of Quetzalcoatl

The reinvention of Quetzalcoatl has become a powerful symbol not just for the indigenous people of Central America, but also for Hispanic and native peoples in North America and South America. Many other indigenous cultures have similar myths of a divine hero who returns in times of need, like the legendary Viracocha of the Inca.

# The Mayan Factor

Argüellés's book *The Mayan Factor* was published just before the harmonic convergence. This is a book of remarkable scope that looks into the mathematics of the Mayan calendar in depth. It jumps from scholarship to speculation and makes several groundbreaking suggestions that define much of the debate about 2012.

## The Thirteen Baktuns as a Map of History

One of the important ideas contained in *The Mayan Factor* is that the thirteen-baktun cycle of 5,125 years can be read as a kind of roadmap of history. Argüellés takes the thirteen baktuns and projects them onto a matrix of the 260-day Tzolkin cycle. Since the Tzolkin is made of thirteen different combinations of twenty glyphs, it divides easily into thirteen columns. When the calendar is read like this, it provides an interesting and compelling picture of the whole of history.

Known history, starting with the Sumerian civilization, begins remarkably close to the calendar starting date of 3114 B.C. Also around this date, the first pyramids were built in Egypt and Stonehenge saw its first wave of construction. At the exact center of the cycle is the birth of the great teacher Gautama Buddha, suggesting a meditative central midpoint. The process of history starts to speed up after this point, with the peak of Mayan civilization occurring halfway through the second half of the thirteen baktuns.

Industrial civilization doesn't happen until the final thirteenth column, and the present time we are in, the final katun, katun 4 Ahau, is represented by the very last square of the 260-day grid.

This idea provides a frame of reference for understanding history as a cycle that has a beginning and an ending. What makes it particularly interesting for us is that the ending is coming up very soon indeed. Conventionally, time just continues forward at the same rate it always has toward an infinite horizon. There is no closure, just origin. The modern view of history is linear and has no concept of a fixed ending and, therefore, no concept of conclusion.

## Accelerating Times

What Argüellés saw was that this idea of an end point provided a powerful tool to explain what made this particular time we are living in unique. The acceleration of modern times is one of its defining features. In 100 years, we have gone from the steam engine to the nuclear bomb. At the same time, population has increased several times over. The power of our communications technology has increased exponentially. The process of industrialization has changed the face of the planet. This time in history is unprecedented, but historians have little to say about what it is that makes it so special. There is nothing in the modern model of time that helps us explain this unique state of affairs. Most importantly, this sense of acceleration is something that pretty much everyone living in the modern world has direct experience of and can feel happening.

This new way of viewing the story of history provides an attractive and useful tool for helping us deal with the ever-increasing demands of contemporary experience. It helps explain some of the most important underlying trends of modern times, psychologically preparing us for the possibility of even greater changes to come.

Seeing history as a cycle with a beginning and an ending gives it a narrative that it would otherwise be missing. In this model history is, literally, a story in whose final chapter we are now living. Like a classic cliffhanger, we are now poised between the possibilities of great global catastrophe and potential transformation.

## The Path Beyond Technology

For Argüellés, this is represented by a transcendence of material technology and the return of a more spiritualized culture that is able to live in harmony and balance with the planet. This is facilitated by the realization that the Tzolkin and its mathematical template of the twenty glyphs represents a kind of harmonically resonant mental structure. He claims that by using the Tzolkin we can evolve our minds from their artificial historical shackles and develop a form of natural telepathy, which is facilitated by using a calendar in tune with the cycles of nature. This is the path beyond technology. For academic Mayanists there is no real evidence for this, but it has been a very popular idea about what makes the Mayan calendar ending in 2012 so important.

## Is the Tzolkin Related to DNA?

In his book *Earth Ascending,* Argüellés draws further interesting parallels between the structure of the Tzolkin and the structures of the I Ching and DNA. He notes that both the ancient Chinese oracle of the I Ching and the modern discovery of the structure of DNA are based upon sixty-four distinct elements.

Argüellés also uses the mathematical structures known as magic squares to show a possible mathematical connection between the sixty-four permutations of the I Ching and DNA and the 260 permutations of the Tzolkin. The magic squares are an 8 × 8 grid in which all of the numbers from one to sixty-four are layed out. This can be accomplished in two particular combinations that make each of the rows and columns add up to a total of 260 every time. Benjamin Franklin was responsible for discovering one of these interesting mathematical curiosities, which have an ancient origin and were highly regarded by mathematicians of antiquity as providing insight into how nature is organized.

**The magic squares of Ben Franklin**

| 52 | 61 | 4 | 13 | 20 | 29 | 36 | 45 | 260 |
|----|----|----|----|----|----|----|----|-----|
| 14 | 3 | 62 | 51 | 46 | 35 | 30 | 19 | 260 |
| 53 | 60 | 5 | 12 | 21 | 28 | 37 | 44 | 260 |
| 11 | 6 | 59 | 54 | 43 | 38 | 27 | 22 | 260 |
| 55 | 58 | 7 | 10 | 23 | 26 | 39 | 42 | 260 |
| 9 | 8 | 57 | 56 | 41 | 40 | 25 | 24 | 260 |
| 50 | 63 | 2 | 15 | 18 | 31 | 34 | 47 | 260 |
| 16 | 1 | 64 | 49 | 48 | 33 | 32 | 17 | 260 |
| 260 | 260 | 260 | 260 | 260 | 260 | 260 | 260 | |

| 64 | 2 | 3 | 61 | 60 | 6 | 7 | 57 | 260 |
|----|----|----|----|----|----|----|----|-----|
| 9 | 55 | 54 | 12 | 13 | 51 | 50 | 16 | 260 |
| 17 | 47 | 46 | 20 | 21 | 43 | 42 | 24 | 260 |
| 40 | 26 | 27 | 37 | 36 | 30 | 31 | 33 | 260 |
| 32 | 34 | 35 | 29 | 28 | 38 | 39 | 25 | 260 |
| 41 | 23 | 22 | 44 | 45 | 19 | 18 | 48 | 260 |
| 49 | 15 | 14 | 52 | 53 | 11 | 10 | 56 | 260 |
| 8 | 58 | 59 | 5 | 4 | 62 | 63 | 1 | 260 |
| 260 | 260 | 260 | 260 | 260 | 260 | 260 | 260 | |

Another way the Tzolkin and DNA are related, according to Argüellés, is that the twenty day signs can be seen to correspond to the twenty amino acids, whose differing combinations make up the DNA code. This mathematical relationship is the springboard for an imaginative leap, where Argüellés suggests that the Tzolkin is more than just a calendar and handy counting tool. His idea is that the 260-day calendar is actually a self-existing template that exists as an organizing principle in nature in the same way DNA does. The structure of DNA has always existed; Francis Crick and James Watson's discovery revealed a fundamental structure of biological nature that was always there, though unknown to us. In a similar way, Argüellés suggests, the structure of the Tzolkin, the 260-day constant, is a fundamental pattern of nature, not a human invention or contrivance.

These two principles have related mathematical properties. Argüellés calls this crossover polarity, meaning both function in a way that creates a kind of weaving together. In the case of DNA, this manifests in its double helix structure; in the case of the Tzolkin, it is manifested in a weave in time marked by a sequence of days called galactic activation portals. This is one of the most important ideas about the calendar Argüellés is responsible for.

## Galactic Activation Portals

This sequence of days within the Tzolkin is actually another discovery of Shearer's, first published in *Beneath The Moon and Under The Sun*. He highlights a series of fifty-two days in the 260-day cycle that form a distinctive pattern on the grid. Each of the days is paired with another three to create a weaving pattern that runs through the Tzolkin.

The galactic activation portal sequence or Loom of the Maya

The picture of the Tzolkin matrix as a grid of thirteen columns comes from one sketch done in pencil on the flyleaf of a Mayan book that was made shortly after the European invasion. This scribbled footnote is called the Buk Xok permutational table and is one of the earliest known examples of a codicil.

## The Loom of the Maya

The pattern of these fifty-two days or galactic activation portals exhibits the property of symmetry in two planes, one vertical and one horizontal, which are both centered on the middle column. This means each of the portal days is connected to three others that are its reflections in these two planes, dividing the Tzolkin into four equal quarters. The significance of this is another interesting mathematical property, where the sum of each of the four linked portal days always adds up to the same number: twenty-eight. In this way, Argüellés shows that the Tzolkin functions like one of Ben Franklin's magic squares

**ALERT**

Any four days anywhere on the Tzolkin would also always add up to twenty-eight when mirrored in this way. There is no real link to any corroborating evidence in the Mayan codexes or elsewhere that shows that they gave any significance to this pattern.

## The Genetic Mirror

The researchers Stray and John Martineau recently uncovered another pattern in the Tzolkin that is based on the same harmonic numbers as the galactic activation portal sequence. It also uses groups of four days that are mirrored in the horizontal and vertical plane and add up to the sum of twenty-eight. However, it emphasizes the numbers one, seven, and thirteen in the Tzolkin. The result reveals a pattern that looks even more like the DNA double helix.

## The genetic mirror sequence

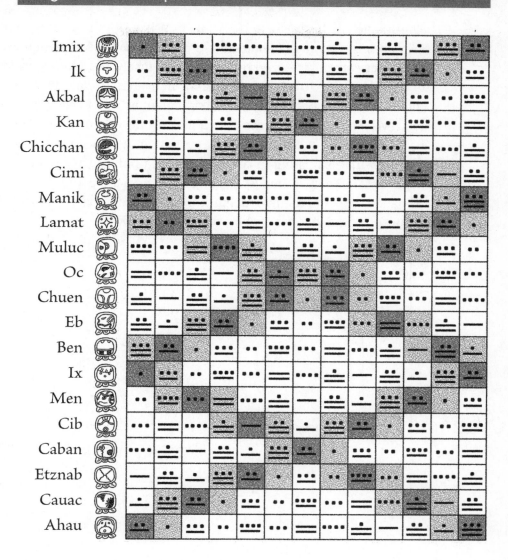

Used by permission from *The Mayan and Other Ancient Calendars* by Geoff Stray, Wooden Books, Glastonbury, UK, 2007 and Walker, New York, 2007.

## The Mathemagic of the Calendar

The magic of the mathematics that transfixes both Shearer and Argüellés demonstrates many interesting properties, but the evidence that any of these were actually utilized by the Maya themselves is pretty slim. Mayanists give no credence to the idea of galactic activation portals, and the idea that there were links between the Tzolkin calendar and I Ching is speculative. However, they are both ways of qualitatively describing time. They both tell us what kind of subjective feeling a moment in time should have. This is a quality that is missing in our modern idea of time, where time is treated solely as a quantity. Argüellés's claims are far reaching and visionary, but the elegance of the mathematical harmony that he demonstrates should not be confused with evidence that these ideas are provable.

## CHAPTER 6

# Dreamspell and the Thirteen-Moon Calendar

If Argüellés had only contributed the ideas contained in *The Mayan Factor* to the debate about 2012, his contribution to modern understanding of the Mayan calendar would have perhaps been more widely recognized. However, he then went on to create a complete alternate calendar system called *Dreamspell*, and to suggest that the world's calendar should change to a new standard based on the number thirteen. This has completely split opinion about his work. This chapter explores how these ideas created an explosion of interest in Mayan calendrics.

## Dreamspell, the Journey of Timeship Earth

The majority of people who have come into contact with a method of reading the Mayan calendar have probably been told, based on their date of birth, that they are something like a Blue Lunar Night or a Red Crystal Serpent. Many of them may then be surprised to find out these terms are not really Mayan in origin, but the creation of the visionary artists Argüellés and his then-wife, Lloydine Burrell. In 1991, based on the work of *The Mayan Factor*, Argüellés and Burrell went on to expand the premise of the Tzolkin calendar as a harmonic matrix, by creating a complete system of reading the signs of the Tzolkin. This became *Dreamspell*: The Journey of Timeship Earth. Essentially, this is a contemporary reworking of the Tzolkin, which they saw as being free of cultural baggage. Some Mayan elders later took issue with this.

*Dreamspell* is based on the concept that the Tzolkin, though a discovery of the Olmec and Maya, is actually a universal constant of time. It is, for the creators of *Dreamspell*, not the calendar's origins, but the harmonic numbers found in the calendar itself that make it important and relevant today. Starting from this premise, *Dreamspell* rewrites the Tzolkin with the goal of creating an accessible and popular system. *Dreamspell* is intended to be usable by anyone, anywhere, living in any of the current cultures of this planet, to regain a connection to natural time.

## Time as Art Replaces Time as Money

One thing Argüellés and Burrell cannot be accused of is exploiting their interpretation of the Mayan calendar for money. The visionary process by which they created or channeled the information for the Dreamspell led them to believe it should be given as a gift to humanity and should not be exchanged for money. Thousands of the quite expensive-looking boxed kits were given away for free, presumably paid for by philanthropic donors. This is because one of the core principles of their system is the need to make a transition between the paradigm of time is money—an idea, they suggest, representative of the time standard the world is currently using—to a paradigm based on time is art. They believe that adopting their version of the Tzolkin would facilitate this. This stand became somewhat diluted later on as the Dreamspell gained in popularity and others wrote their interpretations of it, made calendars based upon it, or created T-shirts, pendants, or other time-is-art paraphernalia.

## Argüellés's Popularity

In the early 1990s, Argüellés's writings were by far the most popular in introducing the concepts of Mayan calendrics to a wide public. *The Mayan Factor,* despite being quite densely written and full of unusual mathematics, made the *New York Times* bestseller list. When the *Dreamspell* box set was released, its combination of oracle and game found an audience eager to embrace it.

**ESSENTIAL**

In *Dreamspell*, colors are attributed to each glyph according to their direction and correspond to those used traditionally. Red represents the east, white represents the north, blue represents the west (though the Maya often preferred black for this direction), and yellow represents the south.

## Explaining Dreamspell

With *Dreamspell*, Argüellés and Burrell take the interpretation of the Mayan calendar put forth in *The Mayan Factor* and rewrite it in a kind of mythological language. This makes their Tzolkin calendar into a fairy tale–like game with the goal of achieving galactic synchronization. Clear and simple interpretations of the meanings of each of the twenty Tzolkin glyphs are given, with just three keywords describing their essences. Each of the glyphs is also given an English name. These are based on the traditional meanings, but in some cases Argüellés and Burrell universalize these. For instance, the traditional alligator or crocodile becomes the dragon. The skull or death becomes the world-bridger.

# The Thirteen Tones of Creation

The thirteen numbers that are attributed to each day sign of the Tzolkin are reinvented as thirteen tones. This is an interesting idea, as there are thirteen black and white notes in a musical octave. (However, it must be noted that the Maya themselves didn't necessarily use tunings that fit to the western scale.) These tones or numbers are also given names that reflect Argüellés and Burrell's interpretation of their functions in this thirteen-note scale. This is called a wavespell, and is directly equivalent to a Mayan thirteen-day trecena. The number one becomes magnetic and the number two becomes lunar. The following table shows the names Dreamspell gives to the numbers and day signs of the Tzolkin, along with the keywords that describe their functions and energies.

|    | Tone Name     | Power     | Action      | Essence       |
|----|---------------|-----------|-------------|---------------|
| 1  | Magnetic      | Unify     | Attract     | Purpose       |
| 2  | Lunar         | Polarize  | Stabilize   | Challenge     |
| 3  | Electric      | Activate  | Bond        | Service       |
| 4  | Self-existing | Define    | Measure     | Form          |
| 5  | Overtone      | Empower   | Command     | Radiance      |
| 6  | Rhythmic      | Organize  | Balance     | Equality      |
| 7  | Resonant      | Channel   | Inspire     | Attunement    |
| 8  | Galactic      | Harmonize | Model       | Integrity     |
| 9  | Solar         | Pulse     | Realize     | Intention     |
| 10 | Planetary     | Perfect   | Produce     | Manifestation |
| 11 | Spectral      | Dissolve  | Release     | Liberation    |
| 12 | Crystal       | Dedicate  | Universalize| Cooperation   |
| 13 | Cosmic        | Endure    | Transcend   | Presence      |

| Seal Name | Power | Action | Essence |
|-----------|-------|--------|---------|
| Dragon | Nurtures | Birth | Being |
| Wind | Communicates | Breath | Spirit |
| Night | Dreams | Intuition | Abundance |
| Seed | Targets | Flowering | Awareness |
| Serpent | Survives | Life force | Sex |
| World-bridger | Equalizes | Death | Opportunity |
| Hand | Knows | Accomplishment | Healing |
| Star | Beautifies | Elegance | Art |
| Moon | Purifies | Water | Flow |
| Dog | Loves | Loyalty | Heart |
| Monkey | Plays | Magic | Illusion |
| Human | Influences | Free will | Wisdom |
| Skywalker | Explores | Space | Prophecy |
| Wizard | Enchants | Timelessness | Receptivity |
| Eagle | Creates | Vision | Mind |
| Warrior | Questions | Intelligence | Fearlessness |
| Earth | Evolves | Navigation | Synchronicity |
| Mirror | Reflects | Order | Endlessness |
| Storm | Catalyzes | Self-generation | Energy |
| Sun | Enlightens | Fire | Life |

The combination of these three elements—the color of the direction, the tone, and the day sign or seal—make up the components of the Dreamspell name or galactic signature, for example, Red Cosmic Serpent. Similar to the ancient Mayan tradition of naming a person after the day on which they are born, this galactic signature is a person's key to playing the game of Dreamspell. The purpose of this is not to win, as in a conventional game; it is to increase synchronization in a kind of cooperative play based around exploring the different harmonics of the calendar system. Doing this is supposed to allow the user to resynchronize with nature. This is a function of using the more natural timing system of the base twenty, vigesimal mathematics used by the Maya. Using the Dreamspell, Argüellés claims, leads to increases in the personal experience of synchronicity and, ultimately, to a kind of telepathy and the liberation of human culture from the materialism of history. Dreamspell is seen as a kind of remedial program in which the keys of the Mayan calendar are represented in such a way that they can become planetary in scope and appeal.

**FACT**

The Dreamspell is designed only as a twenty-six-year long transitional calendar. It runs from the year of harmonic convergence in 1987 to the end of the thirteen-baktun count on December 21, 2012, and then finally to the launching of timeship Earth on July 25, 2013. This event is presented as a kind of interdimensional celebration of planetary awakening.

# The Calendar Controversy

Representatives of the Maya, including Cirillo and Barrios, have spoken against this treatment and the adaptation of the Tzolkin calendar as a universal constant. The greatest point of contention is that the Dreamspell isn't on the same date as the traditional Mayan calendar. This is a very significant fact. When people who have been introduced to Dreamspell as the Mayan calendar discover this, they can become disenchanted with it and confused at the notion of two differing dates. In his defense, Argüellés does not represent his system as the Mayan calendar and never has done. Despite this, it has become a popular misunderstanding perpetuated by many people who have shared Dreamspell information, often innocently.

## Correlation Dates and Calendar Experiments

It seems problematic that, by using a different date, *Dreamspell* is out of line with the remarkable coincidence that the ancient classic Mayan calendar dates and the traditional indigenous Mayan dates are on exactly the same day. This means that not even a single day in this count has been lost for more than 1,000 years. This is a remarkable achievement, and it's difficult for the *Dreamspell* to justify having a different date. This has led to many commentators suggesting that it was simply invented. In a relatively obscure set of essays called *The Rinri Project Newsletters,* Argüellés does address the issue of the start date and refers back to a date he uses as a correlation point. This was taken from a passage in the *Book of The Chilam Balam of Mani,* one of the important postconquest books of Mayan prophecy that were covered in Chapter 4. This date gives a specific Tzolkin date, a Haab date, and a Julian calendar date. This provides a correlation point to synchronize the calendars. It places the *Dreamspell* in the tradition of a continuation of or successor to the now-discontinued Yucatec Mayan tradition of keeping the Tzolkin calendar.

After the end of the classic period and the conquest of the Mexica/Itzá, the Maya in the Yucatán went through a series of changes and innovations in their calendrical practices that led them to drop the Long Count in favor of just recording multiples of the twenty-year katun cycle (the Short Count). They also experimented with changes that included stopping the count of the Tzolkin for thirteen days at the end of a fifty-two year calendar round to account for accumulated leap days. The point of this was that the actual solar year and Tzolkin would then match up perfectly, much in the same way that the 365-day Haab and Tzolkin previously had. Stopping the Tzolkin cycle for even a day is the greatest calendrical heresy imaginable for the traditional Maya of today. The unbroken count of days is one of the most important parts of their core spiritual practice. Yet, this was precisely what happened in the Yucatán after A.D. 1000.

## Explaining the Change

These changes were provoked by a deep-seated desire amongst the Maya to harmonize all possible time cycles, even those of the calendars of their first conquerors—the Itzá, and later, the Spanish. It was a form of syncretism that has led to the survival of Mayan culture through much oppression. Although they lamented the lack of calendrical prowess of the Itzá in their writings, they nonetheless worked at making compromises to accommodate them. The most important calendar to the Itzá was the fifty-two-year calendar round. This progressively gained dominance at the expense of the 360-day tun-based counts, and eventually the knowledge of the Long Count was lost.

## Justifying the Change

To dismiss these changes as adulterations or impure forms of the Mayan Long Count is not necessarily a balanced analysis of the postclassic culture in the Yucatán. One of the purposes of the calendar was to create a harmonized society, and the Maya were just responding to the facts of their situation and taking them into account accordingly. Certainly, at the height of the classic period, the development of the Maya's calendar was at an unprecedented peak. The strength of the Mayan culture at that time meant it was able to resist outside influences sufficiently to achieve this level of coherence. However, caution should be taken in presuming it was simply a better calendar or culture. It may have been different from the classic Mayan culture, but Mayan culture of the Yucatán post A.D. 1000 had some very worthwhile qualities.

## Dreamspell and Mayan Culture after A.D. 1000

The blend of Mexican and Mayan influences can be seen in postclassic Mayan architecture and religious iconography. This society created a fusion that survived long after the Mayan centers elsewhere had been abandoned. Even after the fall of Chichén Itzá, the league of Mayapan rose and kept a form of Mayan civilization strong in the Yucatán until a hundred years or so before the European invasion. At the same time, the pyramids of Tikal and Palenque had been ruins for half a millennium.

There has always been debate and discussion about the calendar in Mayan culture. Inscriptions that deviate from the standard model of the Maya can be found at Palenque, and we have records of priestly gatherings that occurred to properly organize and debate upon the different calendar cycles. *Dreamspell* fits within that tradition of experimentation found within the postclassic Yucatán, although it is not to be taken as the Mayan calendar.

Making conversions from the Gregorian calendar to the indigenous Mayan count has always required a day keeper for interpretation, and there is even a debate about whether the Mayan day begins at sunrise or sunset. If you only know your birthday and want to find your day sign, this makes it more difficult to work out than in *Dreamspell*.

*Dreamspell* is specifically aimed at being a transitional calendar from the apparent disharmony of the Gregorian calendar to something better. It is proposing itself as a new, alternative calendar system, not the re-establishment of an ancient one. The most important thing is to know that this is what it is. Many of those who have used *Dreamspell* have reported positive results. These include a heightened awareness of synchronicity and learning about the Tzolkin calendar in the process of using *Dreamspell*.

Here are some facts about *Dreamspell* to keep in mind:

- It is not the Mayan calendar.
- It is on a different date than the traditional Mayan calendar.
- It doesn't mark leap day.
- It uses midnight as the start of the day; the Maya do not.
- It uses the 260-day Tzolkin as the basis of a modern system.
- Using it can be a good introduction to learning the Tzolkin.
- Some Mayan elders consider it to borrow inappropriately from their heritage.

## The Thirteen-Moon Calendar Change Movement

Argüellés's argument that the rediscovery of the importance of the Tzolkin should be the impetus to reform the world's calendar system is also significant. The calendar we currently use is called the Gregorian calendar, named after Pope Gregory XIII, under whom the last significant reforms occurred. The calendar originated during the Roman Empire and was adopted by the

Catholic Church, which steadfastly protected it as a most sacred treasure of the church. This is because the calendar is used to determine the exact date of Easter, a historically defining debate for the church. What is important to note about this is that the calendar we use was decided upon because of religious and cultural power, not because it was the best or the most accurate. The progressive adoption of the calendar around the world has been a pragmatic one, dictated by the needs of business. The Gregorian calendar is effectively a global calendar by default.

**FACT**

There is some evidence to suggest that the successful reforms of Pope Gregory were partly stimulated by the discovery of the Mayan calendar. This became known in Europe as the devil's calendar because of its "fiendish" accuracy. Its reputation prompted the concern that the Christian calendar should, at least, equal it. It is certainly the case that calendar reform had been stalled for several hundred years before this happened.

The idea of calendar change is very much tied up with a point of view that sees the ending of the thirteen-baktun cycle in 2012 as both a deadline and an opportunity for planetary change. The view is that our planetary crisis of overpopulation, environmental pollution, and global conflict is a by-product of an inaccurate calendar. This might seem somewhat exaggerated, but a calendar is a powerful tool for shaping culture. Our view of time has important consequences for how we behave. The suggestion of the thirteen-moon calendar change movement is that our calendar system treats time as an unlimited commodity. This results in a culture that treats the planet's resources similarly. To be effective, systemic change is required at the root level of a culture. This means we must first change the calendar if we are to be successful in creating a more ecological culture. Change your time, change your mind has become the movement's slogan.

## The Thirteen Moons

The thirteen-moon calendar divides the solar year into thirteen moons of exactly twenty-eight days each for a total of 364 days; the extra day is taken as a day out of time. This day equates to July 25 in the Gregorian calendar. This was the starting date of the Haab calendar that was given in the *Book of Chilam Balam of Mani,* so this is the date that Argüellés took his starting date from. What is useful about the number 364 is that two, four, seven, and thirteen all easily divide into it. This gives a year that can be halved and quartered and that has exactly fifty-two weeks every year. An added bonus of this is that each week starts on the same day of the week. Another strange anomaly of the current system is that its months run independently from its weeks; a new month doesn't start on a particular day of the week. This makes it difficult to work out what day of the week a date will fall upon if it is more than a few weeks in advance.

**ESSENTIAL**

The Gregorian calendar can quite simply be shown to be irrational in structure. For example, the name of the month September means the seventh month, yet it is actually the ninth. This is because originally the Roman calendar had ten months, before the inclusion of extra months for Julius and Augustus Caesar. The names have never been changed.

## Moons and Months

The word *month* has its origin in the word *moon,* but the two meanings have become fundamentally separated. The Romans called them *demeters* and regarded them simply as convenient divisions of the solar year. The word "month" comes from old English, where the moons would still have been counted as part of the calendar. There are two significant cycles of the moon: the sidereal, the time it takes to come back to the same phase, and the synodic, the time it takes to return to the same place in the sky. The sidereal period of the moon is roughly twenty-seven days and the synodic is roughly twenty-nine days. Neither of these corresponds to the moons in the thirteen-moon calendar.

A moon in the thirteen-moon calendar won't specifically start or end on a particular phase of the actual moon. The number of days in one of these moons totals twenty-eight. This is the whole number mean between these two moon cycles, so it is from this that the moon takes its name. It is possible to easily chart the progress of the moon using this calendar, as each phase usually moves backward one or two days each moon. Despite its name, the thirteen-moon calendar is, in fact, a solar calendar.

The thirteen-part year has another advocate: the International Institute of Chartered Accountants. The division of the year into thirteen is mathematically the easiest way to divide it, and it makes accounting much more straightforward than having months of different lengths.

## Leap Day Conundrums

Leap days are ignored in the thirteen-moon calendar because the calendar is primarily designed to be a conversion tool from the current Gregorian calendar. By ignoring these dates, the Dreamspell and the thirteen-moon calendar perfectly synchronize every fifty-two years. It also keeps translation from the Gregorian simple. This idea has also been a major source of criticism for the Dreamspell: It ignores the traditional Mayan idea of counting all days, breaking the sacred count of days.

**Is the thirteen-moon calendar a Mayan calendar?**
Not really. The Maya did use glyphs to track the position of the moon in their inscriptions, but not in this way. They also had a zodiac of thirteen signs that divided the solar year, but this wasn't recorded in their calendar. The Yucatán does seem to have had a calendar that was similar to the thirteen-moon calendar. This was called the Tun Uc, which means "moon" and "seven," probably referring to weeks.

## The Planet Art Network

The idea of calendar change has become the major focus of those using the Argüellés system of interpreting the Tzolkin. The suggestion is that the proposed calendar change is one way we can actually do something about the looming deadline of 2012. Adopting a new, more harmonic calendar means we can practically and psychologically prepare ourselves for a new time. This has become quite a significant social movement that has taken root in many countries. It has become particularly strong in South America, and in countries like Brazil and Argentina it has turned into a populist movement with hundreds of thousands of supporters.

## Organized Advocates

Calendar-change advocates are also part of a broader movement toward ecological living and social change. This is taking form in the creation of new ecocommunities and gatherings called vision councils. These events are organized by a loose alliance of related groups like the Global Eco-village Network, the Rainbow Peace Caravan, and the thirteen-moon–based Planet Art Network. The goal of South American vision councils is to bring together indigenous elders, New Age speakers, activists, and others to share information. Everyone is also encouraged to work together in a process that is facilitated by consensus decision making.

These gatherings are good examples of people living with awareness of 2012 as an organizing principle. The ending of the calendar is a major focal point and is accepted as a cultural norm. In these cases, the end point of the Mayan calendar is acting as a stimulus to catalyze more rapid change than might otherwise happen. The vision councils organize to create a network of new communities and new lifestyles that are more in tune with the planet.

## The Telektonon and Other Work

Argüellés is nothing if not prolific, and has gone on to produce several other developments of his calendrical system. These include *Telektonon*, another board game–like package that Argüellés claims is inspired by the great Lord Pacal of Palenque. Another box set called *7:7:7:7* attempts to integrate Russian plasma physics, Tibetan terma prophecies, and the Argüellés calendar, with some interesting results. He is currently living in Bali and is writing a hefty seven-volume series of books called the *Cosmic History Chronicles,* the last volume of which will be published in 2012. These books focus mostly on the more esoteric aspects of his work.

**ALERT**

Many writers on the Mayan calendar and 2012 refer to Lord Pacal as Pacal Votan. This was a term coined by Argüellés. It blends the identities of two separate figures. One is the historical king, Lord Pacal, whose extraordinary tomb can be found at the Temple of Inscriptions at Palenque. The other is Votan, who was the mythological founder of Palenque.

Some writers on 2012 have made capital from the idea that Jose Argüellés's calendar system is wrong. Calendars in themselves cannot be right or wrong, just more or less accurate or more or less useful. Without Argüellés, it would be difficult to imagine how the subject matter of 2012 would have come to public recognition around the world. Dismissing his work, esoteric and highly imaginative as it is, as disproven is unfair and unhelpful. *Dreamspell* is most certainly a product of the New Age, of which Argüellés was a pioneer, but it is neither wrong nor invalid. It is just not the Mayan calendar.

## CHAPTER 7

# The Pyramids of Time

Many of the ideas associated with 2012 relate to some kind of acceleration of time. In his book *The Mayan Calendar and the Transformation of Consciousness*, Carl Calleman explores another creative way of viewing the Mayan calendar that attempts to explain this phenomenon. His model takes the calendar and maps its cycles to the different levels of a typical Mayan pyramid. The result is another attempt to understand and analyze the underlying processes of history and evolution by using the Mayan calendar.

## The Wave of History

Calleman believes the cycles of time in the calendar are represented in physical form by the sacred architecture of the pyramids. There are certainly some correspondences. Many Mayan pyramids have either seven or nine levels. In Calleman's system, these encode two different forms of calendar cosmology. In the case of the seven-level pyramid, he claims this is a representation of the sacred number thirteen that both the Tzolkin and the thirteen-baktun calendar are based upon.

If you treat these levels as a series of steps, there are a total of thirteen steps in the journey up the pyramid and then back down again. The qualities of each of these numbers can then be applied to this series of steps. Taking inspiration from the Aztec calendar, Calleman links each of these periods to one of the Aztec deities of the Thirteen Heavens. These are the gods traditionally associated with each of these numbers by the Aztecs. His reasoning for choosing Aztec gods is that the Mayan names and attributes for these deities are no longer known.

**ALERT**

Making a direct equivalence between the Aztec and Mayan cultures ignores the fact that the Aztec mythologies tend to be much more dualistic in their tone. Days for the Aztec were either good or bad. The Maya tend to describe days in more subtle ways, with different shades of meaning. The classic Maya may well have seen the gods of these days very differently.

## The Days and Nights of Creation

Each of these gods is seen as a ruling influence on each of the baktuns of the great cycle. The thirteen Aztec gods break down further into two groups. Seven of them have positive qualities and another group of six have more negative ones. These alternate sequentially. The Calleman model divides these into seven days and six nights. The days of the Calleman model are auspicious.

In the days, the development of consciousness pulses forward toward enlightenment. The nights are periods of repose and integration, often characterized by reversals of progress and darker times. Calleman uses this model to analyze history and to give a reading of humanity's progress and setbacks according to the different days and nights. This is a development of the Argüellés idea of the thirteen baktuns as a roadmap of history. What Calleman adds to this is the idea that it happens in seven pulses. These seven waves are interspersed with six necessary periods of consolidation, which he calls the wave of history.

**ESSENTIAL**

A similar structure to the wave of history can be found in the seven days and six nights of the creation story in Christianity, Islam, and Judaism. Calleman presents this as a discovery of how the underlying process of history can be described as a series of waves.

## The World Tree

Calleman has a unique take on what makes the Mayan calendar important. Unlike Argüellés, he doesn't think it is the special harmonics of the calendar system that are responsible for its uniqueness. According to him, the causal agent is not the calendar itself, but a growth process that derives from a world tree lying behind it. This is seen as something like an oscillator driving forward this wavelike progress of the calendar.

The pulses of the world tree are what move history forward in a way that is then coordinated by the different periods of the calendar. The two together create a holistic system of evolution. The idea of time emanating from the growth processes of a world tree is very different to the modern idea of time as a quantity to be spent or purchased. To better understand this idea, we have to go back to the mythological roots of the world tree idea.

## World Trees in Various Cultures

There are many myths of the world tree to be found in different cultures. A notable one is Yggdrasil in Norse mythology. The Maya also have a strong tradition of the world tree. In fact, there is a sacred ceiba tree for each of the four directions that act as a world tree supporting the sky. There is probably one more tree for the center. This is the fifth direction that is represented by the color green. Though not visible in representations of the directions, Mayan myths talk extensively about this central world tree. The terrestrial world of the four directions that we exist in could be seen as a product or fruit of this original cosmic world tree that lies behind it as a primary source.

A good example of the Mayan world tree can be found on the famous inscription on the sarcophagus lid of Lord Pacal of Palenque. This relief depicts the great Lord Pacal reclining and looking upward toward a cross of four arms. It is considered to be one of the masterpieces of Mayan art and was discovered completely intact inside the Pyramid of Inscriptions at Palenque.

## Calleman's Interpretation

Calleman's description of his world tree is something quite different. His idea is that the world tree actually corresponds to a meridian of longitude. This is one of the vertical lines used to circumscribe the world, much like the International Date Line or the Greenwich meridian. This world tree is visualized as a hypothetical midpoint on the planet. From this point, he theorizes that the seven waves of history expand outward organically. So the closer geographically a culture is to the meridian of the world tree, the earlier it will be influenced by the wave of history.

The location of this meridian is placed at the longitude of 12 degrees east. This line bisects Rome and Scandinavia and is noticeably distant from the Maya's world. Calleman's reasoning for the choice of this particular longitude is that he thinks it best fits the observed phenomena of history. This idea of a world tree is very different from anything that has been recorded about Mayan belief and seems to have much more in common, at least in location, with the Norse world tree. Calleman has admitted he is influenced by this idea and that, being Scandinavian, "feels the pulse of the world tree more strongly than most."

# The Nine-Level Pyramid of the Underworld

The second pyramid of time is a nine-level one. This one complements the first pyramid by describing a process of increasing acceleration in time that runs parallel to the wave of history. It is constructed by equating nine different sized cycles of the calendar with each of the nine stories. This is more ambitious than the description of just the thirteen-baktun cycle contained in the previous pyramid.

This pyramid represents, according to Calleman, nothing less than a description of time from the beginning of the universe. The bottom level is a vast cycle of time equal to thirteen hablatuns. Each hablatun is 1.26 billion years, so this cycle is 16.4 billion years long. As the pyramid is climbed, both the length of the cycles and the size of the steps become progressively smaller. At the same time, each step also represents a stage in evolution, so that as evolution progresses, it happens in increasingly smaller periods of time.

The closer we come to the end of the calendar, the quicker the shifts happen. For example, the first level establishes the material elements of the universe. The second level of 820 million years marks the beginning of life. The start of the thirteenth baktun, on the sixth level, sees the establishment of written language. The seventh evolutionary leap, the era of industrialization, happens in just thirteen katuns, or 256 years. We have now reached the eighth level of the pyramid. This corresponds to the last thirteen tuns of the calendar. This is the period of just 12.8 years that we are now living in. The last cycle before we reach the top happens in the final 260 days and equates to the 260-day cycle of the Tzolkin.

In Mayan mythology, in addition to the gods of the Thirteen Heavens, there are also the nine gods of the underworld. Each level corresponds to a Lord of the underworld, so Calleman calls them underworlds. We are currently in the eighth or galactic underworld, in which Calleman sees the advent of telepathy and a transcending of the material framework of life. This will be followed by the brief universal underworld of 260 days that represents the evolution of cosmic consciousness and transcendence into timelessness. In this structure, all levels of the pyramid are added cumulatively until the highest level of creation is reached.

The nine-level pyramid of the underworlds

| | | | |
|---|---|---|---|
| UNIVERSAL | 260 days | | |
| GALACTIC | 13 TUNS 4680 days | | |
| PLANETARY | 13 KATUNS 256 years | | |
| NATIONAL | 13 BAKTUNS 5,125 years | | |
| CULTURAL | 13 PICTUNS 102,000 years | | |
| TRIBAL | 13 KALABTUNS 2 million years | | |
| FAMILIAL | 13 KINCHILTUNS 41 million years | | |
| MAMMALIAN | 13 ALAUTUNS 820 million years | | |
| CELLULAR | 13 HABLATUNS 16.4 billion years | | |

**ESSENTIAL**

There is a nine-day cycle in the Mayan calendar system. Each of these days corresponds to one of the nine Lords of the underworld. This group of gods is collectively called the Bolontiku. These are dark gods who govern the cycles of nighttime. These are the same or similar to the nine who are referred to as returning or descending in the Tortuguero prophecy about 2012.

## Back to the Big Bang

The inspiration for the pyramid of time comes from a remarkable Mayan inscription found at the site of Coba. The carving on this monument records a huge number of cycles, all of which are numbered thirteen. It goes beyond the thirteen-baktun count to include numbers hundreds of millions of times bigger than the known age of the universe. From this, Calleman speculates that we are seeing a temporal scale with increasing stages of acceleration.

Calleman's model uses the nine time cycles within this inscription that have been given names. The total time span of these cycles adds up to 16.4 billion years. This is approximately the current age of the universe, according to the big bang theory. Most estimates suggest this happened about 13.7 billion years ago. This, Calleman suggests, means the Maya actually knew about the big bang and that the monument records this fact. This, unfortunately, ignores the fact that the names of the cycles are not actually from the Maya, but conventions that have been suggested by modern academic researchers.

## Critiques of the Theory

It seems much more likely that the monument at Coba was intended to express the idea of a number so vast that it was beyond comprehension. The sheer size of the inscription is definitely suggestive of the idea that the Maya recognized infinite cycles of time beyond the ability to count. It's an enlightening insight into the Mayan philosophy of time, but not really proof that the Maya calendar refers explicitly to the big bang.

The appeal of Calleman's pyramid is that it shows a model of how time may be accelerating. This gives a framework for interpreting the trends of history in a way that may prove insightful. There are, however, further complications in the detail of this theory.

It ignores the fact that the cycles of the Mayan calendar are very much based around the 360-day unit of the tun. This is very significant because Mayan numbers usually jump by a factor of twenty. However, when the tuns in the Mayan calendar are counted, this rule is broken. This is almost certainly because of a desire to capture the 360-day cycle of the sacred year in the count of days. At this point, it jumps eighteen—the number of the uinals of the year—rather than the usual twenty. This would make a pyramid with one different sized step.

## Outside of Astronomical Time

The tun is very inconvenient for Calleman's theory that the Mayan calendar is specifically measuring something other than a physical measure of time. It is very much associated with a year and it is a fundamental unit of the calendar. In spite of this, Calleman claims that the Long Count does not measure astronomical time at all, but the spiritual evolution of humanity in its path toward enlightenment. He even goes as far as to say that it is not really a physical calendar at all. For him, the loss of the Long Count and its replacement by the calendar round in the postclassic period was responsible for a fall into materialistic consciousness. In his view, it is the Mayan calendar alone that has the true cosmic blueprint encoded in it.

**ESSENTIAL**

The Mayan calendar is a count of days. The unit of a day is a unit of astronomical time. It refers, of course, to the revolution of Earth upon its own axis. This is clearly a physical cycle, not just a spiritual one. The claim that the calendar is not based on any physical cycles overlooks this fact.

# The Debate about the Mayan Calendar End Date

One of the most notable aspects of Calleman's theories is that he disagrees with the established end date of the Mayan calendar of December 21, 2012. Working out what dates the Long Count inscriptions correspond to was the subject of extensive research throughout the twentieth century. It was a search that occupied the professional lives of many dozens of researchers.

## Finding the Right Date

The process of finding the right date involved looking at many different astronomical factors to find the best possible fit. Joseph Goodman suggested a correlation at the beginning of the twentieth century. In 1927, the great Mayan scholar Eric Thompson proposed another correlation that was two days different. In 1950, after further research, he reverted to his original correlation. Opinion then swung back to this original number, which has finally been agreed upon by the vast majority of academics.

The accepted correlation has become known by the rather awkward name of the Goodman-Martinez-Thompson correlation. This is a combination of the names of the researchers who made the most significant contributions to its discovery. This is now widely adopted and fairly uncontroversial.

It is also very significant that this correlation corresponds exactly to the date kept by the traditional indigenous Maya. There has never been any substantial debate about the correlation between the Tzolkin and the Long Count, which is what Calleman questions. There are hundreds of inscriptions and monuments that confirm the established dates.

A complaint about *Dreamspell* has been that it changes the calendar used by the Maya. Calleman has been very vocal in his criticism of *Dreamspell* for this reason. It is ironic that his system does exactly the same thing by changing the end date of the Long Count. Altering this critical point means all of the predicted shifts that he forecasts are tied into an idiosyncratic timetable. Calleman's system ends on October 28, 2011, because it falls on the "auspicious" Tzolkin date of thirteen Ahau, a day that Calleman claims represents completion. This is out of sync with the accepted end date of December 21, which is agreed upon by the consensus of academic experts on Mayan calendrics.

Another reason for picking thirteen Ahau as the end of the calendar is that it represents the energy of enlightenment. It is also the last date in the 260-day cycle in the most commonly used convention. This is important to Calleman, as he believes the calendar is nonphysical. Therefore, the fact that the usual end date falls on a winter solstice in 2012 is not regarded as being particularly significant.

If Calleman had accepted the December 21, 2012, end date, each of the underworlds would have different start and end points. It is unfortunate that rather than increasing the appreciation for the significance of the last cycle of thirteen tuns we are now living in, his theory distracts attention from when they actually happen. The Maya most certainly would have thought they were significant.

It is also not unreasonable to speculate that they may have applied some of the katun prophecies found in the *Books of Chilam Balam* to these last few tuns, as they, too, finish on the auspicious day sign of Ahau.

## An Alliance Between Modern and Traditional

Calleman's ideas do have one very significant backer: the Mayan elder Cirillo. The two men have met and spoken about the calendar, and in 2006 they traveled to India together to visit the Oneness University, the ashram and school of a guru called Sri Bhagavan or Kalki. The avatar of Kalki is a Hindu deity prophesized to return to help humanity achieve enlightenment, in a similar way to Quetzalcoatl. This particular Kalki candidate has a strong interest in 2012 and sees events happening in this year as presaging the enlightenment of humanity.

Cirillo has spoken about us living within the time of twelve baktun, thirteen Ahau. This seems to fit with Calleman's idea of the calendar ending on thirteen Ahau. Calleman and Cirillo have also filmed an interview in which they discuss a prophecy of thirteen Ahau. The prophecy talked about in the interview refers to a katun prophecy and is taken from one of the *Books of Chilam Balam*.

What Calleman and Cirillo have in common is that they are skeptical about the December 21, 2012, end date. This correspondence between a modern and traditional view of the calendar would seem to be significant. Unfortunately, neither presents any evidence that brings the date of December 21 seriously into question.

## Venus Transits

One significant contribution Calleman has made to the debate about 2012 has been raising awareness of the significance of two Venus transit events in the summers of 2004 and 2012. These are very important events that would have had great significance for the Maya. Venus transits are associated with the return of Quetzalcoatl, and it is notable that the second one occurs in the year 2012 itself.

**QUESTION**

**What is a Venus transit?**
This is when Venus passes across the face of the sun from the point of view of Earth. This creates an eclipse-like phenomenon where the disc of Venus can be viewed through a filtered telescope or blackened glass as it crosses the face of the sun. These happen in pairs. Each of these pairs occurs approximately every 120 years. In the Mayan calendar, they are exactly eight Haabs of 365 days apart, which is very significant.

Calleman proposes that each of the pairs of Venus transit events represent breakthroughs in communication. This looks like a credible idea if we examine the last five sets of pairs.

*1518 + 1526: The period between the transits was marked by the circumnavigation of the globe by Magellan.*

*1631 + 1639: The first national postal services began around this time (Denmark in 1624 and Sweden in 1636). This pair of transits were the first to be observed by telescope.*

*1761 + 1769: On these two dates the transit was the focus of the first truly global scientific experiment, as teams of scientists recorded the event simultaneously in many locations.*

*1874 + 1882: These two dates mark the laying of the first telegraph and the invention of the telephone.*

*2004 + 2012: This represents the peak of the global Internet revolution. Is it the beginning of human telepathy?*

Calleman suggests that a communication breakthrough will occur between the Venus transit pair of 2004 and 2012. This will represent the initiation of telepathy on the planet that will offer an opportunity, a divine mirror enabling humanity to return to a state of oneness. It would seem that the continuing Internet revolution would also be a good candidate for a significant communications breakthrough.

**ALERT**

The significance of the next Venus transit in Calleman's system is somewhat undermined by the claim that the calendar finishes in 2011 with the enlightenment of humanity. It seems that if humanity is already enlightened by then, the meaning of the second transit happening a few months later is completely lost.

## The Oneness Celebration

In order to promote appreciation of the transits, Calleman was involved in initiating an event called the Oneness celebration. The first one of these happened on June 8, 2004, the date of the first Venus transit. The basis of the Oneness celebration is bringing people together in meditation on oneness and the fundamental unity of all nature. More events are planned for the second transit on June 5, 2012.

Gatherings like these are fundamental to the popular movement rallying around 2012 and its associated ideas. There are also events planned for the calendar end date and the two solar eclipses that occur on May 20 and November 13 in 2012. They share the hope that by aligning events to these times, these gatherings will catalyze awareness about the importance of the end of the Mayan calendar. This is generally characterized as being a major shift in human consciousness necessary to avert imminent environmental catastrophe.

**QUESTION**

**Are the solar eclipses in 2012 significant?**
The Maya would have certainly thought so. The first eclipse is particularly auspicious, as it is conjunct with the Pleiades. This cluster of seven stars in Taurus had particular significance for the Maya. The Yucatec Mayan name for the Pleiades is Tzab or the rattlesnake's tail. Alignments to the Pleiades are found at many Mayan ceremonial centers.

# Speculations and Interpretations

The idea of the Mayan calendar as a timetable for evolution or map of history is interesting. However, the model put forward by Calleman raises many significant questions. It attempts a comprehensive explanation, but it doesn't accord with the academic consensus on the Mayan calendar.

While the pyramid model may seem attractive as a possible model for showing the acceleration of time, it is speculative. The usefulness of this model is subsequently undermined by the revision of the end date. This idea is not supported by any substantial evidence. It also makes the predicted shift dates out of sync with the accepted chronology of the Mayan calendar.

A good example of the increasing popularity of Calleman's pyramid model is given by the fact that Barbara Hand Clow adopts Calleman's framework throughout her widely read book *The Mayan Code*. Calleman's claims are repeated here without any real questioning of the assumptions behind them. In the eyes of many researchers, the weakness of the calendrical science behind this theory serves to further undermine the reputation of New Age versions of the Mayan calendar.

## Problems with Interpreting the Mayan Calendar

Interpretation and theorizing have been a big part of an attempted understanding of the workings of the Mayan calendar, first with Argüellés's *Dreamspell* system and then with the pyramid model of Calleman. Neither are exact or accurate representations of the Mayan calendar, though both contain insight and interesting speculation.

This is probably necessary as part of a process leading to a greater appreciation and understanding of the significance of this extraordinary calendar system. The difficulty we face is that the western mind is conditioned by a completely different view of time. These ideas represent imaginative ways of attempting to see the world through the eyes of the Maya. In this way, they are probably helpful signposts or stepping stones along the route. However, in no way does either of these models comprise a final understanding of the Mayan calendar.

## Using the Interpretations

What we might take from these insights is an inspiration to further examine the Mayan calendar for clues about how it functions. If these speculations could also be made to accurately reflect the actual cycles and dates that have been established by rigorous academic research, they would be on much stronger ground. In Chapter 9 we will look at a final interpretation of the relevance of the 2012 end date of the Mayan calendar that does stand up to this test and is based on sound archaeological and astronomical evidence.

## CHAPTER 8

# Mayan Calendar Almanac

This section of the book is designed to help facilitate the experience of using the Tzolkin calendar in everyday life. It contains decoder charts for both the traditional Mayan calendar and the modern Dreamspell interpretation. This guide to the energies of each of the twenty day signs can be used to follow the cycle of days and find a person's birth sign.

## An Introduction to Using the Calendar

A calendar remains an intellectual abstraction until it is used. Then it becomes something quite different; it becomes a cultural organizing principle. Pretty much everything in society has a temporal component to it, from a trip to the dentist to an annual holiday. Life is organized and in some ways created by calendars. It is important not just what calendar an individual uses, but also what calendar everyone else is using because, ultimately, it is a shared agreement about how to divide and organize time.

By choosing to use a different standard of time like the Mayan Tzolkin parallel with the usual Gregorian calendar, it is possible to get interesting perspectives on both. Following the different energies of the day signs gives a different feeling to each day, and it also makes you aware of how much subliminal influence a calendar can have on our lives. Only by having some other standard to make comparisons with can this be made obvious.

Some Mayan traditionalists strongly disagree with the Argüellés interpretation of the Tzolkin, arguing that it is made up and an appropriation of Mayan culture. Argüellés's defense is that Dreamspell is intended to be a universalized version of the Tzolkin and that he has never claimed it is the Mayan calendar.

Many thousands of people in dozens of countries around the world are now using the Tzolkin calendar in one form or another. Some have been introduced to the calendar in the traditional way, through meeting a day keeper and being given a reading. From the point of view of the indigenous Maya, this is still an essential experience, but many more people have been introduced to the Tzolkin through books and websites about the calendar, events about it, or friends who already know about it. For the sake of completeness and impartiality, decoding charts for both the traditional Mayan day count and Argüellés's Dreamspell version are presented.

# The Traditional Count

A reading from a traditional day keeper is a form of initiation or baptism, where a person is given her individual day sign, which also becomes her calendar name. Before the European invasion, all the Maya were known primarily by these names. This one-to-one transmission of knowledge has a continuity that goes back at least 1,000 years, but the Maya themselves believe their traditions date back as many as 5,000 years.

Not everyone is able to visit the Mayan highlands where the living traditions are still strong. Those that do, if they are lucky, may get the opportunity to learn directly from someone who has been born into the calendar and whose traditions may stretch back many generations. This unique perspective cannot be recreated through a few paragraphs of reading, which can only serve as a basic introduction.

Few westerners have been accepted into the traditions of Mayan day keeping. Not everyone is suited to such a role; those who are need patience and perseverance to learn the traditional way through a lengthy apprenticeship. The only way to become a day keeper is by living the calendar and immersing oneself in it and the worldview of the Maya.

## Martin Prechtel

One person who has been working in this way with the calendar and is now sharing his knowledge is Martin Prechtel, author of *Secrets of the Talking Jaguar*. Prechtel was raised on a Pueblo Indian reservation in New Mexico. His mother was a Canadian Native American and his father a Swiss paleontologist. He married a Mayan woman and raised two sons in the Mayan village of Santiago Atitlán. After a shamanic apprenticeship he became acting shaman of the community and eventually Nabey Mam, the first chief. The world he describes is a heart-centered one, rather than an intellectual one, where much of the wisdom contained in the calendar comes to a person not by study or contemplation, but by participating in ceremonies and the Mayan way of life. In the traditional communities, learning the calendar is indivisible from learning everyday folklore and the tales of the ancestors.

## Dennis and Barbara Tedlock

Two of the first westerners to be accepted into the Mayan day-keeping traditions were Dennis and Barbara Tedlock, both anthropology professors at the State University of New York at Buffalo. Together, they undertook the traditional 260-day training period to become an *ajk'ij* or day keeper. This involved making offerings of copal incense and candles at shrines and studying the *rahil bahir* or circle of days, as the Tzolkin is known in the Guatemalan highlands. At the end of the training, a large pot called an *olla* is broken. This symbolizes the break with the previous life led by the person being initiated and the entry into the new life of day keeper. Barbara Tedlock's book *Time and the Highland Maya* is an excellent introduction to the rituals and cosmology of Mayan day keeping.

## Different Starts to the Day

One of the things that makes converting the date of the Gregorian calendar into the traditional Mayan Tzolkin more difficult is that there is no certain rule about what time the day begins and what time it ends. For some of the Maya, the day begins at dawn; for others, it begins at sunset. In neither case does it begin at midnight, as the western calendar does. This makes a standardized approach to decoding your day sign more complex because if you are born before dawn, or, in some traditions, after sunset, a different glyph applies. In the case of the traditional calendar, this is one of the reasons a personal introduction remains indispensable.

The debate over starting times is also one of the reasons Argüellés devised his system. He wanted to create a system that gave consistent results for anyone using it anywhere on the planet. For this reason, the day in *Dreamspell* follows the Gregorian start point of midnight. *Dreamspell* was designed to be a transitional calendar that allows an easy introduction to the energies of the Tzolkin. In *Dreamspell,* the definitions of the energies of each day are given in the form of just a few keywords with universalized meanings. The idea behind this is that more people will become engaged in experiencing the calendar, rather than just reading about it.

# New Age Interpretation of the Tzolkin

A number of contemporary western authors offer their own interpretations of the Tzolkin. Two of the first to publish a guide to working with the Mayan day signs and their numbers were Ariel Spilsbury and Micheal Bryner, who created a divinatory card system called The Mayan Oracle. The book that accompanies the cards contains extensive lists of correspondences for each of the energies, attributing crystals, herbs, and astrological signs to each of the glyphs. Each sign also has a poem and affirmation. Most of Spilsbury and Bryner's work was done intuitively from directly working with the day signs; others were channeled. The Mayan Oracle is a general guide that is not aligned to any particular count.

**ESSENTIAL**

You can download a program that tracks the Tzolkin. Time Surfer is a particularly useful piece of software that allows you to follow the traditional Long Count Tzolkin date and Dreamspell simultaneously. Programs like this are very useful for working out significant dates in the past and future and to find interesting patterns. It is easy to use and can be downloaded for free from *www.gaianmysteryschool.com*.

Aluna Joy Yaxk'in, author of *Mayan-Pleadian Astrology,* also explores the Tzolkin. She offers an in-depth analysis of the personality traits associated with each of the twenty signs. Her system takes the dating system of *Dreamspell* but uses the spring equinox as the new-year date, rather than the July 26 date the thirteen-moon calendar uses. Her interpretation is based on the idea that the knowledge of the Mayan calendar originally comes from Pleadian star beings. She also acknowledges the traditional count in her writing.

Kenneth Johnson is an astrologer whose book, *Jaguar Wisdom,* offers interpretations of the traditional Mayan count of the Tzolkin. As well as offering readings of each day sign, Johnson offers information about how to conduct Mayan divination rituals using the Tzolkin. Johnson cites a lot of the Tedlock's work, but is not an initiated day keeper himself, although his book contains a lot of well researched Mayan folklore. Even this very respectful treatment is not approved of by some of the sterner Mayan traditionalists. Johnson does point out Mayan concerns with the uninitiated use of the calendar, but offers the information while cautioning against its abuse.

# Finding Your Day Sign

There are two decoder charts to use to find a day sign. The first one is for finding the Dreamspell interpretation of the Tzolkin. The second one is for finding a date in the traditional Mayan count. The method of reading the charts is the same.

1. Write down the birthday or date to be converted.
2. Find the month number from Table 8-1, the Month Decoder Table.
3. Find the year number. To find a Dreamspell date, use Table 8-2, the Year Decoder Table. To find a Traditional Maya date use Table 8-3, the Traditional Maya Year Decoder Table.
4. Add to these two numbers the number of the day of the month that is being converted.
5. If the total of these three numbers is more than 260, deduct 260 from the total.
6. The result should be a number between one and 260. Look up that number on the Tzolkin chart on p. 98. This is the tzolkin day for the birthday or date to be converted.
7. Each square of the Tzolkin also has a number, from one to thirteen, written in it in Mayan bar/dot notation (see page 13). This is the corresponding number or tone of the date.
8. Read across to the left-hand column. This symbol is the corresponding one from the twenty day signs or glyphs.
9. Look up the meanings of the thirteen numbers and the twenty day signs in the following section. The Tzolkin signature of the date is a combination of both.

Note that when using the traditional Mayan chart, if the year is a leap year, add 1 if the date is after February 29. If you know that a person was born after sunset on the day of their birth, use the following day sign in the traditional Mayan chart.

## TABLE 8-1 MONTH DECODER TABLE

| The Month You Were Born In | Number | | The Month You Were Born In | Number |
|---|---|---|---|---|
| January | 0 | | July | 181 |
| February | 31 | | August | 212 |
| March | 59 | | September | 243 |
| April | 90 | | October | 13 |
| May | 120 | | November | 44 |
| June | 151 | | December | 74 |

## TABLE 8-2 DREAMSPELL YEAR DECODER TABLE

| Birth Year | Birth Year | Number | | Birth Year | Birth Year | Number |
|---|---|---|---|---|---|---|
| 2013 | 1961 | 217 | | 1991 | 1939 | 247 |
| 2012 | 1960 | 112 | | 1990 | 1938 | 142 |
| 2011 | 1959 | 7 | | 1989 | 1937 | 37 |
| 2010 | 1958 | 162 | | 1988 | 1936 | 192 |
| 2009 | 1957 | 57 | | 1987 | 1935 | 87 |
| 2008 | 1956 | 212 | | 1986 | 1934 | 242 |
| 2007 | 1955 | 107 | | 1985 | 1933 | 137 |
| 2006 | 1954 | 2 | | 1984 | 1932 | 32 |
| 2005 | 1953 | 157 | | 1983 | 1931 | 187 |
| 2004 | 1952 | 52 | | 1982 | 1930 | 82 |
| 2003 | 1951 | 207 | | 1981 | 1929 | 237 |
| 2002 | 1950 | 102 | | 1980 | 1928 | 132 |
| 2001 | 1949 | 257 | | 1979 | 1927 | 27 |
| 2000 | 1948 | 152 | | 1978 | 1926 | 182 |
| 1999 | 1947 | 47 | | 1977 | 1925 | 77 |
| 1998 | 1946 | 202 | | 1976 | 1924 | 232 |
| 1997 | 1945 | 97 | | 1975 | 1923 | 127 |
| 1996 | 1944 | 252 | | 1974 | 1922 | 22 |
| 1995 | 1943 | 147 | | 1973 | 1921 | 177 |
| 1994 | 1942 | 42 | | 1972 | 1920 | 72 |
| 1993 | 1941 | 197 | | 1971 | 1919 | 227 |
| 1992 | 1940 | 92 | | 1970 | 1918 | 122 |

**DREAMSPELL YEAR DECODER TABLE** (*continued*)

| Birth Year | Birth Year | Number |
|---|---|---|
| 1969 | 1917 | 17 |
| 1968 | 1916 | 172 |
| 1967 | 1915 | 67 |
| 1966 | 1914 | 222 |

| Birth Year | Birth Year | Number |
|---|---|---|
| 1965 | 1913 | 117 |
| 1964 | 1912 | 12 |
| 1963 | 1911 | 167 |
| 1962 | 1910 | 62 |

**TABLE 8-3 TRADITIONAL MAYA YEAR DECODER TABLE**

| Birth Year | Number | Birth Year | Number |
|---|---|---|---|
| 2013 | 170 | 1961 | 157 |
| 2012* | 64 | 1960* | 51 |
| 2011 | 219 | 1959 | 206 |
| 2010 | 114 | 1958 | 101 |
| 2009 | 9 | 1957 | 256 |
| 2008* | 163 | 1956* | 150 |
| 2007 | 58 | 1955 | 45 |
| 2006 | 213 | 1954 | 200 |
| 2005 | 108 | 1953 | 95 |
| 2004* | 2 | 1952* | 249 |
| 2003 | 157 | 1951 | 144 |
| 2002 | 52 | 1950 | 39 |
| 2001 | 207 | 1949 | 194 |
| 2000* | 101 | 1948* | 88 |
| 1999 | 256 | 1947 | 243 |
| 1998 | 151 | 1946 | 138 |
| 1997 | 46 | 1945 | 33 |
| 1996* | 200 | 1944* | 187 |
| 1995 | 95 | 1943 | 82 |
| 1994 | 250 | 1942 | 237 |
| 1993 | 145 | 1941 | 132 |
| 1992* | 39 | 1940* | 26 |
| 1991 | 194 | 1939 | 181 |
| 1990 | 89 | 1938 | 76 |
| 1989 | 244 | 1937 | 231 |

**TRADITIONAL MAYA YEAR DECODER TABLE** (*continued*)

| Birth Year | Number | Birth Year | Number |
|---|---|---|---|
| 1988* | 138 | 1936* | 125 |
| 1987 | 33 | 1935 | 20 |
| 1986 | 188 | 1934 | 175 |
| 1985 | 83 | 1933 | 70 |
| 1984* | 237 | 1932* | 224 |
| 1983 | 132 | 1931 | 119 |
| 1982 | 27 | 1930 | 14 |
| 1981 | 182 | 1929 | 169 |
| 1980* | 76 | 1928* | 63 |
| 1979 | 231 | 1927 | 218 |
| 1978 | 126 | 1926 | 113 |
| 1977 | 21 | 1925 | 8 |
| 1976* | 175 | 1924* | 162 |
| 1975 | 70 | 1923 | 57 |
| 1974 | 225 | 1922 | 212 |
| 1973 | 120 | 1921 | 107 |
| 1972* | 14 | 1920* | 1 |
| 1971 | 169 | 1919 | 156 |
| 1970 | 64 | 1918 | 51 |
| 1969 | 219 | 1917 | 206 |
| 1968* | 113 | 1916 | 100 |
| 1967 | 8 | 1915 | 255 |
| 1966 | 163 | 1914 | 150 |
| 1965 | 58 | 1913 | 45 |
| 1964* | 212 | 1912* | 199 |
| 1963 | 107 | 1911 | 94 |
| 1962 | 2 | 1910 | 249 |

*=Years marked are leap years. Add 1, if date is later than February 29.

Used by permission from *The Mayan and Other Ancient Calendars* by Geoff Stray, Wooden Books, Glastonbury, UK, 2007 and Walker, New York, 2007.

The Dreamspell or traditional Mayan dates for a particular day can be put together to form a name. With the traditional Mayan calendar, this would include both the Yucatec Mayan form and its translation.

## Tzolkin Chart

|  | | | | | | | | | | | | | |
|---|---|---|---|---|---|---|---|---|---|---|---|---|---|
| Imix / Alligator | 1 | 21 | 41 | 61 | 81 | 101 | 121 | 141 | 161 | 181 | 201 | 221 | 241 |
| Ik / Wind | 2 | 22 | 42 | 62 | 82 | 102 | 122 | 142 | 162 | 182 | 202 | 222 | 242 |
| Akbal / House | 3 | 23 | 43 | 63 | 83 | 103 | 123 | 143 | 163 | 183 | 203 | 223 | 243 |
| Kan / Seed | 4 | 24 | 44 | 64 | 84 | 104 | 124 | 144 | 164 | 184 | 204 | 224 | 244 |
| Chicchan / Serpent | 5 | 25 | 45 | 65 | 85 | 105 | 125 | 145 | 165 | 185 | 205 | 225 | 245 |
| Cimi / Death | 6 | 26 | 46 | 66 | 86 | 106 | 126 | 146 | 166 | 186 | 206 | 226 | 246 |
| Manik / Hand | 7 | 27 | 47 | 67 | 87 | 107 | 127 | 147 | 167 | 187 | 207 | 227 | 247 |
| Lamat / Rabbit | 8 | 28 | 48 | 68 | 88 | 108 | 128 | 148 | 168 | 188 | 208 | 228 | 248 |
| Muluc / Moon | 9 | 29 | 49 | 69 | 89 | 109 | 129 | 149 | 169 | 189 | 209 | 229 | 249 |
| Oc / Dog | 10 | 30 | 50 | 70 | 90 | 110 | 130 | 150 | 170 | 190 | 210 | 230 | 250 |
| Chuen / Monkey | 11 | 31 | 51 | 71 | 91 | 111 | 131 | 151 | 171 | 191 | 211 | 231 | 251 |
| Eb / Road | 12 | 32 | 52 | 72 | 92 | 112 | 132 | 152 | 172 | 192 | 212 | 232 | 252 |
| Ben / Reed | 13 | 33 | 53 | 73 | 93 | 113 | 133 | 153 | 173 | 193 | 213 | 233 | 253 |
| Ix / Jaguar | 14 | 34 | 54 | 74 | 94 | 114 | 134 | 154 | 174 | 194 | 214 | 234 | 254 |
| Men / Eagle | 15 | 35 | 55 | 75 | 95 | 115 | 135 | 155 | 175 | 195 | 215 | 235 | 255 |
| Cib / Warrior | 16 | 36 | 56 | 76 | 96 | 116 | 136 | 156 | 176 | 196 | 216 | 236 | 256 |
| Caban / Earth | 17 | 37 | 57 | 77 | 97 | 117 | 137 | 157 | 177 | 197 | 217 | 237 | 257 |
| Etznab / Mirror | 18 | 38 | 58 | 78 | 98 | 118 | 138 | 158 | 178 | 198 | 218 | 238 | 258 |
| Cauac / Storm | 19 | 39 | 59 | 79 | 99 | 119 | 139 | 159 | 179 | 199 | 219 | 239 | 259 |
| Ahau / Sun | 20 | 40 | 60 | 80 | 100 | 120 | 140 | 160 | 180 | 200 | 220 | 240 | 260 |

# The Twenty Day Signs

The meanings given here are the names of the day signs in Yucatec Mayan. This is followed by the Dreamspell name, then the equivalent name in translation from Yucatec Mayan. There are also three keywords from the Dreamspell describing the energy of the day. The first half of the interpretation of each day relates to the Dreamspell, the second half to the traditional Mayan interpretation.

## IMIX

**Dreamspell:** Dragon; **English translation:** Alligator
**Keywords:** Nurtures, Birth, Beginning
**Color:** Red
**Direction:** East

The Dragon begins the Tzolkin and represents new beginnings and fresh starts. The Maya consider the alligator or crocodile to be a primal being whose qualities represent existence itself. The sign of Imix, the alligator, is about birth and the forces connected to motherhood. It brings forth everything that follows it and sets in motion the story of creation.

## IK

**Dreamspell and English translation:** Wind
**Keywords:** Communicates, Breath, Spirit
**Color:** White
**Direction:** North

The Wind is symbolized by the tongue, the organ of spoken communication. It is also associated with the T-shaped holes that are found in many Mayan temple walls to allow the sacred wind to enter. The sign of Ik represents the breath of the wind as the carrier of divine communication. When speech is harnessed to spirit, the Wind will be able to blow. Ik is a sign of the air and of thought and ideas.

## AKBAL

**Dreamspell:** Night; **English translation:** House
**Keywords:** Dreams, Intuition, Abundance
**Color:** Blue/Black
**Direction:** West

This sign is the house of the underworld, the domain of the Mayan Lords of the night and the dark place from which all dreams come. The Night is the imaginative realm where knowing is intuitive and still connected to the depths of the psyche. From this empty place, creation can spring forth, manifesting our dreams in the waking world. The Maya say those born under Akbal, the sign of the House tend to be domestic in nature.

## KAN

**Dreamspell:** Seed; **English translation:** Lizard
**Keywords:** Targets, Flowering, Awareness
**Color:** Yellow
**Direction:** South

The sign of the Seed governs all the cycles of growth, from placing a seed into the ground through fruition and harvest. By targeting where we sow our seeds, we can ensure the best possible rewards. Those born on Kan, the day of the Lizard, are considered by the Maya to be dynamic, and the day sign has connotations of sexuality that might be expected from such a fertile sign.

## CHICCHAN

**Dreamspell and English translation:** Serpent
**Keywords:** Survives, Life Force, Sex
**Color:** Red
**Direction:** East

Serpent represents the kundalini power of life force. The base level of this energy is the survival instinct in all living things, but this can be cultivated to rise up the spinal column and become the force that drives our enlightenment. Serpent power is the reptilian mind in all its raw vitality. Chicchan people are said to have a strong sense of instinct.

## CIMI

**Dreamspell:** World Bridger; **English translation:** Death
**Keywords:** Equalizes, Death, Opportunity
**Color:** White
**Direction:** North

The World Bridger is the part that endures when a person journeys between the worlds of life and death. It represents the power of transformation and the great opportunity that provides, if the choice is made to embrace it. The Cimi symbol of the skull of death is a great reminder that everyone is born equal and that, in death, all are made equal again. This sign is considered a very auspicious and lucky one by the Maya.

## MANIK

**Dreamspell:** Hand; **English translation:** Deer
**Keywords:** Knows, Accomplishment, Healing
**Color:** Blue/Black
**Direction:** West

The Hand is associated with the healing arts and the creative knowing that comes through touch. Hand is representative of the wisdom of crafts and all that can be accomplished by the craftsperson's knowledge. The sign of Manik, the deer is considered by the Maya to be a powerful and spiritual day sign of high aspirations and ideals. The deer is considered a sacred animal to the Maya and ritual dances are performed to honor it.

## LAMAT

**Dreamspell:** Star; **English translation:** Rabbit
**Keywords:** Beautifies, Elegance, Art
**Color:** Yellow
**Direction:** South

The Star is associated with the planet Venus, a most important deity to the Maya. The Star is the sign of the artist, responsible for beautifying and uplifting with their creativity. Those born under the sign of Lamat, the Rabbit are considered by the Maya to be good gardeners and are likely to have a green thumb. The rabbit is considered to represent the struggle to overcome the material world and achieve spiritual liberation.

## MULUC

**Dreamspell and English translation:** Moon
**Keywords:** Purifies, Water, Flow
**Color:** Red
**Direction:** East

The Moon is the sign of water in all of its aspects, as the Moon governs the tides that cause the waters to ebb and flow. The sign of Muluc also represents the power of purification that water can bring, from life-bringing rains to destructive floods. This is a reminder of the Mayan creation story that says the previous world was destroyed by water. Muluc teaches us not to resist when we need to let go into the flow of life.

## OC

**Dreamspell and English translation:** Dog
**Keywords:** Loves, Loyalty, Heart
**Color:** White
**Direction:** North

The unconditional love of the Dog is the key to this sign. The sensual nature of this sign requires mastery over animal instinct, but when the Dog is trained it becomes the most loyal and trustworthy companion. Oc represents the heart, but the Maya also associate the sign of Oc with misuse of sexuality and even promiscuousness. In Mayan mythology, it was the dog that brought humans the gift of fire.

## CHUEN

**Dreamspell and English translation:** Monkey
**Keywords:** Plays, Magic, Illusion
**Color:** Blue/Black
**Direction:** West

Monkey is a mischievous and playful sign, the trickster of the bunch. Monkey days may not go as they are planned and can be full of unexpected surprises. The sign of Chuen loves to have fun at the apparent expense of others, but also teaches about the nature of illusion when we are taking ourselves too seriously. It is a lighthearted, humorous day sign. The start of the traditional count is celebrated on the day Eight Chuen.

## EB

**Dreamspell:** Human; **English translation:** Road
**Keywords:** Influences, Free Will, Wisdom
**Color:** Yellow
**Direction:** South

The power of free will, represented by the Human's ability to choose, is the key to this sign. Choosing wisely may serve the higher good. If not, the destructive foolishness of the selfish and self-centered man may prevail. Eb influences the unfolding drama of life through playing this key role. The sign of the Road suggests there are many turnings on the road of life to choose from.

## BEN

**Dreamspell:** Sky Walker; **English translation:** Reed
**Keywords:** Explores, Space, Prophecy
**Color:** Red
**Direction:** East

The symbol of Sky Walker can be visualized as two pillars connecting heaven to Earth. This is the role of this prophetic sign that is connected to Quetzalcoatl, the legendary One Reed and archetypal deity of this sign.

Being the hierophant that connects these worlds allows the sign of Ben to be a conduit for prophecy and insight. The Maya associate the Reed with knowledge and authority.

## IX

**Dreamspell:** Wizard; **English translation:** Jaguar
**Keywords:** Enchants, Timelessness, Receptivity
**Color:** White
**Direction:** North

This day sign, associated with the night sky, represents the power of timelessness. The ability to go into trance states to access knowledge from the spirit world is a key to this sign. The jaguar priests were the shamanic elite of the Maya, and Ix is their sign. Those born under this sign can step out of time to receive messages that can then be used for the betterment of oneself and the larger community.

## MEN

**Dreamspell and English translation:** Eagle
**Keywords:** Creates, Vision, Mind
**Color:** Blue/Black
**Direction:** West

The Eagle's soaring perspective means it can see the bigger picture. Sharpness of vision and clear sightedness are able to reveal the larger truth of a situation, transcending the more mundane, Earth-bound outlook of everyday life. The Eagle's eye is a reminder of the planetary mind that modern society has lost touch with. The Maya associated the sign of Men with the sun at its zenith.

## CIB

**Dreamspell:** Warrior; **English translation:** Vulture
**Keywords:** Questions, Intelligence, Fearlessness
**Color:** Yellow
**Direction:** South

The Warrior is forever questing in search of new understanding. This sign is determined, resolute, and proceeds where action is needed without fear. The reverse of this is that the sign of Cib may at times be perceived as being too serious. The Maya see Cib's associated animal of the Vulture as a largely positive bird, providing a necessary part of nature's recycling service.

## CABAN

**Dreamspell:** Earth; **English translation:** Earthquake
**Keywords:** Evolves, Navigation, Synchronicity
**Color:** Red
**Direction:** East

Those born under this sign can use being connected to Earth to navigate through life. The Earth represents a matrix of synchronicity, which can be accessed by being attentive to the signs and willing to go with the flow without resistance. The sign of Caban is also strongly associated with the movement of Earth, especially earthquakes. It is also considered a good day for commerce and trading.

## ETZNAB

**Dreamspell:** Mirror; **English translation:** Flint
**Keywords:** Reflects, Order, Endlessness
**Color:** White
**Direction:** North

The Mirror holds up a surface for us to see our own reflection. This image may be fragmented or appear broken, but in the Mirror's changing facets we have a tool that teaches us about our own endlessly changing natures. The sign of Etznab shows us there is not one true face, but many and that the order of things is constant change.

## CAUAC

**Dreamspell and English translation:** Storm
**Keywords:** Catalyzes, Self-generation, Energy
**Color:** Blue/Black
**Direction:** West

The Storm is a completely self-contained ecosystem. It draws up the waters of the ocean and then transports them over the landmasses. It then drops the water, renewing the cycle. The sign of Cauac shows us how to conserve and nurture energy by becoming self-generating. Cauac is enormously powerful, catalyzing great change in its surroundings, but it renews itself from its own source.

## AHAU

**Dreamspell and English translations:** Sun
**Keywords:** Enlightens, Fire, Life
**Color:** Yellow
**Direction:** South

The Sun is the final sign and is often considered the most auspicious and prophetic of them all: a day doubled. The Sun represents the culmination of the cycle of creation and its very source. The sign of Ahau, the symbol of the Mayan kings, enlightens us with its life-giving rays and governs the growth and fruition of all things. Ahau represents both the furnace of original creation and the brightness of our eventual enlightenment.

# The Thirteen Tones of Creation

The power of the number associated with the day sign is just as important as the sign itself. In fact, the qualities associated with these numbers are considered the more active or dynamic part of the equation, while the day signs themselves are considered more passive or static. The traditional Maya see some of the numbers as luckier than others. The higher numbers are especially auspicious when they appear during divination rituals. One is also a very important number, being associated with numerous mythological figures and gods including Quetzalcoatl, the hero twins, Hunab Ku, and the planet Venus.

Argüellés has associated the thirteen numbers with the thirteen black and white notes of a musical octave. He considers each of the thirteen tones a distinct step or stage in a cosmically aligned process of manifestation or wavespell. The wavespell begins with the unifying influence of one and then progresses through a series of twelve distinct energetic stages before returning to one. This series of energies can be used as a formula for manifestation over a thirteen-day, thirteen-week, or even thirteen-year period.

## Following the Wavespell

One way of experiencing the energies of the Tzolkin is to follow a whole thirteen-day trecena or wavespell and record the experience in a diary. Learning to use a new calendar is probably something many people have not done since they were very young. Adopting a child-like mindset can be very useful for this process. Here are some suggestions for learning the calendar:

- Draw and color the glyphs. This helps activate the right hemisphere of the brain to experience these energies.
- Keep a diary of anything significant that seems like it might relate to the energies of the Tzolkin.
- Meditate on the energies of the day.
- To help familiarize yourself with the meanings of the signs, use the birthdays of friends and family to find out what their day signs are.

These practices help bring attention to the pattern of synchronicities that may begin to evolve as the calendar is studied. Dreamspell is designed as a fully integrated system for following the calendar in this way, but it is also possible to follow the traditional count in this manner. In the beginning, it is probably a good idea to start with one calendar, to avoid confusion. There are many guidebooks available to help do this for both the Dreamspell and traditional counts. Other resources, such as *The Mayan Oracle,* are useful for both.

Using a calendar on a daily basis is different from attempting an intellectual understanding of it. The subjective, personal part of the experience is a crucial component. By experimenting with following a Tzolkin cycle for thirteen, twenty, or even 260 days, you'll gain different insights than you would from approaching the calendar academically. These may be useful in understanding more about the differences between the Mayan experience of time and the one created by the Gregorian calendar currently used by our global society. Ultimately, this may help prepare you for the predicted changes of 2012 by bringing the frequency of the Mayan calendar system into daily awareness.

## The Thirteen Numbers and Their Powers

The numbers begin with the Yucatec Mayan name for the number followed by the Dreamspell name of the tone and the corresponding keywords. The summary gives an idea about how the numbers fit together in the Dreamspell system to create a progression that links the cycle of thirteen together.

| Mayan Number | Dreamspell Tone | Keywords | Description |
| --- | --- | --- | --- |
| HUN (one) | Magnetic Tone | Unify, Attract, Purpose | The first tone represents unity and new beginnings. An intention set on this day will carry throughout the whole thirteen-day period that follows. Each day has its own energetic function that assists in the process of harmonious manifestation in tune with the fractal time wave of thirteen pulses. |
| CA (two) | Lunar Tone of Challenge | Polarize, Stabilize | The function of the second day is to polarize the intention of the first day. This means looking at the challenges to the manifestation of the desired goal. Clearly identifying these obstacles before attempting to move forward is a key to using the wavespell process. |
| OX (three) | Electric Tone of Service | Activate, Bond | After the original intention and its challenge have been assessed, the third stage is to activate and energize the process of achieving the goal. The question to ask at this stage is, "What does the intention serve?" Answering this removes the personal ego from the equation by aligning with the greater good. |

| Mayan Number | Dreamspell Tone | Keywords | Description |
|---|---|---|---|
| CAN (four) | Self-existing Tone of Form | Define, Measure | At the fourth tone, the four corners of a square can be represented. This is the first point that the intention can begin to be defined in the third dimension. A detailed plan of action is required so that form can be given. Write down exactly what you plan to do. |
| HO (five) | Overtone Tone of Radiance | Empower, Command | After the action plan is drawn up, the completed blueprint is now empowered by drawing in the necessary resources to accomplish it. The fifth tone represents the point to focus on gathering what is required. Being in command means taking control of the process by drawing in whatever is necessary. |
| UAC (six) | Rhythmic Tone of Equality | Organize, Balance | Having gathered resources, the sixth part of the thirteen stages is to effectively organize all aspects of the project. Balance is achieved by placing all the elements into the appropriate place relative to each other. Find the order in apparent chaos. |
| UC (seven) | Resonant Tone of Attunement | Channel, Inspire | The seventh step of this process is the mid-point. This is a point at which the space can be created for divine inspiration to be accessed and given room to express itself. At this pause, opening up to a higher source may yield unexpected insights. Inspiration is often unexpected, but by being open to it we encourage the best possibility of recognizing it when it does happen. |
| VAXAC (eight) | Galactic Tone of Integrity | Harmonize, Model | The eighth stage is about testing the integrity of what has been brought together so far. This is an opportunity to try out various solutions in a dry run to explore different possible results. This experimentation and modeling ensures that when the final action of manifestation is taken, the project has the best possible chance of perfect success. |
| BOLON (nine) | Solar Tone of Intention | Pulse, Realize | Upon reaching nine, it is now time to fully engage the pulse of intention to realize the goal that has been set. This takes what has been assembled so far and expresses it with full and complete commitment. Acting without hesitation or second guessing sends a clear message to the receptive universe. This allows the law of attraction to be accessed in an optimal way for the best possibility of success. |
| LAHUN (ten) | Planetary Tone of Manifestation | Perfect, Produce | The tenth tone is the point at which manifestation occurs. By having undertaken the careful preparation in the previous nine steps, all that remains is to focus on perfection. The next three tones will concentrate on recirculating the energy that has been created in this process so that on the first day of the next cycle, everything is ready to begin again. |

| Mayan Number | Dreamspell Tone | Keywords | Description |
|---|---|---|---|
| HUN LAHUN (eleven) | Spectral Tone of Liberation | Dissolve, Release | The spectral tone is about completely releasing what has been created. This is a necessary part of creating in tune with nature, which is always recycling what it has created. This step allows the dissolution of attachment, avoiding the trap of being drawn out of the present moment by lingering on the completed project. |
| CA LAHUN (twelve) | Crystal Tone of Cooperation | Dedicate, Universalize | The twelfth stage is for sharing what we have experienced with others. In the thirteen-day cycle of the wavespell, this is marked by a crystal day gathering, where those who are working with the calendar in this way can meet and share what they have learned. This sharing is an important part of the process and prepares the way for beginning again. |
| OX LAHUN (thirteen) | Cosmic Tone of Presence | Endure, Transcend | The last of the thirteen is a day of meditative awareness, where being in the present moment is the sole focus. These last three stages are what most significantly distinguish the wavespell from other forms of working with intention. Manifestation is only part of the holistic process anchored in the natural time of the here and now. The intended product of following these cycles is personal development and increased awareness. |

Learning and experiencing the basics of the calendar is a direct way of gaining insight into the fundamental pattern of Mayan time. These rhythms, being unattached to the wheel of the year, are different from the days of the week or cycles of the seasons. This count of days is the building block of the Long Count and all the other Mayan calendars.

If 2012 is the end of time, it may be that it marks the ending of the global Gregorian monoculture, as well as the thirteen baktuns. The current global temporal monopoly is unprecedented in history, and the attention the existence of the Mayan calendar brings to the limitations of the current global calendar might mean it is not the only one to run out of days shortly. What is certain is that after 2012, the current cycle in the Mayan count of days ends. The remarkable culture of the classic Maya left no clues about what comes next, so there is a great opportunity for something new to emerge. A global calendar that in some way incorporates the Tzolkin would perhaps herald the beginning of a truly multicultural timing standard for a world needing to renew its vision.

# CHAPTER 9

# The Galactic Alignment

The researcher and author John Major Jenkins may have made one of the most interesting modern discoveries about the Mayan calendar's end date of December 21, 2012. His book *Maya Cosmogenesis 2012* puts forward the theory that the calendar end date is pointing to a very significant astronomical event: the rising of the winter solstice sun in conjunction with the center of the galaxy. This is an event that only happens once every 25,771 years.

## Precession of the Equinoxes

The alignment of the winter solstice sunrise with the center of the galaxy occurs because of phenomena called the precession of the equinoxes. Precession refers to a change in the direction of the axis of a rotating object. From Earth's point of view, the sunrise on any fixed day will rise against a background of stars that changes over time. This cycle is called the precession of the equinoxes because the equinoxes have traditionally been used to measure its progression. They are fixed days that are predictable with relation to the solar year.

**QUESTION**

**What is an equinox?**
The equinox is when the sun is located vertically over the equator. This happens twice a year. The first one, on March 20 or 21, is the spring or vernal equinox for the northern hemisphere and the autumn equinox for the southern hemisphere. The second equinox takes place around September 22 or 23. With the solstices, these days are the four fixed quarters of the year.

Precession is quite a slow process, where the stellar background against which the sun rises moves approximately 1° every seventy-two years. This also creates what is known as the changing ages of the zodiac in astrology. The stellar background for sunrises and sunsets is always found in this 14° wide belt called the ecliptic. The ecliptic is an imaginary circle projected into the sky from the plane of the solar system. This circle is then divided into twelve constellations, which form the signs of the zodiac.

**ESSENTIAL**

Most astrologers think we are currently at the end of the Age of Pisces and are on the cusp of entering the Age of Aquarius in the ages of the zodiac, although there is some dispute about the exact timing. Some astrologers put the date for the beginning of the Age of Aquarius as far forward as the twenty-third century.

Together, the twelve signs create a wheel of the year. The cycle of precession, where the sun's rising and setting points gradually move against the sky, means that the zodiac can also be used to mark a greater wheel of the ages. Each of these zodiac ages lasts 2,160 years, where the rising sun at the vernal equinox will stay within one of the signs. Twelve zodiacal ages make one great year of 25,920 years, an approximation of one precessional cycle.

## The Ecliptic

The ecliptic is the path the sun follows as it moves through the year. Each day, the location of the rising sun appears to move against the background of the stars as it gradually moves its way around the circle of the ecliptic. In a year, the location of the sunrise will have returned to almost exactly the same position in the sky. The difference will be around 0.0138°. Measuring this difference is how we detect precession. Over the whole 25,771-year cycle, these accumulated differences will mean that the rising point of the sun, measured on the spring equinox, will have completed a 360° circle and will have returned once more to exactly the same place in the sky.

**FACT**

The Greeks, and possibly other ancient cultures including the Egyptians and the Neolithic builders of Stonehenge, knew about the precession of the equinoxes. Accurate figures for the rate of precession have only been recorded for the last 150 years. There is a debate about whether the Maya knew about precession. Most conventional academics have suggested they did not, but some are now revising their opinions.

## The Winter Solstice Galactic Alignment

The conjunction of the winter solstice with the galactic equator is not just a one-time event that happens on December 21, 2012. The disc of the sun is one half a degree wide, so it will take about thirty-six years to fully traverse the galactic mid-plane. The conjunction is an event that is happening now and will be happening for some years after 2012. The period of conjunction began around 1980 and will continue until approximately 2018.

The alignment is formed by the location of the winter solstice sunrise crossing the galactic equator. The galactic equator can be visualized as a circle projected onto the sky in a similar way as the ecliptic but in the plane of the galaxy. The circles of the galactic equator and the ecliptic intersect at an angle of 60° to each other. This creates the effect of a cross in the sky.

The classic Maya knew this cosmic cross as the Sacred Tree, and it was extremely important to them. Jenkins believes this is the real origin of the cosmic Mayan world tree depicted on the sarcophagus lid of Lord Pacal. It also corresponds to the cahib xalcat be or four junction roads, the cross-roads of Maya mythology recorded in the Quiché book of the *Popol Vuh*. Importantly, this is the site of the entrance to the underworld, Xibalba.

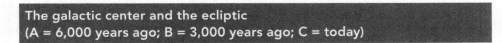

**The galactic center and the ecliptic**
**(A = 6,000 years ago; B = 3,000 years ago; C = today)**

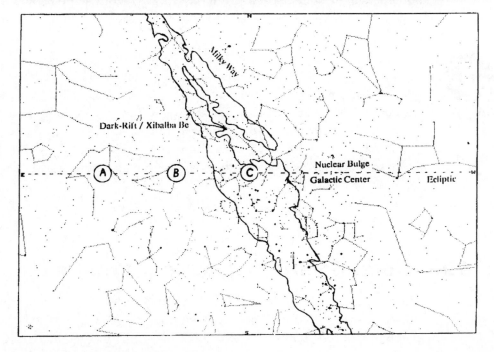

Graphic by John Major Jenkins

**Where is the galactic center?**
In the zodiac, the galactic equator or mid-plane is found at 28° Sagittarius on the cusp of Sagittarius and Scorpio. The true center of the galaxy lies 3° below the ecliptic. This is the gravitational center of mass around which all stars in this galaxy, including our own, orbit.

## Galactic Cycles

Some writers have confused the idea of this galactic alignment with another galactic cycle. This is the much, much longer journey our solar system takes as it moves above and below the central plane of the galaxy. This up-and-down motion happens simultaneously to our very slow orbit around the center of the galaxy. Our star, the sun, is located in one of the arms, sometimes called the Orion arm, that radiate out in a spiral from the center of our galaxy. Our sun travels through and between these spiral arms as it revolves slowly around the galactic center in an orbit that takes about 226 million years.

This means that in the entire lifetime of our planet we have only orbited the galactic center about twenty times. At the same time, our sun also moves up and down in an oscillation toward and away from the galactic equator. This is sometimes confused with the winter solstice/galactic equator alignment of 2012, which is quite different. This cycle takes much longer, passing through the galactic mid-plane about every 35 million years. In this long cycle, the sun is actually moving away from the galactic equator. It will not cross it again for approximately 30 million years.

At the moment, our solar system is moving toward the more densely populated center of our local galactic arm. This means we are entering an area that has more red giant stars. These can be dangerous because they can explode into what are known as type II supernovas. The solar system is currently inside a sixty light-year-wide interstellar bubble that a previous type II supernova explosion has largely cleared of interstellar dust particles. This means our night skies are clearer than they otherwise would be. The galactic alignment of the 2012 era is an optical one, not a physical one. We are not actually crossing the center of the galaxy. It is just that a neat conjunction makes it look like we are, a bit like the hands on a giant clock aligning to cosmic midnight. It is this that Jenkins is bringing attention to. His research suggests that a pre-Mayan culture found at the site of Izapa knew about this conjunction and actually went as far as to align the building of their ceremonial sites to mark the event. This was an event that, for them, was still nearly 2,000 years in the future. To understand the significance of this, we have to look at how the Maya saw the galaxy and what it meant to them.

## The Black Road to the Underworld

There is a dark patch in the Milky Way close to the galactic center. This is caused by an interstellar dust cloud obscuring the light coming from the stars at the core of the galaxy. This is often called the dark rift. For the Maya, this feature marks the black road to the underworld. This is visualized as a celestial mouth, from which deities and kings are born. It is from this dark rift that the winter solstice sun will appear to emerge when it rises on December 21, 2012. This is very significant. The emergence of Xibalba from the underworld is synonymous with birth. The appearance of the sun from the dark rift would be a natural point in the Maya cosmology to measure a beginning or ending point from.

Analogues of the four cosmic roads also appear in the layout of a typical Mayan village. Jenkins theorizes that these—as well as the ceremonial centers built by the Itzá and the Maya—are laid out to reflect this cosmological order. The center axis of the city would be a copy of the celestial order above. The celestial crossroads or cosmic navel represents the place of creation in the Mayan cosmology. It is from this location that all manifested creation emanates; it is the absolute center of the Mayan universe.

## The Death and Resurrection of the First Father

The rising of the winter solstice sun was a significant event to the Maya, and it is recorded as the most important of the four quarters of the year. The winter solstice is still the focus of a midnight ceremony held by the indigenous Maya to mark this event. This belief is also reflected in other ancient cultures. For example, in the Neolithic temple of Stonehenge, the trilith of stones aligned to the winter solstice is the tallest. There is also a myth in the Celtic traditions of the king—a common symbol for the sun—dying the day before the winter solstice, known as the kingless day, to be reborn anew the day after. Jenkins takes a similar myth found in the Quiché Mayan book *Popol Vuh* and applies its symbolism to the Mayan calendar. In this creation story, the First Father, One Hunahpu, represents the birth of a world age.

**ESSENTIAL**

> There are four cosmic roads associated with the Mayan Sacred Tree. Each has a color. The black road is the darker north part of the Milky Way and the white road is the brighter southern part. The arms of the ecliptic, visualized as a double-headed serpent, are seen as green in the east and red in the west.

The story is about his journey to the underworld, where he is tricked and killed by the wily lords of Xibalba. His skull comes to rest in a crevice in a tree. Jenkins equates this to the cosmic world tree of the galaxy and the crevice to the dark rift. This is also seen as the cosmic birth canal or vagina of the galactic cosmic mother. In this place, the skull is able to spit into the hand of Blood Moon, who bears him two sons, the hero twins. They are eventually able to defeat the lords of Xibalba, allowing One Hunahpu to be reborn in an act of cosmic re-creation.

The symbology of this fits well with what will happen in the sky during December 21, 2012, when the winter solstice sun is birthed from the dark rift. The name One Hunahpu is also equivalent to the calendar date One Ahau. This could also be taken to mean First Sun, and Jenkins theorizes that One Hunahpu represents the winter solstice sun.

## The Discoveries at Izapa

The site of Izapa is located in southern Mexico, near the Pacific coast and to the west of the border with Guatemala. This is a very likely birthplace of the Long Count calendar and the site of some very interesting astronomical alignments, one of which seems to point to 2012. Izapa was populated between 400 B.C. and A.D. 100 and was the dominant site in its region. Some of the very earliest Long Count inscriptions, dating back to around 40 B.C., have been found in locations close to Izapa, and would almost certainly have been influenced by it. Unfortunately, no Long Count inscriptions have yet been found at Izapa itself. In *Maya Cosmogenesis 2012*, Jenkins describes many important alignments from this site that relate to different astronomical cycles. The most important of these for its relationship to 2012 is the alignment of the ceremonial ball court.

## The Mayan Ball Game

Ball courts are very common features in Mayan ceremonial sites, and ball games, played with a small ball made of rubber, are common throughout Meso-American indigenous culture. Like most other aspects of Mayan life, the symbology of the ball court and the ball game has cosmological roots.

The game is played with two teams competing to put a small rubber ball through a hoop mounted high at the end of the court, using only their knees and elbows. Two parallel banks of terraces used for spectator seating form the rest of the court.

Jenkins's theory is that the game ball represents the winter solstice sun and the goal ring into which it must be placed represents the dark rift of the Milky Way, which marks the entrance to the underworld of Xibalba. This suggests the ball game represents knowledge of the cycle of precession, and also points toward the calendar end date of December 21, 2012. The ball court at Izapa is aligned east-west with the goal ring in the east. Looking down the court toward the goal, the winter solstice sun could be seen to rise in the background.

**FACT**

Murals found on the great ball court of Chichén Itzá show the primary ball player being decapitated. His head then becomes the game ball. This has given rise to the idea that the captain of one side was sacrificed after a ball game. Jenkins believes this mural actually refers to a high deity and is metaphorical.

At the time the ball court was built, the rising point of the sun was still approximately 30° below the galactic equator. If the symbolism of the ball game and the galactic center is correct, the ball court could be seen as a sort of celestial alarm clock pointing at the conjunction happening in our era. Being able to mark an astronomical event like this, 2,000 years before it happens, is remarkable and shows how important the conjunction was to the Izapans. In effect, they encoded their knowledge of this galactic cosmology into this monument. Their vision of this event was already complete before the rise of the classic Maya some hundreds of years later.

This is quite a convincing application of authentic Mayan and Izapan mythology to the facts of the calendar. Accepting this interpretation means acknowledging the following:

- The Maya were fully aware of the significance of the calendar ending on the day of a winter solstice.
- They were tracking the cycle of precession.
- They were able to formulate the end date of the calendar so that it reflected their creation story.
- This was all worked out before or at the beginning of the Long Count inscriptions, around 50 B.C.

If this is correct, the Mayan mythological jigsaw puzzle is made much more complete. It reveals a picture of a civilization with highly advanced sciences of astronomy and time keeping that, at the least, rival our own.

# The Mayan Creation Event

A conjunction of a solstice or an equinox sunrise and the galactic equator will happen once every 6,442 years. The winter solstice conjunction happens only once every 25,771 years. What makes this even more significant is that it is also the end of a 5,125-year cycle of the Long Count. If you multiply the length of the Long Count by five, you get a total of 25,625 years, very close indeed to one cycle of precession.

Jenkins suggests that each of these five could correspond to one of the five worlds of creation. The Long Count would then be just one-fifth of an even bigger precessional calendar. This neatly ties up the five worlds of creation found in the *Popol Vuh,* with the conjunction of the place of creation and the sun on December 21, 2012. These events happening together, he suggests, perfectly mark the creation event at the ending of a whole precessional cycle.

The Mayan idea of creation may seem quite strange to us, but they attribute creation and birth to the end of a cycle, rather than the beginning. For example, the birth of a child follows its gestation period of approximately 260 days, or one Tzolkin. Each of the Mayan time cycles was named after its last day, not its first. In Mayan prophecy, it was the last day that determined the oracle for the time period.

Cycles that finish on an Ahau day are of particular significance. This happens in the 260-day Tzolkin, at the end of every twenty-year katun and the end of the thirteen baktuns on December 21, 2012, which is the day 4 Ahau. According to Jenkins, this is creation day, when the New Sun emerges from the cave of creation. This is a date that marks the shifting of the world ages and a cosmic re-creation. From this point of view, the thirteen baktuns of the Long Count could be seen as a planetary pregnancy leading to the birth of something entirely new.

By most estimates, precession would take about 200 years of direct observation to calculate, so the Maya may have discovered it as early as the time of the first Long Count inscriptions. Why they did not add their knowledge of the cycle to their calendar may well be explained by the fact that they encoded it into the doctrine of the five worlds of creation, although this cannot be proven.

**FACT**

Astrophysicists have discovered that there is a black hole at the center of our galaxy. Remarkably, the Maya had a place-name glyph associated with the entrance to the dark rift of the Milky Way that translates as "black hole." Jenkins speculates this suggests the Maya actually knew about the black hole at the center of the galaxy.

## The Possible Effects of the Galactic Alignment

Jenkins suggests that as the conjunction completes, we may experience a field effect reversal. This would be similar to what happens when the earth's terrestrial equator is crossed. When water is poured into a sink, in the northern hemisphere it will escape through a plughole by spiraling in a clockwise direction. In the southern hemisphere, this direction of spin is reversed to counterclockwise. When the boundary of the equator is crossed, a null point is reached and water pours directly downward. This is called the Coriolis Effect.

This helps illustrate how very large but diffuse forces can create significant effects on a small scale when polarities are reversed. This field effect reversal may possibly lead to physical effects like changes in the magnetic field of Earth or other disruptions. The effect may also be felt in much more subtle ways.

This idea of a shift in polarity has been interpreted to mean that we may experience either a magnetic or physical pole reversal. Jenkins is not predicting this. Any effect would happen because we are in resonance with the energy coming from the galactic center. We can, Jenkins claims, expect to have our basic orientations inverted and "on the level of human civilization, our basic assumptions and foundational values will be exposed."

Jenkins's theories about the Mayan calendar end date of December 21, 2012, are well researched and backed up by good archaeological and mythological evidence. They also agree with both the academic and traditional Mayan interpretations of the calendar. But acceptance of his theory by mainstream Mayan research has been slow in coming.

Scholars tend to downplay the importance of 2012. This is largely an attempt to resist the onslaught of poorly researched opinion and general hype about the date. In Jenkins's case, this dismissive approach seems mistaken. Of all the contemporary ideas that have been proposed about the meaning of the Mayan calendar and its end date of 2012, his are among the most elegant and are well grounded in credible research.

## CHAPTER 10

# The Fractal at the End of Time

Another interesting theory about 2012 also focuses on the end date of the Mayan calendar, but the inspiration for this hypothesis comes from a very different source from those we've looked at so far. The brothers Terence and Dennis McKenna were on a journey to the Amazon to research indigenous psychoactive plants, when an extended psychedelic experience led them to a new interpretation of the ancient Chinese oracle of the I Ching. This led them to predict a remarkable event for December 2012.

## Psychedelics and 2012

Cultures in central and southern America have a long established history of the use of psychoactive and psychedelic plants for the purposes of divination and healing. The Amazonian drink ayahuasca, for example, has a known history of usage that goes back at least 2,000 years.

Made from a combination of two or more plants that are only moderately psychoactive taken alone, the ayahuasca brew contains an endogenous brain chemical called dimeythltryptamine or DMT. DMT in this form is a powerful psychedelic. Users report visions that often feature animals representing spirits in experiences that can last between four and eight hours. Ayahuasca is widely used by a number of indigenous tribes throughout the Amazon as a sacred plant medicine. It is respected for its potency and is used to heal and also to relate to the spirits of the rainforest. In some cases, it has also been used for sorcery.

**FACT**

The Aztecs have a deity called Xochipilli, whose name means "the prince of flowers." He is responsible for sacred medicines. Statues of Xochipilli show him adorned with at least a dozen different psychoactive plants.

It was ayahuasca that the McKenna brothers, who are both enthnobotanists, were searching for on their Amazonian expedition. They were particularly interested in studying a form of auditory hallucination that had been reported by users of the brew. This led them to create an experiment in which they took ayahuasca in combination with the psychoactive mushroom *Stropharia cubensis*. The result was a protracted and potent visionary experience that is detailed in the book *True Hallucinations*.

This experience inspired Terence McKenna to develop his timewave zero hypothesis. Like Calleman's pyramid model of the calendar, timewave zero also predicts an ever greater acceleration of time toward the Mayan calendar end date of December 21, 2012. In this case, the level of acceleration actually becomes exponential. If the timewave hypothesis is correct, we are heading toward an event in 2012 that will result in the creation of a temporal singularity. This would effectively mean an end to time as we know it.

## Shamanism and the Galactic Alignment

Psychoactive plants may have helped others recognize the importance of 2012. Jenkins speculates that psychedelic plants could have led Maya kings and priests to the discovery of the galactic alignment. Many Meso-American tribes, the classic Maya among them, have a history of using psychoactive plants as part of their culture. These plants include datura, morning glory, tobacco, and psychedelic mushrooms.

Jenkins points to the ready availability of many plants that contain DMT in the Maya's bioregion. He also considers it possible that the Maya made use of toad venom from the *Bufo alvarius* toad. The toad secretes venom from glands behind its eyes and on the back of its legs. These glands can be milked to harvest the venom, which can then be dried into a white powder and smoked or used as a snuff. The psychoactive ingredients contained in this secretion are bufotenine and 5-MeoDMT, a form of DMT. The mouth of a toad is also a Mayan symbol for the entrance to the underworld of Xibalba. It is from this toad's mouth that kings and deities are born.

**QUESTION**

**What is a shaman?**
The word comes from the language of the Siberian Tunga people and means "a healer who cures through trance." According to Men, the Yucatec Mayan word *xaman* means something very similar. Shamans are found in many cultures. They cure ills or find information by going into trance states. These can be created by drumming, chanting, or taking plant medicines.

Jenkins's thesis is that the Maya gained their knowledge of galactic cosmology by taking DMT and going on visionary shamanic journeys to the galactic center. The Mayan understanding of the galaxy, he suggests, was not just a product of deduction or observation, but direct knowledge gained through shamanism. This would certainly help explain the development of the Maya's stunning calendar and astronomical sciences so early in their history at Izapa. McKenna points out that there is a recognized tradition in shamanism of exploring the furthermost boundaries of space and time. For a journeying shaman, the galactic center could provide an essential reference point to orient toward in their astral voyaging to the center of time and space. For these interdimensional travelers, the junction of the galactic equator and the ecliptic would literally have been a crossroads, just as it is described in the Mayan mythology.

# The I Ching as a Lunar Calendar

McKenna's timewave zero hypothesis is constructed around one single fact about the I Ching. The basic unit of The I Ching is the line or yao. Six of these make a kua or hexagram, and there are sixty-four different permutations of these kua that make up the complete oracle. This means the whole system is based upon six multiplied by sixty-four, making a total of 384 lines.

The timewave theory came about when McKenna linked this number to an important lunar cycle. Each lunation of Earth's moon is approximately 29.53 days, and a lunar year of thirteen lunations totals approximately 383.89 days, a figure very close to 384 days. This, McKenna suggests, means the I Ching might in fact be an ancient lunar calendar.

**ESSENTIAL**

A lunation of the moon is the time it takes for the moon to return to the same phase. This is a synodic cycle and is one of the moon's two most important cycles. The other is the sidereal period. This is the time the moon will take to return to the same place in the sky. This is slightly shorter, at 27.32 days.

It is widely accepted that the oldest calendars kept by the Chinese, going back to Neolithic times, were lunar. A calendar based on 384 days or thirteen lunations is a good candidate for basing a lunar year upon because it is just 2.4 hours short of a complete day. By adding one intercalary day every ten lunar years, this calendar will only lose one day every 454.5 years, making it very accurate.

## The King Wen Sequence

The sixty-four hexagrams of the I Ching can be ordered in different ways, but one of the most ancient orders is called the King Wen sequence after the ancient Chinese emperor. McKenna describes this as "the oldest preserved human abstract sequence" because its origins date to the beginning of known history. The hexagrams in the King Wen sequence are placed into pairs, where the second hexagram of a pair is obtained by inverting the first. This series of thirty-two pairs exhibits some very unusual numerical properties that McKenna used to form the basis of timewave zero's mathematics.

## The Mathematics of the King Wen and Timewave Zero

McKenna was curious to find the intellectual principle that lies behind the ordering of the thirty-two pairs of I Ching hexagrams, which was unknown. He theorized that this could be expressed as a first order difference between the hexagrams. This is the number of lines that change between one hexagram and the next. It will always be an integer between one and six. What he found was that an exact 3:1 ratio of odd to even transitions was maintained in the King Wen, and that the number five was excluded completely. This seemed to be a profoundly unusual structure.

McKenna was also struck by the fact that the King Wen sequence contained a singularity: the first and last three positions were a mirror image of each other. This means that if you take the whole sequence, you can reverse it and place it over the original and each hexagram will be paired with its opposite. This backward and forward combination of the first order differences creates closure at the beginning and end of the sequence when it is mapped this way. This creates what can be seen as a single waveform.

## What the Timewave Tells Us

McKenna concluded that the waveform made from the whole sequence of the I Ching could be used as the basic unit to form the hierarchy of a multileveled calendar. Treating the entire sequence as one unit or yao, he further multiplied the wave by six and sixty-four. This creates different layers, still based on the mathematics of the I Ching, which can be used to map every possible level of time from the very large to the very small. A lunar year of 384 days multiplied by sixty-four gives a period of around 67.3 years. This can then by multiplied by sixty-four again, giving a period of 4,306 years. This period is very close to the length of two zodiacal ages—4,320 years. Six of these periods actually give a closer approximation to one cycle of precession than the great year of astrology. This led McKenna to believe that the relationship between the I Ching and the lunar calendar was fundamentally harmonic and could be used as a key to understand the whole unfolding process of history.

**ESSENTIAL**

Like Argüellés, McKenna thinks there is an important relationship between the I Ching and DNA. He equates the wave derived from the King Wen sequence of the I Ching with a physical model of one strand of DNA. McKenna suggests that the flow of energy through our DNA is how we experience the flow of time itself.

By this expansion through multiplication, McKenna was able to apply this highly complex waveform to the whole of the space-time continuum. To achieve this requires twenty-six different levels of the original I Ching wave, each of which is a factor of sixty-four larger than the preceding level. The hierarchy of timewave zero extends in this way to cover a period of 72.25 billion years at the large end, all the way down to the subatomic range of Planck's constant on the microscale. At this point, further subdivisions on the quantum level are no longer meaningful.

## Novelty Theory

The timewave can be read as an index of how much of what is occurring at any given time is novel or new. This could literally be any event that happens. The more unexpected or original, the more novelty the event has. A very novel event could be the invention of the telephone, the Asian tsunami of 2004, or the events of 9/11. The timewave doesn't tell you specifically what will happen or where, but it does describe how novel it needs to be. By looking at the repeating patterns and their corresponding novelty, the idea is that we are able to predict when interesting events will occur but not necessarily what will be happening. The timewave is not deterministic, but it does suggest that change itself can be quantified and predicted.

The accelerating changes in our world over the last few decades contain many good examples of novelty. From the invention of the motor car to the popularity of Facebook, new social and technological forms are appearing more and more rapidly. Change is increasing and this is predicted by the timewave. As a model of time, it embraces the zeitgeist of the modern world far better than the arrow of linear time, with its origins in the medieval world of Christian theology.

## Fractal Resonance

The timewave suggests that different periods of history have resonance with each other. This is because the timewave exhibits self-similarity, one of the defining characteristics of a fractal. This means that different parts of the wave repeat the same sort of pattern but at different scales. For example, some commentators suggest that the timewave for the period of World War II, 1939–1945, closely resembles that for the period 2007–2012. Both are characterized by a major spike toward the end of the period. In the case of World War II, McKenna equates this with the denotation of the first atomic bomb at Hiroshima. In the case of 2012, events are likely to be even more dramatic.

McKenna uses the bombing of Hiroshima as the historical anchor point for the timewave. From this single point, the timewave is projected as an overlay onto history. After this key point, it takes the timewave exactly one period of 67.3 years to reach closure. This made the original end date of the timewave November 17, 2012. When McKenna discovered the end date of the Mayan calendar was just a few weeks later, he simply changed the end point to fit this new insight. This means the original anchor point is somewhat lost, as the whole wave moves forward by twenty-eight days. There is no definitive or empirical reason why the timewave should finish on December 21, 2012. For McKenna, the end of the Mayan calendar just seems to fit in well with the sort of unprecedented event the timewave is predicting.

# The Timewave Predictions for 2012

What the timewave is predicting for its end point at 6:00 A.M. on December 21, 2012, is quite extraordinary. Whereas Calleman and Argüellés are predicting major shifts in consciousness, McKenna's theory predicts events so strange they are literally unimaginable.

## Significant Changes in a Short Span of Time

The timewave predicts that changes that have as great an impact as the invention of agriculture or the Industrial Revolution will happen no less than eighteen times in 2012—and that's only on the last day. In fact, there will be as much change in the last part of that year as was contained in half the previous lifespan of the universe, from the big bang to the birth of the sun. This mindboggling acceleration will increase exponentially. Five of these revolutions will occur during the year, eighteen in the last day, and thirteen in the last second of the timewave.

## Explaining the Theory

This incredible set of circumstances represents a concrescence, where multiple streams of being merge into one unified thing. This is the singularity that waits for us at the end of time. McKenna calls this the eschaton, a sort of strange attractor that is drawing the evolution of the universe toward itself. This represents a totally different form of time that has no past or future; it is comparable only to a state of revelation. This is the fractal at the end of time. It is a vortex of change lying in wait for us that will transform the human experience into something entirely different.

In his rationale for the extraordinary compression sequence that ends the timewave, McKenna observes that the laws of physics themselves seem to vary by their scale in space. Modern science is still working to reconcile the very different laws that seem to operate on the quantum scale and at the cosmological ones. He suggests these laws not only vary by the scale of space but also by the scale of time.

As we approach concrescence in 2012, the fractal scale of the timewave diminishes the closer we get to the end point. As the scale diminishes, McKenna predicts that the physical laws that accompany them will change. Hence, the possibility of huge amounts of innovation and novelty as we get closer to this event, much like a big bang in reverse. What this experience would actually be like is beyond even McKenna's vivid imaginings. Nonetheless, this is what the timewave is predicting.

## Critique of the Timewave

Critics of the theory point out that the anchoring points into history are arbitrary and subject to debate. If you change the anchor point, you change the end date. Nonetheless, since the timewave reaches closure very quickly after the anchor point, it would have to be sometime in our modern era.

In addition, skeptics say the nature of novelty is subjective rather than objective. What might seem to be particularly novel for one person may seem less so for another. Interpretation of the timewave therefore lacks provability, which makes it unscientific. In the case of recent events that are generally agreed to be novel and to have wide significance, the time-wave hypothesis has not been particularly successful in making clear predictions. For example, the events of 9/11 barely scored more than a minor deviation from most of the projections of the novelty curve.

**FACT**

The timewave went through a major revision after the British mathematician Matthew Watkins pointed out an error that threatened to undermine the theory. This subsequently led the physicist John Sheliak to make changes to the mathematics of the timewave to address these issues. He has named this revised waveform timewave one.

## Consciousness and Time

The timewave, for all of its cosmological predictions, actually represents a view of time that is centered on humans. McKenna made no apology for this. He believed that in the hierarchy of time, human perception was exactly in the middle order. This means we are not cosmically insignificant as previously assumed by most science, and our ability to consciously perceive the universe is an important part of cosmic order. The worldview of the timewave is consciousness centered and the existence of an objective physical universe, apart from its perceiver, doesn't figure. McKenna speculates that the world itself may come to be seen as a "fluctuation of a vacuum domain, albeit a long lasting one," a spontaneously arising artifact of consciousness itself.

As a hypothesis, timewave zero has some very compelling qualities. It challenges the idea of linear time in a more radical way than has ever been done before. It also provides another useful model that points to a possible cause for the acceleration of time that many people are experiencing. It does these things with many brilliant insights about the relationship between the I Ching, DNA, and the nature of time itself.

**ESSENTIAL**

In many ways, the timewave is the quintessential 2012 theory, containing dramatic consciousness-expanding revelations with a mind-blowing psychedelic apocalypse at the end. It is a big idea. The timewave doesn't just predict the end of history; it predicts the end of time.

Where it appears more flawed and limited is when it is taken literally as a predictive model. Novelty is open to interpretation. Different anchor points create different timewaves. Nor is there is any way to subject the hypothesis to scientific proof.

If the claims contained in the timewave theory had only attempted to explain the span of human history, perhaps it would be manageable and easier to accept. Instead, the scope of the theory is so encompassing that it either describes events that will reveal the purpose of the universe or it will fail.

The events at the end of the timewave also stretch credulity beyond any reasonable breaking point. By the calculations of McKenna, we are about to be sucked into a whirlpool of novelty from which there will be no return. He hypothesized that this event may be caused by the collision of two universes impacting. This, he suggests, may be happening in such a way that all matter and antimatter will be totally destroyed, leaving just a photonic shell in its place. This could represent the liberation of all beings from the burden of time, as we would emerge from the 2012 event into a new universe composed entirely of light.

What McKenna has done with the timewave is to paint a remarkable picture of the possible, rather than the probable. First published in 1975, the timewave is actually one of the earliest attempts at explaining what might happen in 2012, and it is still one of the most original. The timewave is a pioneering attempt to describe the indescribable and will probably remain a high watermark of the human imagination until it is either proven or disproved in 2012.

## CHAPTER 11

# Surfing the Galactic Superwave

One of the more devastating possibilities regarding 2012 comes from a theory that the galactic alignment the Maya may have been targeting could also be the due date for a major cosmic inundation. Scientists have long known that some galaxies appear to be exploding from the core out. Astrophysicist Paul LaViolette suggests that not only is this much more common than previously thought, but our own galaxy may also be in the middle of this process and a giant galactic superwave may well be about to arrive.

## Galactic Superwave Theory

Astronomers have noted that between one in five and one in seven spiral galaxies appear to be in the process of exploding. The core nuclei of these galaxies can often be seen to glow as brightly as the whole galaxy itself. This can completely mask the features of the spiral arms in telescope images. These violent eruptions are huge in scale and can become more than 100,000 times brighter than our own galactic core. These actively exploding spiral galaxies have been called Seyfert galaxies, after their discoverer, the astronomer Carl Seyfert.

According to LaViolette in his groundbreaking book *Earth Under Fire*, astronomers are now realizing that these explosions are not confined to a particular type of galaxy, but occur in all spiral galaxies on a periodic basis. About 80–85 percent of the time a spiral galaxy will appear quite normal, but in the remaining 10–15 percent they are actively erupting. These explosions radiate out from their galactic cores and, in some cases, can engulf the entire galaxy. The length of the explosions can last from hundreds to several thousands of years.

**FACT**

LaViolette does not agree with scientists who believe there is a giant black hole at the center of the galaxy. He thinks there is a massive and highly dense star that is in the process of matter creation, rather than annihilation. He claims the general relativity equations for a black hole at the galactic center would lead to a breakdown in the structure of space and time.

### No Warning

If one of these galactic superwaves was heading in our direction, we wouldn't even be able to see it. Light takes thousands of years to reach us from the center of the galaxy, so the first we are likely to know about it may be when it arrives. The consequences for our solar system could be far reaching, and for life on Earth, possibly quite dramatic. The superwave would bring with it a huge amount of interstellar matter. This would then be attracted into the gravitational field of the sun and the dust would form a shroud around our star.

To understand how this might affect our star, we can look at the T-Tauri class of star. These have substantial dust clouds around their equatorial planes. The dust cloud causes the T-Tauri stars to behave quite differently than our sun. These stars flare intensely, anywhere from between 100 to 1,000 times the amount our sun does. They also put out a much greater solar wind, luminosity, and ultraviolet radiation than the sun does, although if the dust cloud were absent, the star itself would be of a similar size.

If our sun started to behave like a T-Tauri star, the resulting increase in solar activity would be dramatic. Average temperatures would increase substantially. In addition, the direct effects of the flares themselves could wipe out global communications systems or create effects similar to a massive airborne nuclear explosion. A reasonably sized galactic superwave event could be responsible for triggering a significant extinction cycle. A major superwave event could reduce life on Earth back to a bacterial soup.

## Supernova Triggers

If we can't see the superwave coming, how can we go about finding out if one is likely to arrive? LaViolette suggests that we may be able to detect the motion of a galactic superwave by looking for a pattern in supernova explosions. He theorizes that as the superwave passes, the unstable blue supergiant stars that are prone to this kind of explosion might be triggered by the gravitational tide of the wave. By looking for a pattern in supernova explosions, we might be able to detect the aftereffects of the bow shock front from a passing galactic superwave as it moves through the galactic arm.

By looking at the dates that recent supernova have been observed, LaViolette shows that it is possible that all four supernovae recorded within historical times may have been triggered by the same galactic superwave. Each of these supernovas occurred at a different distance to our planet and was observed on a different date, but by analyzing and comparing these times and distances it is possible to tell if it was likely that they may have been triggered by the same superwave event horizon. The Crab Nebula supernova explosion was recorded by the Chinese in A.D. 1054 and was clearly visible to the naked eye at that time. The remnant of this event is the famous Nebula and is approximately 6,585 light years away. LaViolette calculates that if a superwave triggered this supernova, it would have passed our solar system about 14,000 years ago. The three other significant supernovae of recent times—Cassiopeia A, Tycho, and Vela XYZ—also fit quite closely into this model. All four correspond to a possible galactic superwave trigger that would have passed our solar system about 13,400 years ago.

## Analyzing Supernova Data

This period of 13,400 years quite closely corresponds with the last major mammalian extinction on Earth. It is also very close to one-half of a precessional cycle ago. LaViolette's theory is that galactic superwaves pass us once every precessional cycle. There is also the possibility, he believes, of a 13,000-year recurrence interval. If that proves to be true, it means that a significant superwave event could be imminent. Conventional scientific opinion suggests that superwave events are much less frequent than this, but LaViolette presents some interesting evidence to back up his claim.

## Cosmic Rays and Ice Core Samples

Scientists have developed a technique for estimating the amount of cosmic-ray particle radiation that the planet is exposed to. When cosmic radiation hits Earth's atmosphere, the rays react to create tiny quantities of a rare radioactive isotope called beryllium-10, which then falls to Earth. By taking samples of ice cores at the polar ice caps, scientists are able to see how much beryllium-10 is concentrated in the layers that are formed each year. This can be used to interpret how much exposure there has been to cosmic radiation. There are cosmic-ray peaks that appear around 14,150 years ago; 36,800 years ago; 60,500 years ago; 89,500 years ago; and 103,500 years ago. This pattern corresponds quite closely to the length of the precession of the equinoxes. LaViolette believes that passing galactic superwaves could have created these cosmic-ray influxes and suggests that there is a definite and predictable relationship between the occurrence of superwaves and Earth's precession.

## The Great Flood and Ice Melt

Many stories from around the world recount the tale of a great flood. It appears in the Bible as the story of Noah, and the Maya believe that the last world was destroyed by it. They called the flood Hun Yecil, meaning the "inundation of the trees," as the deluge happened so quickly all the trees were swept away with it. Flood stories are extremely widespread, appearing in the mythologies of more than ninety different cultures on all of the populated continents of the planet.

## Reinterpreting Atlantis

One of the most famous flood stories is probably that of Atlantis. The original story of Atlantis and the flood was told in Plato's *Timaeus* dialogue. LaViolette believes the story is actually an allegory and wasn't intended to be read literally. The clue for this is that Poseidon (Neptune) was given all the seas as his dominion as well as Atlantis, which was his only land territory. LaViolette's theory is that Atlantis wasn't a continent at all but the vast ice sheet that once covered North America. Hence, being water, it was really still part of Poseidon's domain. The myth of Atlantis wasn't intended to be read as the sinking of a continent but as the melting of the ice sheet, which was responsible for the great flood. The timing of the sinking of Atlantis is around 9,600 B.C., which coincides with the climatic warming that occurred at the end of the last Ice Age, known as the Younger Dryas.

According to LaViolette, the Atlantis flood was triggered by the large amount of cosmic dust injected into the solar system by the superwave event that happened 2,000 years previously. This dust altered the sun's radiance, resulting in a substantial change of climate on Earth.

The dialogues also refer to two previous attacks of Atlantis upon Greece, which in LaViolette's interpretation would be two previous floods. These correspond to the glacier wave flooding associated with the superwave that happened 14,000 years ago and the species extinction peak of 12,700 years ago.

LaViolette's view is that the ancient Greeks had encoded a sophisticated astronomical knowledge in these myths. For example, it appears that the cycle of precession is encoded in the Great Year of the Greeks that lasted 26,000 years. It consisted of two epochs, both of which ended in widespread disaster. The great summer or *ekpyrauses* lasted for half the cycle and ended in combustion; the great winter or *kataclysmos* lasted the other half and ended in deluge. LaViolette estimates this deluge phase of the great year corresponds to the point at which precession will have brought the galactic center to its southernmost point. This will occur approximately 270 years from now, so very close to our epoch. The orientation of our planet to the galactic center also means that any galactic superwave that does arrive is likely to cause maximum damage.

## Superluminal Gravitational Waves and the Asian Tsunami

In his 1983 doctoral dissertation, LaViolette suggests that the arrival of a galactic superwave event may be preceded by a gravitational wave. The initial intensity of a galactic nuclei explosion may cause the gravitational wave to actually reach superluminal speeds. This could be as much as sixty-four times the speed of light, giving the wave a head start on the electromagnetic component of the blast. LaViolette has predicted that a superwave impact may be experienced as a gravitational wave impact first, followed by a major gamma-ray burst.

QUESTION

**What is a gravitational wave?**
Gravitational waves are emitted by neutron stars, black holes, and probably the galactic center. They have two important and unique properties: They don't need any type of matter to be propagated and they can pass through any intervening matter without being dissipated. This makes them different from electromagnetic radiation, which may be blocked out by interstellar dust, whereas a gravitational wave will pass through unimpeded.

Remarkably, the massive earthquake that caused the Asian tsunami of 2004 was followed just forty-four hours later by an enormous gamma-ray burst. The magnitude of both of these events was extremely unusual. The earthquake on December 26 measured 9.3 on the Richter scale. That's ten times bigger than any other earthquake in the last twenty-five years. The gamma-ray burst that followed on December 27 was the largest ever recorded by a factor of 100. The outburst was so powerful it released more energy in a tenth of a second than the sun emits in 100,000 years. Both of these events are categorized as Class 1 events. The probability of two such events falling so closely together is in the order of 5,000 to one against. Given this, LaViolette suggests that the Asian tsunami may have been caused by a gravitational wave impact.

**FACT**

The gamma-ray outburst came from a star called SGR 1806-20, located about 10° northeast of the galactic center at about the same distance to the center of the galaxy as our sun, approximately 26,000 light years. The star is just 20 miles wide, but its weight is 150 times the mass of the sun. During its active phase, it was 40 million times brighter than our star.

These two very unusual events happening in close proximity almost exactly fit LaViolette's description of a superwave impact. The gamma-ray burst from SGR 1806-20 was by far the largest ever recorded, but a galactic nucleus explosion could possibly contain more than 100,000 times even this vast amount of energy. The idea that a gravity wave emanating from thousands of light years away may have caused an earthquake and tsunami of the severity of December 26, 2004, is very sobering. This idea shatters the image of our galaxy as a calm and stable place where small incremental changes happen over vast epochs. Change may instead be abrupt, unforeseen, and transformative. It is unfortunate that not one of the three major gravitational wave–detecting telescopes was online at the time of the tsunami, which means that the gravitational wave hypothesis can be neither confirmed nor disproved for this event.

## Geocosmic Cycles and Magnetic Pole Reversal

The possibility that a pole shift will happen in 2012 is a popular idea that will be investigated further. LaViolette's research does point to a link between geocosmic cycles and magnetic field changes. The last really major disruption to Earth's magnetic poles happened around 12,700 years ago, about the same time as the proposed superwave impact. As a result, Earth's north magnetic pole moved to a location in the equatorial mid-Pacific for between ten and fifty years. This event was called the Gothenberg magnetic flip after the city it was discovered in. During this period, Earth's magnetic field fluctuated massively in step with the eleven-year sunspot cycle. This happens to a much smaller extent in a typical sunspot cycle, but during this period the peaks were hundreds of times more intense, approaching the levels found in T-Tauri stars.

**ESSENTIAL**

The last complete magnetic pole reversals are thought to have happened approximately 20,000 and 100,000 years ago. They have happened many times before; in one case the magnetic poles were reversed for hundreds of thousands of years between 2.4 million and 730,000 years ago.

For Earth's magnetic poles to fluctuate in this way, the whole of the planet's magnetic field must be overwhelmed by an enormously powerful outside source. A superwave may provide a suitable catalyst for this kind of extreme reaction from the sun. A pole reversal would require a solar flare many hundreds of times larger than the biggest ones recorded in modern times. Larger galactic superwaves may cause complete field reversals, where the magnetic pole actually flips 180 degrees and then stabilizes for some period of time in this position.

# Precession, 2012, and Superwaves

It seems remarkable that both Jenkins's galactic alignment theory and LaViolette's galactic superwave theory both relate to the precession of the equinoxes. Can this really be a coincidence? Or is the galactic alignment of 2012 actually pointing to an incoming superwave? A large superwave event may well fulfill some of the more apocalyptic prophecies relating to 2012.

LaViolette has an explanation for why superwaves and precession seem to go hand in hand. The sixteenth-century astronomer Nicolaus Copernicus was the first to theorize that the gravitational influences of the sun and the moon on Earth combine to cause Earth to wobble slightly on its axis. This wobble then appears to transcribe a very long circular path in the sky that we call the precession of the equinoxes. LaViolette's alternate view is that galactic superwaves themselves may play the most important role in determining the period of Earth's precession.

He suggests that a superwave might produce a very strong gravity potential wave that could entrain Earth. The result for the planet would be a tidal pull that would pull it toward or away from the galactic center, setting up the 25,771-year cycle. These forces would be greatest when Earth's poles are pointed closest to the direction of galactic center. This idea would also explain why the periods that LaViolette associates with possible superwave impacts accord so well with those of precession. It would also explain why the conjunction with the galactic center is of such importance.

## Critique of LaViolette's Theory

This would neatly tie up the relationship between the end of the Mayan calendar, the galactic alignment, and its association with catastrophe. However, the traditional theory has not been disproved and there are some other new ideas about what might be causing precession that also need to be examined before jumping to a conclusion. These will be examined in the next chapter. It is also possible that a galactic superwave event may not be as damaging as LaViolette thinks. Small events of a similar type seem to happen about every 500 years and don't tend to trigger major cycles of climatic change. However, the possibility of a more major gravitational wave impact is significant enough that it would be wise not to discount it.

## Facing the Odds

At the moment, our galactic core is relatively quiet, but the gamma-ray burst and tsunami of 2004 may be cosmic warning signs that a really big event is on its way. LaViolette is not predicting that a superwave will definitely arrive in 2012, but he considers it possible that the end of the Mayan calendar does foretell this. He certainly thinks that one will arrive sooner or later, probably sooner.

His current estimate is that there is a 90 percent chance of a superwave event in the next four centuries. He thinks we should prepare for this and that in the great scheme of galactic evolution, intelligent species evolving on other planets have almost certainly had to face such a challenge. The year 2012 may be, from this perspective, a cue for us to evolve the ability to reach beyond our solar system as quickly as possible in order to find other civilizations that have successfully surfed one of the really big galactic superwaves.

In support of galactic superwave theory, LaViolette points to an impressive fifteen predictions made by the theory that have subsequently been verified. However, widespread acceptance by the scientific community has not been forthcoming. This lack of enthusiasm may be a result of his wide-ranging multidisciplinary approach, especially regarding his interpretation of the Atlantis myths. For mainstream science, any mention of the mythical continent is still very much taboo. Despite this, *Earth Under Fire* remains essential reading for anyone seriously interested in 2012 and the geocosmic cycles that we are all subject to as residents of this planet.

## CHAPTER 12

# Plasma Changes in the Solar System

The increasing amount of plasma that has been entering our solar system over the last couple of decades has been receiving a lot of attention in the run up to 2012. A Russian team of scientists, headed by the planet physicist Dr. Alexey Dmitriev, has been following this phenomenon. Their research suggests that this influx of plasma may be responsible for some of the recent dramatic climate changes.

# The Role of Plasma in Recent Solar System Changes

A team from the Siberian Russian Academy of Sciences has been investigating changes in the heliosphere, the electromagnetic envelope that surrounds our solar system. The heliosphere acts like a giant protective sheath surrounding our sun and the entire solar system as we travel through space. Normally, it functions as a giant deflector, protecting us from a potentially harmful influx of cosmic radiation and keeping conditions within the inner solar system relatively stable. However, it is now being bombarded with so much radiation that an unprecedented amount is breaking through. This is reaching our sun and all of the planets of the solar system, including our own.

**QUESTION**

**What is a plasma?**
A plasma is a partially ionized gas and is sometimes called the fourth state of matter. The behavior of plasma is quite unlike those of solids, liquids, and gases. In nature, plasmas are usually found in gas-like clouds, as in the case of interstellar nebulae. Other examples of plasmas include ball lightning and the phenomenon of the aurora borealis.

The increase in incoming interstellar plasma, Dmitriev suggests, is dramatically impacting the behavior of our sun and its solar system. "Strong evidence exists that these transformations are being caused by highly charged material (in) interstellar space which have broken into the interplanetary area of our solar system," Dmitriev wrote in 1997.

## Changes in Interstellar Space

For much of the twentieth century, space was visualized as a near vacuum. The astronomical reality, it is now being discovered, is actually quite different. Our solar system moves through something called the local interstellar space medium (LISM).

The LISM is not uniformly empty at all, but has greater and lesser amounts of plasmic flux density created by the presence of highly charged particles. The amount of energy within empty interstellar space is actually highly variable. Scientists are now coming to realize that space has more in common with our terrestrial oceans, with their complex tides and currents, than was previously recognized.

The quantity of plasma we encounter in the LISM is a critical variable for what happens in the wider behavior of our solar system. This increased influx of energy is, according to the research of the Russian Academy of Sciences, the fundamental cause of the multiple magnetic and climatic changes that have recently been observed in the sun and across all of the planets. Dmitriev even goes as far as to say the consequence of the increase in this interstellar plasmic energy is far more important, in his opinion, than human greenhouse gas emissions are in the creation of our planet's current global warming crisis.

## Changes in the Heliosphere

The heliosphere itself has exhibited a dramatic change in behavior over the last ten years. The transition through this increased plasma flux has expanded the heliosphere's bow shock wave in front of the solar system more than ten-fold. Dmitriev gives an extensive catalogue of changes he claims this has caused within the solar system.

### RECENT PLANETARY CHANGES

- Significant physical, chemical, and optical changes observed on Venus; an inversion of dark and light spots detected for the first time and a sharp decrease of sulfur-containing gases in its atmosphere
- The first stages of atmosphere generation on the moon, where a growing sodium-based atmosphere that reaches 5,500 miles in height has been detected
- Changes in the atmosphere of Mars, including a cloudy growth in the equatorial region and unusual growth in ozone concentration
- Significant melting of the Martian polar ice caps
- A doubling of the magnetic field intensity on Jupiter after the series of impacts from the fragments of the Shoemaker-Levy comet in 1994; also, the appearance of large auroral anomalies, excessive plasma generation, and radiation belt brightening
- The creation of an ionic flux tube between Jupiter and the volcanic regions of its moon, Io. This stream of plasma is millions of miles in

length and is 1 million amperes in strength. It is affecting Jupiter's magnetic field and intensifying its plasma genesis.

- Reporting of auroras and a visible increase in brightness on Saturn
- Abrupt large-scale growth of magnetosphere intensity and an increase in brightness on Uranus
- A change in light intensity and light-spot dynamics on Neptune
- A growth of dark spots on Pluto

**ESSENTIAL**

Dmitriev notes that Uranus and Neptune, which are magnetically conjugate planets, have both undergone major magnetic pole shifts of more than fifty degrees each in the last decade. Earth is magnetically conjugate to Jupiter, so he theorizes that the dramatic changes on Jupiter could well have consequences for our planet.

The claim of a direct causal link between the increase in plasma entering the solar system and recent planetary changes is still very controversial, but Dmitriev's research is quite comprehensive and is backed up with extensive scientific references. It seems likely that the increase in this cosmic energy does have some role to play in influencing climate, but it may be one of many contributing factors, rather than a sole cause. Dmitriev himself points out that planetary changes are complex affairs with many interdependent factors. It is the total sum of all these influences that actually determines what happens.

## Changes to the Sun

There have also been some recent dramatic changes to the sun. The Ulysses spacecraft sent by NASA to measure the magnetic field of the sun found the magnetic fields of the poles enormously diminished. The magnetic poles of the sun usually reverse at the end of an eleven-year sunspot cycle. At the end of the most recent cycle, the poles only moved to the sun's equator and did not completely invert. This behavior alters everything that was previously believed about the sun's magnetic field. Effectively, the sun no longer has a single north or south magnetic pole; instead, it has four poles located in the equatorial regions.

## X-Ray Flares

After the peak of the last eleven-year sunspot cycle in 1999, the sun has had a number of extremely large x-ray flare events. One of these, on April 2, 2001, was so large that it went off the scale completely. The previous scale ran to X-20 as the highest category, but this solar flare had to be categorized as an X-22 event. The x-ray burst was not in the direction of Earth, but a much smaller x-ray flare in 1989 was responsible for knocking out the whole Canadian power grid. If the X-22 event had hit Earth, possible consequences could have included major power outages, interruption of the Internet, damage to telecommunications and GPS satellites, and even the wiping of computer hard drives. The most powerful flare observed since then happened on November 4, 2003. It lasted eleven minutes and produced an x-ray flux of at least X-28, although some reports suggest it was much larger even than that.

**ESSENTIAL**

The data gathered by the Ulysses spacecraft showed that the sun's magnetic field interacts with the rest of the solar system in a much more complex fashion than previously believed. NASA scientists determined that the polar magnetic field is much weaker than previously observed and the amount of cosmic dust entering the solar system is thirty times more than expected.

## The Carrington Event

These recent events, though very significant, are not actually the largest solar flares ever recorded. That honor goes to a flare that happened on September 1, 1859. This has become known as the Carrington event after Richard Carrington, the young English astronomer who saw the event as it happened from his private observatory.

It was a remarkable piece of luck that he happened to be observing the sun at the particular moment that the flare erupted, because the event lasted for less than five minutes. In that time, a huge knot of sunspots appeared and generated a plume that was by far the biggest observed in the 160 years records have been kept.

Before dawn on the following day, a huge firework display of auroral lights bathed Earth, reaching as far south as the Caribbean. The rainbow-hued lights were so brilliant that it was said to be possible to read by them as if it were daylight. The Carrington event also caused major disruption to the telegraph system worldwide.

Conventional astronomy suggests that a flare of this size may only happen once every 500 years or so, but even greater flares have been observed on other stars. Some of these stellar megaflares have emitted quantities of radiation that would be likely to cause major loss of life on Earth.

# The Maunder Minimum

Sunspot activity has been broadly increasing since the Maunder minimum period from 1645 to 1715, when there were very few sunspots. At a typical peak of the sunspot cycle, there may be as many as 1,000 spots a year, but during the Maunder minimum the number of spots dropped as low as one or two a year for a thirty-year period. This was also the peak of what has been called the Little Ice Age. This was a period of approximately 400 years, from the fifteenth to the nineteenth centuries, when the drop in temperature was so great that the winter mortality rate in Europe increased dramatically. In London, the river Thames froze over completely every winter. The edge of the Atlantic ice pack moved southward during the Maunder minimum and glaciers started expanding.

## Sunspot Cycles

The general increase in the sun's activity has been consistent for more than 100 years, but it seems to have reached a peak in sunspot cycle 22 from 1986 to 1996. Sunspot cycle 23 began in 1996 and ended in 2008. The cycle was six months late and weaker than normal.

Cycle 24 was due to start in March 2008, but it is more than a year late already. As of July 2009, the first significant sunspot system has finally emerged. This is the longest period that the sun has been spotless for more than 100 years. Considering the maximum of this cycle is due in 2012, this might seem to suggest that the peak of the cycle may again be less than the recent average. Yet, generally this cycle is still predicted to be 30–40 percent more intense than the last one, although NASA has recently downgraded its projections for cycle 24 on the basis of the slow start to the cycle. The official prediction of the NOAA Space Weather Prediction Center is a peak of ninety sunspots in August 2012. There are also some predictions that delay in the cycle may cause the sun to suddenly burst into violent activity with another series of x-ray megaflares in the X-20+ range, or even cause another Carrington event.

**FACT**

The Maunder minimum was named after the astronomer Edward Maunder, who measured and photographed sunspots at the Greenwich Royal Observatory. It was his studies of this unusual period in history that led to his discovery of the important eleven-year sunspot cycle.

NASA's THEMIS satellite found that a 4,000-mile-thick layer of solar particles has gathered and is rapidly growing within the outermost part of the magnetosphere, a protective bubble created by Earth's magnetic field. This is causing a breach in the planet's magnetic defenses. This gap in the magnetosphere is more than four times the size of the Earth itself. This is not a problem at solar minimum, but at peak solar activity it could allow up to twenty times more plasma to impact Earth, making some of the worst solar storms in decades possible.

## Solar Shutdown

The sharp downturn in the sunspot cycle may mark the point where solar activity significantly decreases as the sun enters the beginning of another minimum period. The result of this would be dramatic cooling; in some ways, it could have worse consequences than global warming. The lack of activity in solar cycle 24 has prompted concerns about this.

This shift in global temperature could have a substantial impact on the agricultural belts of Europe, North America, and Russia, which are responsible for a substantial part of the world's current food supply These are vulnerable to a downward temperature change of more than a few degrees.

Greater decreases in temperature are certainly possible if the sunspot cycle fails to gain momentum.

For Europe, the possible collapse of the Gulf Stream and its underwater equivalent, the Atlantic warm convector, could signal a massive change in climate. The warming these currents provide prevents European countries from being as cold as those on the equivalent latitudes in North America. Without them, some of the most populated parts of the European continent would be under Arctic conditions.

# Cosmic Rays and Climate Change

Dmitriev is not the only scientist who thinks this influx of cosmic rays has a major part to play in the recent increases in global temperature. Henrik Svensmark is the head of Center for Sun-Climate Research at the Danish Space Research Institute. In his book *The Chilling Stars: A New Theory of Climate Change*, he suggests that when cosmic radiation, especially protons, hit Earth's atmosphere, the reaction they cause has the effect of creating clouds. The more cosmic rays there are the greater the cloud cover.

A shutdown in solar activity and a decrease in the magnetic field of the sun leave our planet more open to the influx of plasmic energy from outside the solar system. This then leads to an increase in cloud cover and the kind of climate change we are now seeing. Svensmark predicts we could be about to enter a new Maunder minimum–like period and that global temperatures are about to rapidly cool.

Dr. Nir Shaviv, an astrophysicist, also thinks cosmic rays affect our planet's climate. By reconstructing the temperature on Earth over the past 500 million years, Shaviv thinks he has found that changes in the amount of cosmic rays are responsible for more than two-thirds of Earth's temperature changes, making it the most important driver of climate change over long periods of time.

Shaviv hypothesizes that the sun's passage through the spiral arms of the Milky Way appears to have been the cause behind the major Ice Ages over the past billion years. He has correlated variations in the cosmic-ray flux to the solar system's orbit around the center of the galaxy and through its spiral arms. In the more crowded spiral arms, like the Orion arm, which our Sun is currently in, there is a higher density of cosmic rays. Shaviv agrees with Svensmark that the result of this increase is that Earth becomes cooler.

Both Svensmark and Shaviv are considered climate skeptics who dispute the extent to which the creation of greenhouse gases is contributing to the current climate change. The year 2012 is significant in the context of research into cosmic rays because:

- It coincides with the next predicted solar sunspot maximum, and recently discovered breaches in Earth's magnetosphere make us more vulnerable to solar-flare events.
- The effects of increased cosmic dust and radiation entering the solar system will be likely to accelerate by 2012.

According to these scientists, whether the planet cools or heats up depends on the balance of solar activity and cosmic radiation.

**FACT**

The study of meteorites that have hit Earth during its passage through the arms of the Milky Way have shown up to 10 percent more cosmic-ray damage than those that sustained damage elsewhere. Shaviv believes that kind of cosmic-ray variation could alter global temperatures by as much as 15 percent. This would be sufficient to turn the Ice Ages on or off.

It is not necessary to agree with their views on climate change to share their conclusion that an increase of cosmic radiation may cause significant changes. Svensmark points out that it is actually well established and uncontroversial that solar activity has a direct influence on the eleven-year variation of stratospheric pressure levels found in the upper atmosphere. The electromagnetic fields of our planet are highly sensitive and respond to a range of influences from solar wind to tropical storms. A ten-fold increase in cosmic radiation is likely to affect these fields and the upper and lower atmosphere of the planet in ways that may be unpredictable. The debate is to what extent and how these changes will manifest.

## CHAPTER 13

# Earth Changes and the Pole Shift

In the approach to 2012, Earth is undergoing a variety of major geophysical changes unprecedented in scale and effect. The causes of some of these appear to be manmade, but others appear to be responses to changes in the behavior of the sun and an increase in cosmic radiation. There is widespread speculation linking these events with a planetary catastrophe in 2012, possibly a reversal of Earth's poles.

# Earth Changes

The fact that Earth's climate is in a state of rapid change is now well established. Climate change is a notoriously difficult area in which to make accurate predictions. One of the major problems is that science has become very specialized, which makes assessing all the different factors that act on a system as large as a planet challenging. While the unusually high concentration of carbon dioxide in the atmosphere is certainly having some effect on climate, the influence of solar activity and cosmic rays on global temperature may be equally, if not more, important. If the sun's behavior changes, Earth's climate is likely to respond. Assessing these trends and the balance of probabilities is a matter of fierce debate.

Other important changes are also happening. There appears to be an increase in the number and severity of extreme weather events such as tropical storms, flash flooding, droughts, and tornadoes. There is also evidence that major geophysical events like earthquakes and volcanic activity appear to be increasing substantially. For instance:

- In the last fifty years, the number of tornadoes has doubled and there has been a dramatic increase in the geographical area in which tornadoes are found.
- The number of recorded earthquakes in the last century has increased by 500 percent and measurements of volcanic activity are up by at least 200 percent. This may be at least partly due to the increase in the number of seismic and volcanic detectors around the world. The spread of humans into what were once remote parts of the world may also be a factor. (Reference: Micheal Mandeville *www.earthchangesbulletin.com*)

## Increase in Plasma

The increase in plasma entering our solar system affects our planet in a variety of ways. The incoming plasma is magnetized to the poles of the earth and concentrates in these regions, creating the effect of the polar auroras. The radiation belts around the planet and Earth's magnetic field are also affected. Scientists from the Russian Academy of Sciences are predicting wide-ranging and various changes for our planet. The direct effects of increasing cosmic rays include:

- Increased plasma generation in the ionosphere
- Increased magnetic storms in the magnetosphere
- Increased number of cyclones in the atmosphere

**FACT**

K. M. Hiremath, from the Indian Institute of Astrophysics in Bangalore, has studied variations in the Asian monsoons and concluded that there is a causal connection between solar activity, incoming cosmic rays, and rainfall. He has also found a significant connection with the cycles of El Niño.

# The Magnetic Pole Shift

Dmitriev's point of view on the pole shift is that it is already happening. In fact, he believes that the shift actually began in 1885. In the last 100 years, Earth's magnetic south pole has traveled almost 560 miles toward, and into, the Indian Ocean. The magnetic north pole has moved more than 170 miles between 1973 and 1994 in the direction of Siberia via the Arctic Ocean. The rate of the magnetic pole's movement has also increased in the last century compared with fairly steady movement in the previous four centuries.

**FACT**

Earth's magnetic field is not uniform and is becoming less so. There are a number of areas called world magnetic anomalies that generate a substantial magnetic field independently of the two poles. The four most significant ones are in Canada, Siberia, Antarctica, and Brazil. These anomalies have recently undergone significant growth.

Oregon State University researchers investigating the sediment record from Arctic lakes have been able to use carbon dating to track changes in the magnetic field. They found that the north magnetic pole has shifted significantly in the last 1,000 years. It generally migrated between northern Canada and Siberia, but has occasionally moved in other directions. The causes of these magnetic changes are related to changes in behavior of the electrical flow in the iron at the core of the planet. This, in turn, is influenced by incoming plasma at the poles of Earth.

Dmitriev thinks the movement in the magnetic poles and the growth in magnetic anomalies indicate something very dramatic is going on in the core of our planet. The scale of these changes indicates something beyond even the magnitude of the Gothenburg magnetic flip event that happened around 12,700 years ago, when the magnetic poles migrated to near the equator. He believes the signs suggest a complete magnetic pole reversal is already underway.

**ESSENTIAL**

Earth's magnetic field has decreased by around 10–15 percent in strength since it was measured by Carl Friedrich Gauss in 1835. Fluctuations in the magnetic field are cyclical, and a downward trend has been observed for around the last 4,000 years. Most scientists believe this trend could just as easily reverse.

Dmitriev estimates the speed of this process will increase to around 125 miles or more a year in the near future, and that we should prepare for the consequences of this in a globally coordinated way. The appropriate response, he says, should be to draw up a "global, ecology-oriented, climate map which might reveal (the location of) these global catastrophes."

# The Impact of Technological Civilization on the Biosphere

One of the most important and unpredictable variables in the process of rapid magnetic change that Dmitriev reports is the effect our industrial and technological civilization is having on our planet. The extent of human impact on the biosphere is now so great that we are impacting the electromagnetic skeleton of the planet. More than 30 percent of disturbances in the magnetosphere are now caused by electricity production, transmission, or consumption.

For example, the Van Allen radiation belts over the eastern United States have moved inward from more than 200 miles above the surface of the planet to slightly more than 6 miles. This is caused by the massive amount of energy being transmitted between the power stations around the Great Lakes to the eastern seaboard. The transmission route runs along one of Earth's magnetic meridians, and the frequency of electricity transmission in the United States is at 60Hz, which is resonant with the ionosphere.

**QUESTION**

**What are the Van Allen radiation belts?**
These are two belts of plasma surrounding Earth that are held in place by the planet's magnetic field. The inner belt extends 200–6,000 miles from Earth's surface and has a high concentration of protons. The outer belt extends 12,000–26,000 miles and is made of electrons.

This is just one of the many ways in which we are changing our electromagnetic environment, potentially with unforeseen consequences. This may well dramatically complicate the changes that already appear to be happening as a result of the extra-solar energy shift. Dmitriev regards these events as irreversible and fundamental. Possible outcomes, he predicts, may include a major reorganization of life on Earth. He concludes that the combination of the manmade technological impact on the planet and the increase of plasma saturation coming into the solar system mean we are entering a period of rapid and unstoppable geophysical change.

# Changes in the Magnetic Field Affecting Nature

Some species and habitats are more sensitive than others to the effects of these changes. Unfortunately, some of those animals and insects that may be most severely affected occupy key ecological niches in the world's ecosystem.

## Bees

The rapid decline in bee population, known as colony collapse disorder (CCD), may be a symptom of the change in the earth's magnetic polarity. While some scientists believe that bees find their hives by following polarized lines of light in the sky, research at National Tsing Hua University of Taiwan into magnetic reception in bees has shown the presence of magnetite. This suggests they have magnetic homing senses.

Changes in Earth's magnetic field and the influence of manmade electromagnetic pollution are possible causes of the dramatic bee decline. A survey commissioned by the Apiary Inspectors of America found losses of more than 30 percent in the bee population from CCD. Some scientists estimate that life on Earth is so dependent on bee pollination that the current human population would be unable to feed itself just eight years after the collapse of the bee colonies.

## Whales

Whales may also have a biomagnetic sense, which allows them to navigate by sensing Earth's magnetic fields. Whales following magnetic field lines could beach themselves in areas where the field lines intersect with the coast.

A study in the United Kingdom by Margaret Klinowska found a correlation between local magnetic field lines and sites where whales were stranded on shore. The biomagnetic theory may also explain why there are multiple-species strandings. The use of underwater sonar has also been implicated in whale beachings.

## Frogs

The weakened magnetosphere allows more ultraviolet light to penetrate through the atmosphere to the surface. Frogs and other moist-skinned amphibians are among the species most sensitive to these increases in ultraviolet radiation. There has been a recent sharp decline in frog and other amphibian populations in both tropical and temperate climates.

## Humans

*New Scientist* magazine has reported research showing how human behavior is influenced by changes in Earth's magnetic field. Oleg Shumilov of the Institute of North Industrial Ecology Problems in Russia looked at activity in Earth's geomagnetic field from 1948 to 1997 and found that it grouped into three seasonal peaks every year: one from March to May, another in July, and the last in October. He also found that geomagnetism peaks matched up with peaks in the number of emotional disorders such as depression, anxiety, mood swings, and even suicides in the northern Russian city of Kirovsk.

## Responding to the Electromagnetic Crisis

If the rapid increase in manmade electromagnetic emissions is left unchecked, it seems likely there will be an increase in consequences for human health and the health of the biosphere. The combination of a number of other geophysical effects converging in 2012 may mean that this impact is compounded. These effects include:

- Weakened magnetosphere
- Solar maximum due in 2012
- Increase in interstellar plasma and cosmic rays
- Movement of the magnetic poles

One possible scenario is that at the solar maximum around 2012, a massive solar eruption on the scale of the Carrington event could pass through the weakened magnetosphere of Earth. This could massively impact our global communications systems and computer networks and dramatically accelerate the changing motion of the magnetic poles. If the magnetic flux of the flare event is of sufficient magnitude to overwhelm the ring main of Earth's magnetic field, it could theoretically produce a rapid magnetic pole shift.

The sun's recent behavior does suggest that major solar eruptions are quite likely at the next solar maximum. The Carrington event megaflare happened at the end of the 300-year-long solar shutdown of the Maunder minimum period. This was followed by more than 100 years of increased solar activity on the sun. During this period, the strength of the sun's magnetic field more than doubled. The recent decline in the sun's polar magnetic field may mark the end of that warm period.

It may be that during the shift to a colder period, the sun's behavior goes into oscillation between less and much greater activity, increasing the likelihood of megaflare events. It is also possible that a Carrington event megaflare could signal the beginning, as well as the previous ending, of one of these periods of much decreased solar activity and colder temperatures on Earth. The flare that caused the shutdown of the Canadian power grid in 1989 was rated as an X-20 event; a Carrington event flare could be more than twenty times that size. Additionally, the substantial hole in the Earth's magnetosphere detected by NASA's THEMIS probe means that our planet is much more vulnerable to incoming solar radiation than was previously realized.

# Electromagnetic Disruption

In the event of a really large solar event, not only might our electromagnetic infrastructure be damaged, but the resulting impact on the biosphere may require us to act to stabilize the electromagnetic field of the planet. This may require turning off sources of electromagnetic disruption that are currently considered essential services.

Some of the major industrial sources of electromagnetic pollution include:

- Electricity power grids
- Mobile phone networks
- Satellite communications networks
- ELF communication systems
- Radar
- Microwave networks like WiFi and CCTV monitoring systems
- Auroral research projects like HAARP

## Power Lines

Power lines lose energy in the process of transmission. Where power lines are very long, they can lose as much as 40 percent of the total energy transmitted. This electromagnetic energy leaking out into the atmosphere has a very pronounced effect on the ionosphere and can cause it to warp and bend. Many major power lines transport currents in the range of 750 megavolts and some carry up to 1,500 megavolts. Extremely low frequency

(ELF) waves from power lines are probably the biggest source of manmade electromagnetic radiation into Earth's atmosphere. ELF pollution has been doubling every decade for the last thirty years, and the average intensity of the manmade ELF magnetic fields is now more than ten times stronger than the natural planetary and cosmic background. Other significant contributors to ELF pollution include radar stations and hydroelectric power plants.

## Electromagnetic Warfare

The electromagnetic spectrum has been used in the past for more than energy transmission and communication. On July 4, 1976, a radio mast in Kiev started emitting a complex harmonic ELF signal based around 11Hz that spread across the world. This powerful signal upset radio communications everywhere and was named the Russian woodpecker after the buzz-saw sound it made. The intention behind this was to deliberately broadcast frequencies that were damaging to human health and mental well-being. These transmissions ended after the fall of the Soviet Union, but they illustrate how much influence ELF signals can have. ELF waves will penetrate anything and everything, which is why ELF transmissions are used for submarine communication.

## HAARP and Disruption of the Ionosphere

The highly controversial High-Frequency Active Auroral Research Program (HAARP) is the most versatile and largest radio-frequency radiation transmitter in the world. The HAARP Ionospheric Research facility based in Alaska is a high-power transmitter and antenna array operating in the high-frequency (HF) range. The transmitter is capable of delivering up to 3.6 million watts to an antenna system consisting of 180 antennas arranged as a rectangular array.

HAARP's research focuses on plasmas and the relationship between the sun's energy and events on Earth. There have been some claims that HAARP could perform significant weather-control experiments. Radio operators monitoring HAARP transmissions noticed a correlation between RF output from the station and the growth of hurricanes Katrina and Rita into dangerous storms in 2005. This may be coincidental, but the ionosphere is delicate. High-energy physicist Dr. Elizabeth Rauscher has predicted that if a big enough hole is punched through it, it could pop.

A major breach in the planet's ionosphere, on top of its already weakened magnetosphere, could change the effect of a major solar event from severe to potentially disastrous. The ionosphere is part of a complex system responsible for stabilizing the planet's atmosphere. The hole in the ozone layer, which has been caused by the human production of chlorofluorocarbons (CFCs), is an example of the kind of negative impact human activity can unexpectedly have on the sensitive upper atmosphere.

Even radical action to reduce the electromagnetic impact of humans may not stabilize a magnetic pole shift already in progress. Failure to take action, however, may accelerate the rate of change, which may prove seriously undesirable. A final possibility is that manmade electromagnetic tinkering with Earth's magnetic field may actually induce or catalyze such an event.

## Magnetic Versus Physical Pole Shift

In a physical pole inversion of the planet, the planet actually rolls over on its axis. A physical pole shift would likely be catastrophic for the global ecology. One probable consequence would be major crustal displacement, as the flip causes tectonic plates and continents to collide with each other.

Patrick Geryl, author of *How to Survive 2012,* strongly believes a complete magnetic pole reversal will inevitably trigger a disastrous physical pole shift, simply because Earth's core is iron and therefore will respond to the new polarity. This is an overly simplistic view that is not supported by scientific or historical evidence.

There is no evidence that this has happened during previous magnetic pole shifts and nothing to indicate why it should happen this time. An event like this has happened once before in the geological record, but not for many hundreds of millions of years. His belief that a pole shift is certain in 2012 has led Geryl to conclude that the only reasonably safe places to be in such an event will be in special unsinkable ships or deep underground, high up in a major mountain range. Even then, survival is not guaranteed.

Geryl believes Earth reversing its direction of spin will initiate the pole shift. This idea comes from Greg Braden's book *Awakening to Zero Point,* in which he examines a scenario where Earth's rotation actually slows, momentarily stops, and then reverses in the opposite direction. This theory would require an unknown force to negate Earth's spin, slow it to a halt without tearing the crust of Earth from its mantle, and then reverse the force so that Earth spins in the opposite direction. The forces responsible for the miniscule slowing Earth is already undergoing would in no way be adequate to do this, nor would any other known force in our solar system.

## The Schumann Frequency

Another idea put forward in Braden's *Awakening to Zero Point* is that the fundamental frequency of the earth is shifting upward. This change in planetary vibration is said to be responsible for creating the current Earth changes. The frequency Braden is talking about is called the primary Schumann resonance. This is a function of the amount of time it takes for electromagnetic waves to travel around the planet. It is calculated by dividing the speed of light by the circumference of Earth.

**ALERT**

The kind of massive tsunami in the movie *2012* would probably only be induced by a physical pole shift rather than a magnetic one. An event of this magnitude could possibly trigger a wave of water a mile and a half high that could circumnavigate the globe. Very little of human civilization would be likely to survive.

The primary Schumann frequency is 7.8Hz, and varies slightly with changes in the ionosphere. Neither the speed of light nor the circumference of Earth is changing, so the primary Schumann resonance is not going to fundamentally alter either.

Despite the scientific inaccuracy, Braden should be given credit for articulating ideas whose popularity seem to come from their resonance with many peoples' intuitive perceptions of the changes happening on our planet. The vibrations of our planet are changing, but in a much more complex way unrelated to the Schumann frequency.

The notion of Earth reversing its direction of spin mirrors in some ways the much more subtle change of polarity represented by the winter solstice meridian crossing the galactic equator. The science may be wrong, but the notions of a pole shift and an ascending planet tap into the popular psyche in a powerful way. Better science can reveal much more and help us get a clearer view, but the value of new ideas and speculations like these is that they get people to ask important questions.

The mechanism of a magnetic pole reversal is not well understood and the consequences are difficult to quantify, but they are likely to be some significant ones, including major climatic disruption.

- Some scientists think that the poles can spontaneously migrate from one orientation to the other over the course of a few decades to a few thousand years.
- Others think the geodynamo at the earth's core first turns itself off spontaneously and then restarts itself with the magnetic north pole pointing either north or south.
- External events such as an asteroid impact are not thought to cause magnetic field reversals. The ages of impact craters do not line up with the timing of previous reversals.
- The mainstream scientific opinion is that the current wandering of the magnetic poles does not foretell a magnetic pole shift and no such event is likely in our immediate future.

The historical record shows, however, that magnetic pole shifts are quite frequent events over a geological time scale and it is inevitable that one will happen sooner or later. This could be as long as a few thousand years away but it will certainly happen at some point, as it has happened many times before. In the last 25 million years, the poles have inverted once every 250,000 years, on average. In the last million years, the inversions have happened closer to once every 125,000 years. Estimates for the amount of time a magnetic field reversal would take to complete vary widely, from 5,000 years to a couple of months.

## Magnetic Field Drops to Zero

As the magnetic field inverts, the strength of the magnetosphere would likely drop to zero. This would mean our main planetary defense against incoming cosmic radiation would be removed. There is a theory that these periods of magnetic cancellation are responsible for jumps in evolution because the massive increase in cosmic radiation triggers genetic mutations.

An extended period of magnetic cancellation and increased exposure to the solar wind could also result in major disruption to life and possible species extinction. In some ways, a rapid pole reversal may be more desirable than a slower one. At least a functioning magnetosphere provides protection from the solar wind.

## The Chandler Wobble

A good indicator of the possibility of changes in the physical poles of Earth is an effect called the Chandler wobble. This is the change in the spin of the earth on its axis. It's named after Seth Carlo Chandler, an American astronomer who first discovered the wobble back in 1891 after thirty years of observations. The effect causes Earth's physical poles to move in an irregular circle. This wobble has a seven-year cycle. The wobble:

- Produces a very small ocean tide, the pole tide, which is the only tide not caused by bodies outside Earth
- Has varied in amplitude since its discovery, reaching its largest size in 1910 and fluctuating noticeably from one decade to another
- Is caused by fluctuating pressure on the bottom of the ocean, caused by temperature and salinity changes and wind-driven changes in the circulation of the oceans, according to the Jet Propulsion Laboratory

Independent researcher Micheal Mandeville of *www.earthchangesbulletin.com* has been exhaustively analyzing trends in seismic and volcanic activity from around the world. Using a very detailed statistical analysis, Mandeville claims to have found correlations between the position and motion of the pole with increases and decreases in earthquakes and volcanic eruptions. These correlations are sufficiently consistent, he claims, to conclude that the Chandler wobble stresses Earth's crust, which in turn creates a cycle of earthquakes and volcanic activity.

## The Anomaly of the Wobble

For a six-week period beginning in November 2005, there was no discernable wobble motion in Earth. The track of the spin axis began to slow down, and by about January 8, 2006, it ceased nearly all relative motion. Mandeville suggests that the anomaly in Earth's wobble could be a response to the massive earthquake and the devastating tsunami of December 26, 2004.

After an initial earthquake that measured 9.3 on the Richter scale, a cluster of several thousand earthquakes followed, including dozens of earthquakes greater than 6.0 in magnitude and at least three above 7.0. This caused substantial uplifting, down-warping, and lateral movement in the two tectonic plates that could have ruptured their mutual junction.

The scale of this tectonic activity is by far the greatest on the planet in the last twenty years. Mandeville theorizes this could have caused warping that pushed the Indian continental plate deep enough down into the liquid mantle of Earth to cause a measurable drag on the spin of the equator.

Another contributing factor to this anomaly may be the shifting location of the magnetic north pole, which is currently migrating toward the north spin axis of the wobble. During the past eighty years, for unknown reasons, this rate of drift has been accelerating. The change of the wobble and the drifting of the pole may be seen as symptoms of the early stages of a pole reversal. However, neither of these events necessarily means a complete inversion is imminent or likely.

## Alternate Theories

An extended wandering of the poles, also known as a geomagnetic excursion, remains more likely than a complete reversal. The most compelling evidence that a complete pole reversal may be about to occur comes from Dmitriev's theory that incoming interstellar plasma is responsible for current planetophysical changes. The poles of both Uranus and Neptune have had polar shifts of at least fifty degrees within the last decade. If this is due to the influx of interstellar plasma into our solar system as Dmitriev believes, our own planet is being subjected to these same conditions.

It is not necessary to insist that a pole shift must be about to occur in 2012 to conclude that Earth is entering a period of major geophysical change.

There are many contributing factors to this, including increasing cosmic radiation, climate change, and the technological impact of humanity.

On the other hand, the combination of the weakening of Earth's magnetosphere, the large increase in interstellar plasma, and the solar maximum due in 2012 may produce large-scale effects for life on Earth. Given these circumstances, the possibility of a sudden magnetic pole shift cannot be completely discounted, but it is far from inevitable. However, most scientists think a magnetic pole shift is highly unlikely in the near future and that it would be gradual, rather than sudden.

## CHAPTER 14

# Atmospheric Plasma and UFOs

The role that plasma plays in the behavior of our planet's climate is remarkable enough, but scientists and researchers have shown that plasma vortexes can be found in tornadoes and in many unusual atmospheric phenomena that appear to be increasing in frequency. Recently declassified government documents have shown that many UFO sightings may also be related to atmospheric plasmas.

# Self-Luminous Formations

There are many names given to the glowing plasmas that are found in the atmosphere, and there are a broad spectrum of these self-luminous effects that include ball lightning, upper atmospheric effects called sprites and elves, earthquake lights, the aurora borealis or northern lights, and glowing orb-like balls of light.

Dmitriev chooses to call all of these natural self-luminous formations (NSLFs) or vacuum domains. For simplicity, they are referred to here as plasmoids, which is defined simply as any coherent structure of plasma and magnetic fields. Plasmoids have been proposed to explain natural phenomena as diverse as ball lightning, magnetic bubbles in the magnetosphere, objects in cometary tails, and structures found in the solar atmosphere.

## Anomalous Behavior of Plasmoids

Plasma physicist Dr. T. Matsumoto has shown that atmospheric plasmoids exhibit various anomalous behavior such as hopping over land, skimming across water surfaces, and passing unchanged through glass, water, and air. Changes in atmospheric pressure and other conventional meteorological explanations are unable to explain these anomalies.

Matsumoto describes plasmoids as possessing these unique properties:

- They emit a wide range of electromagnetic waves.
- They have the ability to penetrate solid objects.
- They are able to draw dust in and bring it to rotation.
- They form electric, magnetic, and gravitational fields around them.
- They are able to divide themselves into several parts.
- The frequency of their occurrence rises abruptly with peaks of solar activity.

## Tornadoes

The mechanics of tornado formation are not well understood. Spectators close to funnel clouds, the swirling vortices that do not reach the ground, have reported little or no wind surrounding the funnel cloud while it is airborne. But when a tornado touches the ground, it can have devastating effects, easily destroying houses, lifting cars into the air, and displacing objects and people—in some cases, for miles. Many viewers also report seeing lights at the center of tornadoes.

There has been an ongoing scientific debate on the nature of these reported sightings of tornado lights. Some meteorologists have denied that they exist at all and have tried to explain them as just anecdotal folklore based on the exaggerated descriptions of untrained observers. The meteorologist and chemist Dr. B. Vonnegut and photographer James R. Weyer settled this last point definitively when they were able to photograph two luminous tornadoes. Their photos were subjected to rigorous scientific scrutiny: The original negatives were analyzed using equipment called an isodensitracer. The results of this densitometric study concluded, "The luminous pillars constitute a genuine exposure and are not an artifact of either exposure or development."

**ALERT**

In the United States, an average of 800 tornadoes are reported nationwide each year, resulting in eighty deaths and more than 1,500 injuries. The most violent tornadoes are capable of wind speeds of 250 mph or more. Damage paths can be in excess of 1 mile wide and 50 miles long. A tornado in Broken Bow, Oklahoma, carried a motel sign 30 miles and dropped it in Arkansas!

## Luminous Eye Phenomena

Dmitriev's department of the Russian Academy of Sciences has made an extensive study of the effects of tornadoes, collecting reports of a wide variety of luminous eye phenomena in tornadoes that have been witnessed by observers. These include:

> *"[a] Ball of fire . . . lightning in a funnel . . . yellow shining surface of [a] funnel . . . incessant lightning . . . [a] fiery column . . . glowing clouds . . . brilliant shine . . .[a] brilliant luminous cloud in a funnel . . . beaded lightning . . . exploding fireballs . . . [and] a rotating band of deep blue light."*

The conclusion of their research has been that these plasmoids are fundamentally inherent to tornadoes and that it is the vortexes created by these plasmoids that are responsible for creating the funnel clouds, not the other way around.

This is quite different from the conventional meteorological explanation of a tornado, known as the Brooks model. This states that tornadoes are a thermodynamic effect produced by a parent storm cloud. However, Dmitriev cites examples of tornadoes appearing without any clouds overhead. In cases like these, what appeared to be a parent cloud actually formed around the central vortex as the tornado progressed. In the electrogravidynamic model of Dmitriev, the tornado is actually caused by the rotating central tube of plasma. This model has the advantage of being able to explain many of the anomalous behaviors that occur in and around tornadoes that the conventional Brooks model cannot.

Effects of tornadoes that are better described by the plasma vortex model include:

- Funnel clouds are seen to travel over the surface of the earth in jumping movements, suggesting that other forces besides atmospheric pressure are causing them.
- When a tornado is just slightly above the ground no lifting effects are seen, but as soon as it touches the ground levitation begins. The area inside the tornado has been measured to have a lower air pressure, but this does not occur beneath the cloud.
- As tornadoes cross rivers, they have been seen to form trenches in the water, sometimes up to twenty feet deep. This suggests that they are sources of powerful, anomalous gravitation.
- Tornadoes have been observed to emit pitches or hissing noises whilst airborne, indicating very high levels of electrostatic charge.
- Tornadoes can transport objects and even living creatures over long distances without damaging them. This suggests that the lifting power of a tornado is being caused by levitation, not by suction and rotation.
- Many types of luminous phenomena have been associated with tornadoes. Lights have been seen both before a tornado appears and inside its central vortex.

## Microcomets and Miniature Black Holes

Dmitriev has attempted an alternative explanation of how tornadoes and their funnel clouds arise. He suggests they may originate in small atmospheric holes made in the upper ionosphere by tiny microcomets. These holes are well documented and have been seen and recorded in the ultraviolet spectrum. The cause of this is thought to be incoming helium nuclei from the sun that react with the upper ionosphere to create miniature black holes.

These mini black holes of spinning gravitational waves create a vacuum effect and a pulsed heat release. This, in turn, produces a wide variety of self-luminous phenomena, depending on a number of variables. Self-luminous formations or plasmoids as proposed in the Dmitriev model are luminous effects created by the combined forces of electromagnetism and gravity because of these cosmic collisions.

It is an elegant theory, but a hugely controversial one for conventional meteorology. The incidence of these formations, he believes, is related to solar activity. Similar storms found on other planets are thought by Dmitriev to be created by the same mechanism and increase in frequency when the sun is most active. Essentially, tornadoes on Earth can be seen in this model as a sympathetic response to similar storms on the sun.

# Plasmic Weather Phenomena

Tornadoes are just one example of plasmoid activity in the atmosphere, which also creates a wide range of other very interesting weather effects. The incidence of these phenomena seems to be increasing significantly in frequency and scale. Many of these types of effect were unknown until recent times.

## Sprites, Elves, and Blue Jets

These are all transient luminous event (TLE) atmospheric phenomena that are observed at high altitudes above thunderstorms. Passengers aboard planes have recorded some of the best footage of sprites. These plasma effects can be both huge in scale and spectacular in intensity.

Sprites are usually reddish in color and are among the oldest known of these phenomena, first reported more than 100 years ago. Sprites appear at heights of between 30 and 55 miles up in the atmosphere as glowing plasma-conducting columns up to several miles in length. Sprites typically last milliseconds, just long enough to easily be perceived by the human eye. They are often carrot shaped and scatter radio frequencies.

**QUESTION**

**What is ball lightning?**
Ball lightning is another atmospheric plasmoid effect that appears as a glowing, hovering ball of light that moves slowly near the ground before disappearing or exploding. The ball usually measures around a foot in diameter, although two park rangers in the Australian outback reported seeing one in 1987 that was at least 300 times the typical size.

Elves are a related type of discharge found at around 55 miles and above that are described as an enhanced airglow in an expanding doughnut-shaped ring. Elves result from an especially powerful electromagnetic radiation pulse (EMP) that emanates from lightning discharges. Elves last for less than a thousandth of a second, which makes them virtually impossible to see with the naked eye.

Blue jets are a strange new type of effect that typically consists of an upwardly moving, bluish beam emission from cloud tops, known as jets. These occur below 30 miles in altitude and last up to a quarter of a second.

Other effects associated with these three phenomena include gravity waves that generate upper ELF signals of around 300kHz and horizontal magnetic field variations in the frequency range of the earth-ionosphere cavity resonance.

## Thermal Plasmas

Dr. Massimo Teodorani and his associates have extensively researched anomalous plasma formations that have been seen in the valley of Hessdalen in Norway. For more than two decades, many eyewitnesses in the valley have observed and reported flickering, pulsing lights that change shape. Teodorani's team of Italian astrophysicists joined a team of Norwegian engineers lead by Professor Erling Strand in a joint study using radar, photography, video, radio spectrum analyzers, and spectroscopes.

The phenomenon observed by the team of scientists could be broken down into two groups: 95 percent are thermal plasmas and 5 percent are unidentified solid objects. The plasmas emit long-wave radio frequencies and appeared when there were disturbances in the geomagnetic field.

The summary of their research makes the following conclusions:

1. Most of the luminous phenomena are thermal plasma.
2. The light balls are not single objects but are constituted of many small components that are vibrating around a common center.
3. The light balls are able to eject smaller light balls.
4. The light balls change shape all the time.
5. The luminosity increase of the light balls is due to the increase of the radiating area. However, the cause and the physical mechanism with which radiation is emitted is currently unknown.

## Large-Scale Natural Self-Luminous Formations

Plasma effects in the atmosphere are not confined to the small scale. They also appear as very large-scale spheres that have been reported by Dmitriev. These are also described by Susan Joy Rennison in her book *Tuning The Diamonds*, which makes a detailed argument for a relationship between the increase in these new electromagnetic phenomena of all scales and a shift in human spiritual evolution. These formations vary in size from around 30 feet across up to 2 miles in diameter. In one case, on a data gathering expedition in the Altai mountain range of Russia, scientists from Dmitriev's team measured a large-scale formation that was nearly 5 miles wide. The Belokurikha flame, another large-scale self-luminous plasma recorded by Dmitriev, appeared in the Belokurikha mountain range as a giant auroral-like flame structure reaching up several miles toward the ionosphere.

### Lights in the Sky

Though the incidence of these events does appear to be increasing at a significant rate, luminescences in the atmosphere have been recorded for as long as historical records have existed. Lights in the sky have been seen preceding and accompanying earthquakes and volcanic eruptions, before and during tropical hurricanes, in the development of thunderstorms, and above tectonic fault lines.

"Actually, there's no large-scale high-energy event in the depths of the earth or on its surface which would not be accompanied by luminous objects," Dmitriev remarks. The conclusion of his research paper on tornadoes states: "Hundreds of thousands of these natural self-luminous formations are exerting an increasing influence upon Earth's geophysical fields and biosphere. We suggest that the presence of these formations is the mainstream precedent to the transformation of Earth; an Earth which becomes more and more subject to the transitional physical processes which exist within the borderland between the physical vacuum and our material world."

## Project Condign and UFOs

Project Condign was the name given to a top secret UFO study undertaken by the British Government's Defense Intelligence Staff (DIS) between 1997 and 2000. This was declassified and released to the public in 2005 after a request under the Freedom of Information Act by the UFO researchers Dr. David Clarke and Gary Anthony.

The report looked into all reported sightings of UFOs over the previous three decades. Between 1967 and 1997, there were 100–750 credible incidences a year in British air space alone. The project came to the remarkable conclusion that the phenomenon was indisputably real, but that they weren't dealing with physical craft. Instead, the report concludes that the UFO phenomenon is caused by highly charged atmospheric plasmas. These were named unidentified aerial phenomena (UAPs) by the DIS.

In a high-energy state, the UAPs are visible to the naked eye, but in a lower energy state they may only be visible in the infrared spectrum or on radar. The UAPs generally have a magnetic field about 5,000 times weaker than Earth's, but the UAP's field is pulsed and rotating, which seems to provide them with their source of propulsion.

The UAPs were also capable of flying in formation and quite frequently formed complex geometric arrangements of three to five balls that gave a very good approximation of the underside shape of a classic UFO. These balls were able to move synchronously and were observed to be able to join and then part again. When flying in formation, light in between the balls of plasmas often appears to be blocked, giving the appearance of a solid craft.

## UFOs

The power of these UAPs is so great that close proximity to their plasma fields can seriously harm a vehicle or person. The Project Condign report notes that scientists in the former Soviet Union have taken a particular interest in the UFO/UAP phenomena and are pursuing related techniques for military purposes. Several Russian and Chinese aircraft have been destroyed chasing UFOs.

**FACT**

Parts of the Condign Report are still classified and have not been published. These include the relationship between UAPs and solar sunspot cycles, various drawings, and photographs. However, the report does include the admission that the significance of ley lines and Earth energy grids were investigated as part of the report's study.

The effects of proximity to these UAP plasmoids can be wide ranging in the people who encounter them:

- 75 percent of people felt odd or dizzy or reported tingling sensations.
- 65 percent saw vivid images and/or said they experienced pleasant vibrations.
- Only 40 percent said they experienced fear or terror.

The Condign Report also notes that there are significant neurological effects on humans who encountered the UAPs. Contact with UAPs created serious perceptual and temporal distortions. The Condign Report's conclusion after three years of gathering and processing data is that there is "no evidence that they (UAPs) . . . represent any hostile intent" and that "further investigation should be made into the applicability of various characteristics of plasmas in novel military applications."

### Russian UFO Research

Extensive research on these plasmoids has also been carried out by the Russian Academy of Sciences in a department headed by V. G. Azahazha. They concluded that these phenomena are highly mobile high-energy plasma vortexes, which they call UFOs. Their studies showed that these plasma UFOs exhibited the following behaviors:

- Gradual growth
- Splitting into two or more separate parts
- Dissolution to invisibility
- Disparate bright lights merging into larger formations (often reported as small craft joining the mother ship and forming a row of portholes)
- Disappearance, accompanied by a smell
- Rotation, nonlinear motion
- Weak thermal radiation
- Translucence, haloes, blackness
- Beamed light emissions

The beamed light emissions are explained by the Russian scientists as "discharge, or leakage paths" that allow the plasma to "float off" and to change direction, seemingly at will.

## Are Plasmas Alive?

Given the remarkable properties of these plasmas, scientists have been debating whether they could be considered a form of life. The ability of plasma to self-organize so impressed the great physicist David Bohm, who was one of the primary research partners of Albert Einstein, that he remarked he frequently had the impression that plasmas were alive and that they had many of the properties of organic life. Modeling has shown that plasmas can imitate the functions of a simple cell, having a semipermeable cell wall through which they can "feed" by absorbing other less-organized plasma. In fact, plasmas were named after their similarities with living blood cells.

## Helical Dust Structures and Inorganic Life

V. N. Tsytovich, another scientist based at the Russian Academy of Science, has shown how plasmas can self-organize when exposed to electrical charge. Tsytovich has developed his observations into a theory of what he calls inorganic life. The principal location of these is in the helical dust structures that have been seen to form around stars and in interstellar space.

In a gravity-free environment, these plasma particles bead together to form string-like filaments, which will then twist into helix-shaped strands closely resembling DNA. These structures are electrically charged and are attracted to each other. They are able to "feed" by assimilating other less-organized plasmas through their boundary walls. They can "reproduce" by amoeba-like splitting, and each of the plasma's offspring retains the capacity for self-organizing, growth, and further reproduction. According to Tsytovich, "they are autonomous, they reproduce, and they evolve," behavior fulfilling enough criteria, in his opinion, to be considered a form of life.

**ESSENTIAL**

A much wider range of environments found in our universe suit the conditions for plasma-based life forms to exist in than those that support carbon-based life forms; 99.9 percent of matter in our universe is plasma. Inorganic life could exist in much hotter and colder conditions than organic life, such as solar atmospheres, planetary ionospheres, or interstellar space.

The conclusion of Tsytovich's report is groundbreaking in scope. He not only believes we need to widen our definition of what comprises life to include plasmas or inorganic life, but also that organic carbon-based life itself may possibly be derived from these plasma life forms. Tsytovich and other scientists have proposed that plasma life forms may, in fact, have been responsible for catalyzing the development of organic carbon-based life on Earth.

## Plasma Cells and the Foundation of Life on Earth

The work of Mircea Sanduloviciu of Cuza University, Romania, has been cited by Jay Alfred, author of *Dark Plasma Theory* and commentator on the esoteric applications of plasma science, as further evidence of the connection between these self-organizing plasmas and the foundation of life on Earth. Sanduloviciu has developed a theory that plasma spheres arising within electric storms were the first cells on Earth. Sanduloviciu believes that the emergence of these plasma spheres is a prerequisite for the evolution of biological cells and that cell-like self-organization can occur in a few microseconds. Like the Tsytovich helical dust structures, Sanduloviciu found that the spheres could replicate by splitting into two. Under the right conditions they also got bigger, taking up neutral argon atoms and splitting them into ions and electrons to replenish their boundary layers.

**FACT**

The most remarkable feature of these plasma cells is probably that they can communicate information by emitting electromagnetic energy, making the atoms within other spheres vibrate at a particular frequency. These cell-like spheres could be at the origin of other forms of life we have not yet considered.

Tsytovich has pointed out that plasma life forms could possibly develop under terrestrial conditions. For example, a plasma bubble forming at the end of a lightning strike could act as a mold for organic elements to form a primitive biological cell. The more highly ionized atmosphere of Earth in its distant past would give this kind of scenario a higher probability of success.

Tsytovich concluded, "These structures can have all necessary features to form inorganic life. This should be taken into account for formulation of a new SETI (Search for Extra-Terrestrial Intelligence)-like program based not only on astrophysical observations but also on planned new laboratory experiments, including those on the ISS (International Space Station). In the case of the success of such a program one should be faced with the possibility of resolving the low rate of evolution of organic life by investigating the possibility that inorganic life 'invents' organic life."

# Plasmic Effects Expected to Increase Toward 2012

The number of plasmic and plasmoid phenomena of all kinds observed on our planet appears to be increasing as we approach 2012. This could be directly related to the increase in interstellar plasma that our solar system is encountering. As this combines with the next solar maximum due for 2012, the amount of plasmic effects in Earth's atmosphere are likely to increase even further. Matsumoto has shown that their frequency is correlated with increases in solar activity.

The range of their effects varies from small orbs that are barely visible all the way up to giant atmospheric effects more than a mile in diameter. The aurora borealis is a plasmic effect on a planetary scale and is even more dramatic seen in the ultraviolet part of the spectrum.

The existence of highly organized and high-energy atmospheric plasmas that resemble flying craft is now recognized and openly acknowledged by many governments. These display complex behavior and appear to be the source of the majority of credible and reliable UFO sightings. An explanation of the apparent intelligence these plasmoids exhibit is less easy to explain by any conventional scientific model. In the next chapter we will investigate the role plasma may play in one of the other great mysteries of our time—the phenomenon of crop formations.

## CHAPTER 15

# Crop Circles and Orbs

The story of plasma isn't quite finished yet. Some researchers believe that plasma may be responsible for the phenomenon of orbs, glowing balls of light that are increasingly appearing in digital photography. They have also been linked with the mysterious phenomenon of crop circles, and some scientists now think that plasma vortexes may be the true makers of crop circles.

## Orbs in Folklore

Accounts of self-propelling luminous phenomena are common to the folklore of many cultures. These balls of light are often seen to move but don't emit heat, and one conventional scientific explanation is that they are a product of ignited marsh gas, most likely slowly leaking methane. While that may explain orbs that appear near marshes and swamps, the incidence of orbs is much more widespread than that. Orbs used to be considered fairy denizens of the woods.

The floating ghost lights often inspired awe and fear in those who encountered them. They usually hovered close to the ground or between the trees. They were considered both intelligent and powerful and were to be treated with respect. Reports have persisted in more recent times, especially in areas of strong geomagnetic energy, like those above earthquake fault lines.

There are a large number of folk names given to floating orbs around the world. In English, these include corpse light, fair maids, merry fires, fox-fire, friar's lantern, hinkypunk, hobby lantern, ghost light, jack-o'-lantern, kitty-with-a-wick, peg-a-lantern, pixy-light, spunkie, and walking fire.

## Orbs in Digital Photography

A more recent occurrence is the presence of orbs in digital photography. These "faeries" are usually invisible to the naked eye but appear, sometimes in profusion, when photos are taken. There are several possible explanations for this. First, more pictures are being taken now because digital photography makes it so easy. Second, the optics of digital cameras are more suited to capturing orbs than those of conventional film. Third, a percentage of orb phenomena are caused by simple physical reasons:

- Solid orbs: dry particulate matter such as dust, pollen, etc.
- Liquid orbs: droplets of liquid, usually water, e.g. rain
- Foreign material on or within the camera lens and body

These factors do not quite account for some of the more unusual properties of these orbs, nor do they explain why orbs tend to appear under certain circumstances and not others. In addition, many of the orbs that appear in digital photos show complex internal structures, with patterns much like those of snowflakes. In addition, they often have cell-like membrane structures around their edges. Orbs appear in many millions of digital pictures and it has been estimated that as many as one-third of all digital photos contain anomalies that are orb-like in appearance.

## Factors Influencing the Appearance of Orbs

The number and density of orbs in photography is correlated with a number of certain conditions. A greater number appear:

- At the beginning of lightning storm activity, which tapers off once the frontal boundary passes
- When a low-pressure zone passes over or barometric pressure is dropping
- When a Tesla coil device is being operated
- Around high-power electricity cables and towers at night
- In crop circle formations
- At gatherings of people focusing intentional energy, including ceremonies and meditations

## Photographic Orbs and Plasma

David M. Rountree, AES, has a BSEE in microwave technology and a master's degree in electronic engineering. In 1992, Rountree formed an organization called Scientific Paranormal Investigative Research Information and Technology (S.P.I.R.I.T.) and began collecting, building, and focusing instrumentation to search for the cause of paranormal phenomena. He has been studying the phenomenon of orbs closely and has named them unified field plasmoids.

Rountree developed a theory that the orbs he was capturing in his photographs were composed of plasma. He hypothesized that a camera flash could render them photographic. Around 1990, he saw an orb without the help of photographic equipment. He reported it was three dimensional and slightly fluorescent, which led him to theorize that some orbs could attract electrons to make themselves more visible. These electrons, by their very nature, needed to discharge themselves, so they headed for the ground. Once an orb hit the ground, it would "effectively disappear in thin air from whence it came," Rountree reported.

From studying these experiment results, Rountree discovered that orbs can even transfer energy between themselves when they meet each other. Using an EMF meter, Rountree was able to monitor fluctuations in the background EMF and photograph the conditions of a location in conjunction with the spike.

He began associating certain orbs with increases in EMF at a site. "I now had evidence that suggested certain orbs were possibly plasma energy, emitting EMF radiation as a by-product of their existence. This is due, I surmised to electron movement around the 'skin' of the orb, creating a wide spectrum of electromagnetic radiation."

## Orbs and Meditation

The appearance of orbs seems to relate not only to atmospheric and electrical conditions, but also to human intention. Researchers Kris and Ed Sherwood have conducted guided meditations specifically designed to connect with the energies of the orbs. They have conducted these light-ball visualizations at sacred sites and in crop circle formations around the English countryside.

The Sherwoods have been remarkably consistent in sighting orbs. Ed has taken digital photographs while Kris has been meditating, and the resulting photos sometimes show hundreds of orbs, many of them bright and well defined. In some cases, motion blurs suggest the orbs are moving faster than the shutter speed of the camera. In other pictures, very luminous objects appear to be hovering above peoples' heads. The results were particularly noticeable inside crop circle formations. Kris Sherwood concluded, "The genuine crop circle phenomenon has demonstrated its ability to be psycho-interactive with those giving their attention to it."

Human-created crop formations have been documented by a number of different groups of circle makers since 1978. This has been interpreted in some media reports to mean that all crop formations are hoaxes, deliberately created to fool people into thinking they are some kind of supernatural phenomenon. This ignores the fact that readings taken in crop formations of unknown origin have consistently shown marked differences from readings taken in crop formations of known human origin.

**QUESTION**

**What are crop circles?**
The term crop circles, also known as crop formations, was first coined by researcher Colin Andrews to describe patterns created by the flattening of cereal crops such as wheat, barley, rapeseed, rye, and corn. These often take the form of intricate geometric patterns. The majority of crop circles recorded in the last twenty years have appeared in the west of England.

It also does not take into account the reports of many human circle makers, allegedly responsible for the "hoax" crop formations, who say they have often witnessed anomalous lights and floating luminous orbs in fields they were working in. This has led to the speculation that crop formations may be an interactive phenomenon and that human circle makers can attract the attention of the genuine circle makers with their activity. It may be possible that a form of communication between the symbology of art and circle-making activities may be occurring in these cases.

**ALERT**

In August 1996, a video showed a number of balls of light hovering over a field, apparently causing a crop formation underneath them. The video later turned out to be a hoax, created by a video editor who happened to spot the crop formation when it was freshly created and used computer animation to create the orbs.

It is estimated that between 10 percent and 80 percent of crop circles are manmade. Even researchers who think it is at the higher end of that scale admit there is no way to tell how formations were constructed in at least 20 percent of formations. These remain resolutely mysterious, and some other form of explanation is needed.

## Plasma Vortex Theory of Crop Circle Creation

The first scientific attempt to explain the appearance of crop circle formations was put forward by Terence Meaden, a physicist and meteorologist with master's and doctorate degrees from Oxford University and a Fellow of the Royal Meteorological Society. In addition, Meaden is the founder of the tornado study group TORRO, which collects, analyzes, and publishes data on the incidence, strengths, and origins of tornadoes and severe storms.

**FACT**

Crop circles are not new. The earliest recorded image resembling a crop circle is depicted in a seventeenth-century English woodcut called the Mowing-Devil. The image depicts the devil with a scythe cutting a circular design in a field. The accompanying pamphlet states that the farmer, disgusted at the wage his mower was demanding for his work, insisted that he would rather have the devil himself perform the task.

TORRO also studies the ball lightning and other phenomena associated with these events. One of his major areas of research has been the study of tornadoes and plasmoids. Being very familiar with properties of atmospheric plasma, Meaden hypothesized that a whirlwind or tornado could potentially generate a plasma vortex that could account for the delicate and precise way that crop stalks appeared to be laid down in circles, as if from above. The plasma vortex theory could also explain the anomalous lights that were associated with crop circles as friction-generated plasmoids created by a plasma vortex.

A professor in Japan was able to produce laboratory results that seemed to corroborate Meaden's whirlwind-created plasma vortex theory. Using electrostatic discharges and microwave interference, a vortex modeled on interactions between a spinning electrical field and Earth's magnetic field was simulated, showing that it was theoretically plausible.

Meaden's theory was a promising way to explain the phenomena of the more simple circles that appeared in the 1980s. However, as much more complex formations started to appear, the idea that these could credibly be created by a simple whirlwind was dispelled.

The plasma vortex theory was still embedded in the traditional meteorological notion that whirlwinds generate plasmas, rather than the other way around. There was simply no convincing way to argue that more complex crop circles were being created by a combination of merely wind and electrical charge. Meaden had always contended that the causes were more complex, but the whirlwind-based plasma vortex theory had hit a major roadblock.

## Levengood's Gravitational Vortex Theory

The plasma vortex theory took a back seat for a while, until Dr. William Levengood redeveloped it into a much more radical and encompassing view. Levengood attempted to explain the microwave energy and other residues he had found in grain samples taken from crop formations. In fourteen years of scientific investigation on crop circles, Levengood has examined more than 250 crop formations in detail. Since 1992, he and his team have been involved in extensive on-the-ground surveillance and the collecting of samples and electromagnetic and other readings from crop formations. These samples are then sent to Levengood for analysis in his private laboratory based in Michigan, where he compares the grain collected from in and around the circles with control samples taken from edges of the fields the formations were found in.

## Exploded Nodes

One notable characteristic of grain samples taken from the formations was the incidence of exploded nodes. Wheat stems taken from crop formations revealed a massive number of expulsion cavities at their stem nodes. This effect suggests they were subjected to an internal pressure so sudden and powerful that it blew holes through the node points of the stem walls as the internal sap rapidly expanded. Levengood concluded that this could be characteristic of electromagnetic radiation, probably microwave, emanating from the epicenter of the formation.

Typical crop samples taken from formations include the following characteristics:

- Stalks are very often bent up to ninety degrees without being broken, particularly at the nodes, which are like joints in the wheat stems.
- Stalks are unusually enlarged, stretched from the inside out by something that seems to heat the nodes from the inside. Sometimes this effect is powerful enough to literally explode the node, blowing holes in the node walls and causing sap to leak from the stalk.
- Stalks are left with a surface electric charge, suggesting the force that flattened the crops was electrical.
- The thin bract tissue surrounding the wheat seed shows an increase in electrical conductivity, consistent with exposure to an electrical charge.

**ESSENTIAL**

Researchers claim their watches, mobile phones, batteries, and cameras are often affected during the examination of crop circles. There are no explanations for these occurrences, other than the influence of strong EM field distortions. Physical effects on people who enter crop circles have been reported. While some feel elated, others feel nausea, headaches, dizziness, tingling sensations, pain, and giddiness.

## Growth Rates

The germination of some seeds found in crop formations has accelerated growth and vigor. There are also significant reductions in the growth rates of seedlings germinated from the wheat seeds taken from formations; seedling heights are 35 percent shorter than controls. These results, Levengood concludes, strongly suggest rapid heating, such as would be caused by the exposure of the plants to microwave radiation or unusual electrical fields.

## Presence of Meteoritic Material

Levengood's laboratory analysis of samples from crop formations also notes the presence of a gray dust of hematite or iron oxide, which is of a type found in meteoritic material. This suggests to Levengood that the formations were created by a close encounter between a meteoritic system and a plasma vortex. The vortexes described in Levengood's theory are created much higher in the atmosphere than those proposed by Meaden's theory. Beginning in the ionosphere, where there is an abundance of microscopic meteoritic material, the Levengood vortexes are drawn down to the surface of the earth, apparently to areas of significant electromagnetic charge. This could be related to underground geomagnetic fields in the locations where the circles are found. Measurements taken by Levengood and his team in recently made formations have shown elevated magnetic levels that quickly dissipate, suggesting that a charge has somehow been released. Levengood has found that these plasma vortexes are subject to seven boundary conditions:

1. Transient microwave heating
2. Wind-shear turbulence
3. Electric fields produced by the vortex
4. The influence of the Earth's electric field
5. Magnetic fields produced by plasma
6. Thermal gradients
7. Convective turbulence

The inherent instability of the vortexes means a small change in any one of these conditions will result in a change in the total geometry and characteristics of the crop formation. Unlike Meaden's theory, Levengood's model allows for the creation of complex shapes and geometries. His theory is also supported by the fact that the traces of hematite and microwave energy are not found in those circles that are known to have been deliberately manmade. Levengood and his team have probably provided the most complete and comprehensive model of how crop formations could be made, but their research has neither been accepted by the scientific community nor widely covered in the news media.

Levengood's critics have focused on the fact that correlation is not causation. They also point to his self-expressed caution that "node size data cannot be relied upon as a definite verification of a 'genuine' crop formation." There has yet to be an independent replication of Levengood's work.

It remains a fact, however, that Levengood is a well-established scientist with an outstanding research record. His conclusions provide one of the most satisfyingly scientific explanations of the possible origin of these mysterious crop formations. Of course, Levengood does not attempt to explain why the formations seem to represent a symbolic language or interpret what kind of intelligence lies behind this phenomenon; instead, he focuses on the physics of how such a thing could possibly be accomplished at all.

## CHAPTER 16

# The Symbolic Language of Crop Circles

Crop formations have undergone a distinct and measurable evolution in complexity over the past thirty years. Beginning as simple circles, they have evolved to represent complex pictograms, fractal patterns, and even geometric demonstrations of mathematical concepts like the number pi. Some researchers also believe that they encode information about significant planetary alignments in the run up to 2012 and even, possibly, messages from extraterrestrials.

## The Evolution of Crop Circle Formations

Many of the initial formations in the 1980s were simple circles—hence the title crop circle—and consisted of singular or multiple circles, sometimes arranged in geometric patterns. The precision of the outlines in these crop circles and the spiraling weave patterns of crop stalks within the formations made them stand out from the typical wind-created downing that happens naturally in many wheat fields. At this level of complexity, Meaden's whirlwind vortex theory was a very credible contender theory in explaining how these intriguing formations could occur.

The first major evolution in the complexity of crop formations happened in 1990 with the first pictograms. These were often comprised of a series of geometric shapes arranged around a central shaft or bar. Containing perfectly straight lines, right angles, and circles within circles, the complexity of these circles required a more sophisticated explanation than the Meaden theory could provide.

## Fractal Crop Formations

The next significant level of evolution in crop formation design occurred in June 1996 when a formation appeared near Alton Barnes in Wiltshire, England. It consisted of a series of eighty-nine circles arranged in a pattern that seemed to strongly suggest the double helix structure of the DNA molecule. A large number of circles of changing scale were laid out with a remarkable degree of exactitude in the formation. Videographer Peter Sorenson was living just a few hundred feet away from the field in which it appeared; as the first person to discover it, he seized the opportunity to film the formation at dawn before anyone else had a chance to enter. His footage shows the crop formation to be executed very precisely with tightly woven circles with well-defined edges.

The DNA double helix crop circle formation

The Julia-set crop circle formation

©Andreas Müller, cropcirclescience.org

## Stonehenge Fractal Mystery

One of the most enduring mysteries associated with crop formations is related to the appearance of a large crop circle within sight of Stonehenge in broad daylight. The formation was in the bass clef–like shape of a Julia-set fractal that appeared in full view of the busy A303 road within a thirty-minute period one Sunday afternoon in July 1996.

Tourists spotted the 900-foot formation just after 6 P.M., and a pilot, a gamekeeper, and a security guard confirmed it had not been there half an hour before. The complex curving arc, precisely composed of many circles of changing scale, was certainly a relative of the double helix DNA formation that had appeared earlier that summer near Alton Barnes. The undetected, near instantaneous appearance of such a large formation in an area with so many potential observers has defied any attempted explanation.

## Windmill Hill

Three weeks later, at the end of July, another even more spectacular Julia-set fractal appeared at the Windmill Hill megalithic site, near Avebury stone circle. This time the formation was larger, had three spiral arms, and contained 194 circles! The geometric relationship between the two was very clear.

The symbolic language of crop circles seems to evolve by establishing a motif, then expanding upon it with further formations that become increasingly elaborate. Skeptics have suggested that this can be accounted for by the fact that hoaxers are getting better and improve throughout each season. But no hoaxers have ever claimed to have made either of these stunning formations. Much smaller manmade designs have taken many hours to complete, often with elaborate equipment. These manmade formations often leave telltale signs of crop damage and tracks left by their makers into and out of the formation.

# Message Crop Formations

The study of crop formations has attracted geometers and mathematicians enthusiastic to interpret the shapes and measurements of the formations in attempts to crack their symbolic code. The most fruitful of these endeavors has been the interpretation of astronomical messages in the crop circles, mostly related to cycles of the sun, moon, and other planets. Some articulate the geometric relationships inherent in these cycles. Others seem to explicitly contain messages.

## The Missing Earth

One of the message crop formations is the so-called missing-Earth formation that appeared at Longwood Warren, Wiltshire, in 1995. An orbital ring containing sixty-five circles surrounded a series of concentric circles or orbits, complete with circles for planets. This was widely interpreted as being a map of our inner solar system on a certain date. It seemed to show the orbits of the asteroid belt (the orbital ring), the orbits of Mars and Venus, and the position of Mercury with the sun clearly marked at the center. The proportions of the orbits were remarkably accurate. The one exception was that although Earth's orbit was shown in the formation, Earth's position was not!

This led many interpreters to suggest that the formation was foretelling a catastrophic end to our planet on a specific date. One possible date corresponding to the alignment shown was on the inferior conjunction of Venus on January 16, 1998. The lineup also occurred again in June 2004, during another Venus loop (the sixty-five day period where the planet goes retrograde and appears to move backward in the sky as observed from Earth) and four days before the Venus transit. No apocalypse happened, but it was one of the first of many crop formations that appear to be drawing our attention to the importance of Venus with highly complex messages about its cycles.

Other significant astronomical cycles that have been shown to be encoded within crop formations include the eighteen-year Saros eclipse cycle and the nineteen-year Metonic cycle of the moon. Specific dates of lunar and solar eclipses and specific planetary conjunctions have also been found. Researcher Paul Vigay noted that it seems that the geometric language of astronomical time is a particularly favorite subject matter for the creators of crop formations.

**The missing-Earth and pi crop formations**

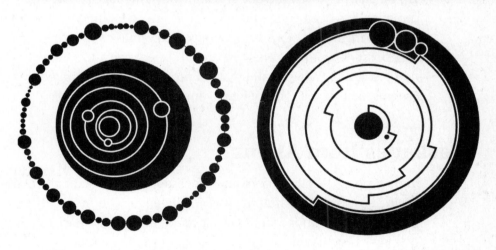

©Andreas Müller, cropcirclescience.org

## Pi in the Fields

Probably the most outstanding crop formation of the 2008 season was found in a barley field at Barbury Castle in Wiltshire. The now-famous image of a rotary encoder or ratchet design was at first a seemingly mysterious message, but after more than a week of attempted interpretations, a retired physicist-engineer from North Carolina by the name of Mike Reed managed to decode it.

What he discovered was that the formation represented the value of the mathematical constant pi to a value of ten decimal places. The number is so exact that the tenth digit is even correctly rounded up.

A small dot near the center of the formation represents the decimal point and the numbers are drawn into the crop using 36 degrees of rotation to represent a digit. The first digit, "3," was represented with $3 \times 36 = 108$ degrees of rotation, while the second digit, "1," was drawn with $1 \times 36 = 36$ degrees of rotation. The third digit, "4," was drawn with $4 \times 36 = 144$ degrees of rotation, and so on. "The code is based on ten angular segments, with the radial jumps being the indicator of (the end or start of) each segment," Reed concluded.

Since pi is a universal mathematical constant formed from the ratio of the circumference of any circle to its diameter, once the code has been cracked it can be interpreted by anyone speaking any language anywhere. The pi crop formation has been called the most complex ever found. It is certainly one of the most ingenious. Anyone wishing to communicate in the most universal form possible would do well to match the elegance and simplicity of this geometric solution. When mathematical proofs are demonstrated in corn fields, it seems likely some form of intelligence created them.

## Messages from Aliens?

Some crop circles have contained messages that specifically claim to have originated from an extraterrestrial intelligence. The first of these appeared in the field next door to a radio telescope at Chilbolton. The formation was instantly recognizable as a clear response to the message to extraterrestrial intelligence that was broadcast from the Arecibo radio telescope in 1974. The message looked strikingly similar, but on closer inspection revealed several significant differences.

The Chilbolton crop formation's reply to the image broadcast by the Arecibo telescope has been altered so that:

- The human figure has a far larger "alien" head.

- The building block elements of life now include silicon, in addition to the original elements listed.
- There is an extra strand added on the right side of the DNA double helix.
- The diagram that depicts our solar system has been changed to show Earth, Mars, and the moons of Jupiter as being inhabited.

Whoever created this formation certainly went to a great deal of trouble to encode this information. At the bottom, the original Arecibo picture had included an outline of the radio telescope itself and its dimensions. In the reply, this had been replaced by a strange multiarmed fractal that would seem to be the aliens' telescope. A much larger version of this image had previously appeared as a crop formation in its own right in the very same field!

An even more explicitly alien crop formation appeared at Crabwood in 2002. This contained a giant image of a typical gray alien face, with an elongated skull and enlarged eyes. This was rendered into the crop as a series of lines, much like an old black-and-white television image. The effect was both striking and haunting. At the bottom right-hand side of the image was a disc that contained what appeared to be a binary code message of some kind. This data disc turned out to be exactly that. Read from the inside outwards, it contained a binary code that could be translated into the computer language ASCII. The message reads:

*"Beware the bearers of false gifts and their broken promises. Much pain but still time. Believe: there is good out there. We oppose deception. Conduit closing."*

It's worth noting that the binary code is in ASCII, a computer language invented by scientists in the 1960s, which translates into the western alphabet. No other crop formation has done anything like this. All other binary encoded information relates to dates and astronomical information that is universal and not specific to one language. The crop circle researcher Vigay, one of the researchers responsible for decoding this message, noted this and the fact that the frame of the picture is uneven and not at exactly ninety degrees, which is unusual considering the precision of the rest of the formation. He was left with the impression that the Crabwood formation was an extremely elaborate hoax.

## Crop Formations and the Mayan Calendar

Researcher Stray has done some remarkable work correlating the geometries of different crop formations with the underlying number harmonics of the Mayan calendar system. These correlations are so extensive that numbers related to nearly all of the known cycles that were being tracked by the Maya have been represented in a type of crop formation. Here are some notable examples of the correspondences:

- **13—Tones:** A thirteen-fold star appeared at Huish, Wiltshire in July 2003. This formation is almost identical to a diagram created by Argüellés in *The Mayan Factor* to illustrate the thirteen-baktun cycle.
- **20—Solar seals:** A Mayan design of a circle with twenty "G" symbols, the Mayan sign for the Milky Way, with thirteen sectors inside the circle, appeared in Waylands Smithy in 2004.
- **33—Symbols in the Tzolkin:** A sun formation with thirty-three divisions in its outer circle appeared in Silbury Hill, Avebury, Wiltshire, in May 1998.
- **52—Calendar round:** A formation with fifty-two circles in the tail appeared in Beckhampton, Wiltshire, in 1998. According to the crop circle researcher known as Red Collie, the alien face formation at Crabwood in 2002 contains the fraction of 104/2. This is a key number of the Mayan calendar system expressing the relationship between the calendar round and the Venus round.
- **65—Venus round:** A pentagram with thirteen scales between each pair of arms, making a total of sixty-five scales, appeared in Silbury Hill, Wiltshire, in 2002. The pentagram is the figure traced out by Venus over five of its 584-day cycles, which adds up to exactly eight 365-day Haabs. Sixty-five Venus cycles equal one Venus round, which is exactly the same length of time as two calendar rounds.
- **260—The Tzolkin:** A grid of 780 squares appeared in Etchilhampton, Wiltshire, in August 1997. Three Tzolkins of 260 days each equals 780

days. This is also equivalent to one synodic period of Mars. Crop circle researcher Michael Glickman noted that this formation appeared exactly 780 weeks before the same week in August 2012. Of this he said, "I am convinced that what is being predicted is a dimensional shift . . . which culminates in 2012. By that point, we will fully occupy an entirely different level of being."

- **360—The Tun/Haab:** A formation with twenty outer circles and eighteen inner squiggles appeared in Avebury Trusloe, Wiltshire, in 1999. These numbers represent the eighteen uinals of twenty days each in the yearly Haab calendar.
- **400—The baktun:** A grid of 400 squares appeared in East Kennett, Wiltshire, in 2000. There are 400 360-day tuns in one baktun.

## Mayan and Aztec Designs in Crop Circles

Another distinct evolution happened in the complexity of crop formations when Mayan- and Aztec-style designs began to appear around 2001. These incorporate some of the classic motifs of Mayan and Aztec art, like the Mayan "G" shape, which is commonly found on Mayan ceramics and statues. The first of these appeared in Wakerley Woods, Northamptonshire, in 2001

**The Aztec Pizza crop formation**

©Andreas Müller, cropcirclescience.org

and was named the Aztec Pizza, because it looked like a cross between the famous Aztec sunstone and a pizza. It incorporates eighteen "G" glyphs into its design, which is the Mayan symbol for the Milky Way. Stray has pointed out that eighteen is also a key number in the Aztec sunstone.

## The Mayan Wheel

The evolution of these designs continued to progress over the next few years, reaching a new high point in 2004 with the Mayan Wheel formation that was found at the ancient megalithic site of Silbury Hill, Wiltshire, in August 2004. This formation was considered by many to be the finest of that summer and was widely reported in the world's media, where it was named the doomsday crop circle. This was because it seemed to evoke a deep resonance with the 2012 end date of the Mayan calendar, although no detailed analysis or interpretation (other than mentioning the formation's Mayan appearance) was offered in the coverage.

**FACT**

The crop formation with the largest area and the most circles was found at Milk Hill, near Alton Barnes in Wiltshire in August 2001. It consisted of a six-armed Julia-set fractal with thirteen major circles in each arm. The total number of circles in the formation was 409 and it measured more than 800 feet in diameter.

The formation does seem to contain a number of symbols that are related to 2012. Firstly, around the edge are double-G glyphs, called jaguar snouts by the Maya, a symbol that represented the entrance to the underworld. This is found at the dark rift at the center of the galaxy, from which the winter solstice sunrise will appear to emerge on December 21.

Some interpreters have suggested that the formation also represents the four completed worlds in the Mayan creation story and the current fifth one. The previous worlds are represented by the outer rings, which are divided into four equal parts by a broad dark space in between. The open circle at its center, surrounded by two wings, represents our current fifth sun.

## The Secklendorf Formation

Most crop formations are still found in the west of England, and the majority of those are concentrated in the crop circle country of Wiltshire, within a 15-mile radius of Avebury stone circle. However, increasingly more complex crop formations are being found on mainland Europe and elsewhere, such as Canada. In 2008, a particularly impressive example was found at Secklendorf in Germany. The formation has a star tetrahedron in the central circle and a complex ring of orbits and planet circles surrounding it. This has been interpreted by Collie as showing near-future orbital locations for Earth, Venus, and Mars on the forthcoming Venus transit of June 6, 2012. It also shows the orbital locations for Earth and Venus on the calendar end date of December 21, 2012.

The Secklendorf formation seems to contain a map of multiple alignments of Venus in the approach to 2012. Each of these six dates is a significant conjunction:

**The Secklendorf and the 2012 crop formations**

©Andreas Müller, cropcirclescience.org

- March 27, 2009, inferior conjunction of Venus with the sun
- October 29, 2010, inferior conjunction of Venus with the sun
- August 16, 2011, superior conjunction of Venus with the sun
- January 11, 2012, superior conjunction of Venus with the sun
- June 6, 2012, inferior conjunction of Venus with the sun, Venus transit (represented by the star tetrahedron at the center of the formation, with the position of Mars also shown by the smallest circle on the outer ring)
- December 21, 2012, three months before superior conjunction of Venus with the sun (end of the fifth sun/thirteen baktuns)

## The 2012 Crop Formation

In July 2008, once again near Avebury in Wiltshire, a more complex version of the missing-Earth–type formation appeared. This time it contained the orbits of all nine planets, not just the inner ones. The planetary alignment that the formation points to is almost exactly the calendar end date of December 21, 2012. There is some debate about the precise date that is being described; some researchers think it is a slightly better fit for the positions of the planets on December 23. Nonetheless, this is still remarkably close and the clearest connection between 2012 and the crop circle phenomenon that has so far been recorded.

All nine planets appear there precisely as they will be located in space at the winter solstice, with one exception—Pluto, which is now considered to be a dwarf planet. While the positions of the inner terrestrial planets are marked with a small doughnut and the outer gas-giant planets with a large doughnut, Pluto is marked with a medium-sized ring, which immediately brings attention to it. It is also thirty degrees—or about twenty years of its orbit—ahead of its expected location. This has led to lots of speculation about what this could mean. A favorite explanation is that the orbit of Pluto has somehow been disrupted by the gravitational influence of a body like the legendary Niburu, sometimes called Planet X, returning to our solar system.

Crop circles and 2012 seem to be linked in multiple and often mysterious ways. There appears to be a significant link between the numbers expressed in crop circles and those in the Mayan calendar. There are also a number of dates relevant to 2012 that have been decoded from messages in crop formations, including one almost exactly describing the end date of the calendar on winter solstice 2012.

The theoretical link between plasma vortexes and the creation of crop formations may well be linked to an increase in the amount of available plasmic energy our solar system is currently experiencing. We may be seeing the culmination of a process of cosmic evolution much longer in the making than the very rapid one mirrored in the summer fields.

**QUESTION**

**What is Niburu?**
The name Niburu comes from the ancient Sumerian and describes a planet that is hypothesized to exist on an extremely long orbit, only entering our solar system every few thousand years. The arrival of Niburu, the wanderer, is seen as a time of great change. The return of such a planet would likely cause significant disruption to any other planet whose orbit it came close to.

Study of UFOs and crop circles has been largely relegated to the paranormal fringes and extremes of science, but now the common thread of plasma may link them to a range of vitally important subjects from climate change on Earth to much greater cosmic weather patterns throughout our galactic neighborhood. The year 2012 may turn out to be a catalytic point, when all these phenomena come together in a more integrated understanding of our place in the universe.

## CHAPTER 17

# Planet X and Nemesis

One persistent source of speculation about 2012 is that it heralds the return of a wandering planet or star into our solar system, possibly causing massive disruption to all of the planets. This is sometimes referred to as Planet X or Nibiru. Alternately, some scientists suggest our sun may have a hidden twin, sometimes called Nemesis, that could be responsible for cyclically disrupting the peace.

## The Search for Planet X

The quest to find the hypothetical Planet X has a long and colorful history in astronomy. The American astronomer Percival Lawrence Lowell first popularized the idea that there was a planet beyond the orbit of Neptune at the start of the twentieth century. He believed that discrepancies in the orbits of Uranus and Neptune could be accounted for by the existence of a large, yet-to-be discovered planet located beyond the orbit of Neptune.

This followed in the footsteps of a long tradition of planetary discovery by studying the irregularities in the orbits of the outermost planets. It was perturbations in the orbit of Saturn that led William Herschel to search for and find the planet Uranus. In 1843, the mathematician John Couch Adams discovered perturbations in the orbit of Uranus. In 1846, this led to the discovery of Neptune by Johann Gottfried Galle of the Berlin Observatory.

**FACT**

The famous Lowell Observatory in Flagstaff, Arizona, is named after Percival Lowell, who founded it specifically to search for Planet X. Certain of its existence, he became obsessed with finding it. After his death in 1916, his widow Constance sued the observatory for the share of Lowell's estate he had dedicated to continuing the search and the work was abandoned for the next decade.

In 1930, it seemed that Lowell had been vindicated by Clive Tombault's discovery of Pluto. Tombault was hired by the Lowell Observatory to examine thousands of photographs of the night sky, continuing the search for Planet X. He found the new planet just six degrees from one of the two positions that Lowell had suggested as likely locations for the discovery. The new planet was named Pluto partly because it contained the initials of Percival Lowell. The astronomical symbol for the planet is a combination of the letters 'P" and "L" in recognition of this fact.

## The Demise of Planet X

In 1978, the mass of Pluto was found to be only 60 percent of that of Earth's moon, far too small to be the perturber of Neptune's orbit, showing that it couldn't be Planet X. In 1993, data analyzed by the astronomer Myles Standish from Voyager 2's fly-by of Neptune in 1989 showed that Neptune had a mass that was 0.5 percent smaller than had previously been calculated. When that change in mass was taken into account, the supposed discrepancies in the orbit of Uranus disappeared. This effectively ended the search for another large planet near the orbit of Neptune.

# The Outer Planets

Pluto's status in the solar system has declined in recent years. Much smaller than any of the other planets and not much bigger than the largest of the asteroids, astronomers began to question whether Pluto should be considered a planet at all. As the power of telescopes rapidly increased during the 1990s, more trans-Neptunian objects (TNOs) of a similar size to Pluto were discovered just beyond its orbit in what is known as the Kuiper Belt.

**QUESTION**

**What is the Kuiper Belt?**
Named after astrophysicist Gerard Kuiper (rhymes with "viper"), the Kuiper Belt is an area of space on the edge of the solar system near the ecliptic plane. The Kuiper Belt extends some 5 billion miles from the sun, a little more than fifty times the distance between Earth and the sun. More than 800 Kuiper Belt objects have been found.

## The Tenth Planet

In 2005, Caltech astronomer Mike Brown discovered the biggest of all of the objects found in the Kuiper Belt so far. The object, initially called 2003 UB313, was named Eris after the Greek goddess of chaos and discord, because of its extremely eccentric orbit. Eris is slightly bigger than Pluto. A NASA press release announced her discovery as the finding of a tenth planet, but this was never formally confirmed.

In reality, Eris presented a further challenge to Pluto's continuing status as a planet. In 2006, the International Astronomical Union controversially reclassified Pluto, Eris, and their largest neighbors as dwarf planets. The new 2006 definition of a planet defined them as bodies that have "cleared their neighborhoods." Both Eris and Pluto still have significant debris in their orbits. Not all astronomers agree with this and there has been a public campaign to restore Pluto to full planet status.

**ESSENTIAL**

Since the International Astronomical Union changed the rules about what constitutes a planet in 2006, there are now only officially eight planets in the solar system. However, there also eight TNOs of such size that they have now been designated dwarf planets. These are, in descending order of size, Eris, Pluto, Makemake, Haumea, Sedna, Orcus, Quaoar, and Varuna.

## The Discovery of Sedna

Over the last fifteen years, the Kuiper Belt has been quite extensively charted, though it is possible that several more large objects remain to be found, possibly including something as large as Pluto. It was long thought that beyond the Kuiper Belt lay largely empty space. Then, in March 2004, Brown's team at Caltech found a body at least half as large as Pluto much further out. They named it Sedna, after the Inuit sea goddess. The discovery of this object has changed astronomers' theories about the composition of the outer solar system. Sedna's extremely elongated orbit ranges 76–1,000 astronomical units (one AU is equivalent to the distance between the sun and Earth). This 10,500-year orbit is so eccentric that Sedna spends only a small fraction of its orbital period near the sun, where it can be easily observed.

Brown believes this area will now be a rich hunting ground for new planetary bodies. He noted in his 2007 Lowell lecture, "Sedna is about three-quarters the size of Pluto. If there are sixty objects three-quarters the size of Pluto, then there are probably forty objects the size of Pluto. . . . If there are forty objects the size of Pluto, then there are probably ten that are twice the size of Pluto. There are probably three or four that are three times the size of Pluto, and the biggest of these objects . . . is probably the size of

Mars or the size of the Earth." Discoveries in the outer solar system in the near future may completely rewrite the map of our local neighborhood. According to Brown, there may be fifty or more objects that once would have been considered big enough to be classified as planets.

**QUESTION**

**Could there be another Earth-sized planet yet to be found in our solar system?**
Astronomers have not excluded the possibility that an Earth-like planet could be located further out than 100 AU with an eccentric and inclined orbit. Computer simulations have suggested that a body roughly the size of Earth was ejected outward by Neptune early in the solar system's formation and may currently be in an elongated orbit between eighty and 170 AU.

# Nibiru and the Destroyer

None of these strange and wonderful objects can claim to be the Planet X that Lowell was looking for, but in popular usage, the name Planet X has now come to mean any unknown planetoid on the far edge of our solar system. Some researchers think this object may be dangerous to us. This hypothetical planet is predicted to periodically swing into the heart of the solar system, causing great damage and disruption when it does.

## Zechariah Sitchin

The concept of a theoretical planet called Nibiru has been popularized by the writer Zechariah Sitchin, from his personal interpretations of ancient Sumerian texts. Sitchin has published a number of books, including *The Twelfth Planet,* that claim the Sumerians believed there is a planet unknown to modern astronomy that follows a highly elliptical orbit, reaching the inner solar system roughly every 3,600 years. Part of his theory lies in an astronomical interpretation of the Babylonian creation myth the Enuma Elish, in which he replaces the names of gods with hypothetical planets. Some interpreters of Sitchin's work believe that a return of Nibiru is timed to coincide with 2012, though Sitchin himself doesn't agree with that timing.

Sitchin also claims that Nibiru is home to a technologically advanced human-like alien race called the Anunnaki, who have visited Earth in the past to mine for gold, which they need to maintain the atmosphere on their planet. These beings, Sitchin claims, created humanity by genetically experimenting with primates and crossing them with Anunnaki DNA.

## Recent Critiques

When Sitchin first wrote his books, he was one of only a handful of specialists who could read the Sumerian language, but since the publication of the *Sumerian Lexicon* in 2006, it has been possible to check Sitchin's translations. Both individual words and larger portions of ancient texts have been found to be incorrectly translated.

Mike Heiser, who has a PhD in Hebrew Bible and Semitic Languages from the University of Wisconsin-Madison, has been particularly critical of Sitchin's work. He claims Sitchin's associations of gods with planets is flawed. For example, Sitchin associates Nibiru with the Babylonian god Marduk. However, Marduk is normally associated with the planet Jupiter in the Babylonian cosmology. Conventional Sumerian scholars believe the Sumerians only knew of five planets, not twelve. Heiser also cites the Chicago Assyrian Dictionary, a resource that contains an exhaustive compilation of all cuneiform material known to the present day. It has no references to Nibiru being a planet beyond Pluto and the Anunnaki gods are never associated with it.

## The Return of the Destroyer

Marshall Masters, a former CNN science reporter, also believes Planet X will return in 2012. In his documentary *Surviving 2012 & Planet X,* he points to a number of scientific reports that he claims have been later suppressed or covered up because they indicate the government knows about the existence of a rogue planet that is on a collision course with the inner solar system due in 2012.

Masters claims that low-level seismic activity and planetary changes on Earth are being created by the influence of Planet X. Most of Masters's historical support for the impending return of the destroyer comes from a book called the *Kolbrin Bible,* which claims to be based on earlier ancient Egyptian records called The Great Book. These supposedly contain accounts of previous visits of the destroyer that resulted in world cataclysms.

Although both Masters's and Sitchin's versions of Planet X are based on questionable sources and interpretations, they have some similarities to a much more scientific theory that supports the idea that cataclysms on Earth, including periodic mass extinction events, may be triggered by the gravitational influence of an unseen body on the edge of our solar system. This theory, however, doesn't require a planet or brown dwarf to come charging into the orbits of the inner planets. The secret of how this might happen may be found in a far distant region of our solar system called the Oort cloud.

# The Secrets of the Oort Cloud

The Oort cloud is a far distant conglomeration of frozen objects that surrounds the solar system between 900 billion and 4.5 trillion miles from the sun. The edge of the cloud is thought to be a massive 1.5 light years from the sun, more than a third of the way to the nearest star to the sun, Proxima Centauri. Most comets are thought to originate from this region. These comets spend millions of years in the Oort cloud until they are deflected into an orbit that takes them into the inner solar system where we can see them. The source that causes these comets to be deflected is currently of intense interest to astronomers.

Measurements of the regularity and distribution of comets coming from the Oort cloud have shown patterns that cannot be accounted for by the gravitational influence of our galaxy, known as the galactic tide. It is the edge of the Oort cloud, trillions of miles away from the inner solar system, that is currently the subject of much study and many speculations, some of which are very relevant to life on our planet.

## The Supergiant

Dr. John Murray of the U.K.'s Open University suggests there is another planet in deep space at the edge of the Oort cloud. Murray has been studying the motions of long-period comets. By analyzing the behavior of these comets, Murray has detected what he believes are tell-tale signs of a single massive object that has deflected all of them into their current orbits, and he calculates there is only a one in 1,700 chance that this is a coincidence. In a research paper published in the Monthly Notices of the Royal Astronomical Society, he has suggested that the so-far unseen planet is a supergiant, several times bigger than the largest planet in the solar system, Jupiter.

**FACT**

Some astronomers believe there is a theoretical size limit to gas giants. This would be roughly equivalent to about thirteen times the size of Jupiter, meaning that if Jupiter was much larger, the forces of gravity would start a chain reaction of deuterium fusion that would lead it to become a light-emitting proto-star.

The orbit of this supergiant would be approximately 3,000 billion miles (32,000 times further away than Earth) and it would take as many as 6 million years to orbit the sun. Such a distant planet would be slow moving and difficult to detect despite its huge size. What is probably the most interesting part of Murray's hypothesis is the remarkable suggestion that the planet orbits our sun in the "wrong" direction, counter to the orbits of all the other known planets. This has led Murray to believe that it did not form in this region of space and that it could be a planet that "escaped" from another star. He has even been able to calculate that the predicted supergiant lies in the constellation of Delphinus.

## The Search for Nemesis the Death Star

Some of the theories currently being investigated by science seem to outdo the imaginings of the most extreme conspiracy theorists and doomsday prophets. One particular idea that has been gaining a lot of momentum is that the sun is one half of a binary system and that we have a yet-to-be discovered companion star.

Richard A. Muller dubbed this hypothetical star Nemesis. Nemesis is theorized to be orbiting the sun at a distance of between 50,000 to 100,000 AU, somewhat beyond the Oort cloud. The existence of this star was originally postulated as part of a hypothesis to explain an apparent cycle of mass extinctions in the geological record.

**ESSENTIAL**

More than half of all stars throughout the galaxy are part of a binary system, which are thought to be created when two or more stars are born out of the same interstellar dust cloud. Binary stars orbit around a shared common center point in space. The smaller of the two stars has the larger orbit.

## Mass Extinctions

In 1984, paleontologists David Raup and Jack Sepkoski published a paper claiming they had identified a statistical pattern in species extinction rates over long periods of time. Using evidence from the fossil record, they were able to identify twelve major extinction events over the last 250 million years. The average time interval between extinction events was determined to be 26 million years. Two of the identified extinction events could be shown to coincide with large impact events. Raup and Sepkoski were not able to identify what might be causing the supposed periodicity of these events, but suggested there might be an astronomical explanation.

In response, Muller came up with the idea of Nemesis, named after the Greek goddess of retribution, as a death star whose orbital interactions with our solar system periodically caused showers of comets to be thrown toward the inner planets. The more Muller examined the hypothesis, the more plausible the possibility seemed.

During the passage of Nemesis through or near the Oort cloud, the star's gravity would dislodge millions or even billions of comets from their once-stable orbits, which would then head toward the inner solar system, pulled in by the sun's gravity. The few that inevitably collided with Earth would be likely to result in mass extinction events.

## The Red Dwarf Hypothesis

The exact nature of Nemesis, if it exists, has yet to be determined. Muller's preferred candidate is a common red dwarf star with magnitude between 7 and 12 that would be visible through binoculars or a small telescope. More than 3,000 red dwarfs that fit into this category have been catalogued, but their exact distances are not yet known. Red dwarfs are the most common type of star found in the galaxy. They are small and relatively cool in comparison to our sun. Some astronomers think it likely that any red dwarf so close to our solar system would be more conspicuous than this and would have been discovered already.

**QUESTION**

**If the sun has a companion star and we are part of a binary system, why can't we see the other star?**
If it is a red dwarf, it has probably already been discovered and catalogued, but it has not been recognized as a companion to the sun. This is because its proper motion, or movement across the sky, may be very small, as it may be moving away from or toward us. If it is a brown dwarf, it may be relatively close but still difficult to detect visually. The next generation of orbiting telescopes may be able to discover it.

## The Brown Dwarf Hypothesis

Other astronomers, including Daniel Whitmire, Albert Jackson, and John Matese, argue that the unseen companion to the sun is much more likely to be a brown dwarf. These are unborn stars that briefly ignite but then quickly die. The initial ignition dust cloud that surrounds them makes them very hard to see and even the most powerful telescopes could miss such a star, even if it were very close to our solar system. Brown dwarfs are very common, and if one were orbiting somewhere around the outer edge of the Oort cloud it would be a good fit for the perturber sending comets toward us.

Matese studied eighty-two Oort cloud comets and found that approximately a quarter have an anomalous distribution in the sky that can best be accounted for by a large body that has not yet been detected. The best fit for Matese's data is either a brown dwarf or the capture of large extra-solar planets from a passing star encountering the sun. Such an object would also help to explain Sedna's highly unusual orbit. Matese also predicts this object could periodically send showers of comets into the inner solar system.

## The Black Dwarf Hypothesis

The astronomer P. R. Weissman considers the likely mass of the perturber means it could be a black dwarf. These are hypothetical stellar remnants, created at the end of the life cycle of a normal star when the processes of nuclear fusion shut down. It then no longer emits significant heat or light. The time required for a star like our sun to reach this state is calculated to be more than 13.7 billion years, longer than the current age of the universe. Therefore, the existence of an actual black dwarf would be likely to force a revision of the big bang theory. Detection of a black dwarf would be very difficult indeed. It is theoretically possible its thermal radiation could be detected in the infrared spectrum, but it is more likely that it would be found by its gravitational influence alone.

**ALERT**

Matese and Whitman have suggested that the supposed extinction cycle might be caused by the solar system oscillating across the galactic plane of the Milky Way, a different sort of galactic alignment from the one happening in 2012. These oscillations may lead to gravitational disturbances in the Oort cloud with the same proposed consequences as the orbit of Nemesis.

# WISE: The Telescope That Could Solve the Mystery

A telescope that might be able to resolve the question of our potential companion star is scheduled for launch by NASA in November 2009. The Wide-Field Infrared Survey Explorer (WISE) is by far the most powerful midinfrared telescope ever assembled, with far greater sensitivity than any previous mission or program. WISE is scheduled to survey the entire sky, looking for nearby stars that are cooler and dimmer than the sun. According to NASA, "WISE will find many such Brown Dwarf stars in the solar neighborhood, most of which have yet to be discovered. Some may even be closer to the Sun than any other star previously known."

In the next few years, advances in the capabilities of telescopes like WISE mean that if there is a companion star to the sun and it is a red or brown dwarf, we may well discover its location, possibly by 2012. We will then likely know if it really is the hypothetical death star, responsible for the apparent cycle of mass extinctions that seem to occur every 26 million years on Earth. If we do not find it, it may mean that there is still a companion to the sun to be found, but that it is either a black dwarf or a supergiant planetoid, both of which would be much more difficult to detect.

Most importantly, the perturber of the Oort cloud, whatever it turns out to be, shows that a Planet X or Nemesis doesn't have to charge into the inner planets of the solar system to potentially cause catastrophic change to our planet. It may be that the death star has already influenced the course of life on Earth by periodically sending comet showers toward our planet. Urgent further study is required to find out if this really is the case and, if it is, when the next inundation is due.

# CHAPTER 18

# The Binary Star Theory

Periodic mass extinctions may have been caused by a yet undiscovered binary companion to our sun. This may also provide a new explanation for the precession of the equinoxes, the cycle responsible for the galactic alignment of 2012. This theory is supported both by new scientific thinking and by ancient knowledge interpreted from India's Vedic calendar.

# The Change from a Geocentric to Heliocentric Worldview

In the last chapter, the evidence for a possible binary companion to the sun was presented. In this chapter, this idea is expanded upon to include the possibility that this yet undiscovered star may be responsible for producing the effect of the precession of the equinoxes. This would link the star to the mechanism responsible for the galactic alignment of the 2012 era, when the winter solstice sun can be seen to rise in conjunction with the center of the galaxy. Redefining precession as a heliocentric phenomenon based on the motion of the sun around another star would also revolutionize the science of astronomy in a shift equal to that caused by the theories of Copernicus.

Copernicus's explanation of the cycle of precession was part of a revolutionary new model of our solar system that moved the center of the known universe from Earth to the sun. The irony of this is that the motions described by Copernicus to create the modern heliocentric or sun-centered model of the solar system are all actually geocentric or Earth centered.

### COPERNICAN MOTIONS OF EARTH

- The first motion of Earth proposed by Copernicus was the rotation of the planet on its axis to produce the twenty-four hour day.
- The second motion was the orbit of Earth around the sun that created the 365-day year.
- The third motion was the wobble of Earth on its axis to produce the effect of the precession of the equinoxes. A century after Copernicus introduced his theory Sir Isaac Newton suggested that this was an effect caused by the combined gravity of the sun and the moon.

In Copernicus's model, the sun doesn't move. However, we now know that the sun orbits the galactic center and oscillates up and down in relation to the plane of the galactic equator. The binary star theory introduces heliocentric motion, the idea that the solar system is moving in a curve through space in relation to its companion. This, it suggests, is the cause of precession, not Earth wobbling.

## The Change from a Heliocentric to a Galactocentric Worldview

One of the great successes of the Copernican heliocentric solar system was to remove the need for epicycles. In the Earth-centered worldview founded by the ancient Greek astronomer Ptolemy, this complex idea was used to describe the strange looping motions seen in the planets as they traversed the sky. Similarly, the binary star model dispenses with the need for the complex and fragmented mathematics required to support the lunisolar theory of precession.

The binary star theory asks us to take an imaginative leap that is equal to the one that Copernicus asked the medieval world to take. At the time, Copernicus's theory had not only scientific but also theological consequences, as the world was to lose forever its unique place at the center of creation. In a similar way, the binary star theory of precession displaces the sun from the center of the modern worldview. This new perspective may have just as dramatic an effect on our culture as the Copernican revolution had in its time. Instead of being important members of a small and exclusive club of less than ten planets, we now have to learn to live with the mindboggling vastness of the galaxy, where we are just one solar system out of countless billions. These may be the first steps from a heliocentric perspective to a galactocentric or galaxy-centered cosmos.

## Walter Cruttenden and the Binary Research Institute

Walter Cruttenden describes himself as an amateur archaeo-astronomer. After a successful career in finance, he has dedicated himself to promoting and refining the binary star theory of precession. In 2001, he founded the Binary Research Institute (BRI). He has written a book on the subject called *Lost Star of Myth and Time* and made a documentary film called *The Great Year*. The BRI also holds an annual Conference on Precession and Ancient Knowledge (CPAK).

## Rate of Change of Precession

If lunar and solar gravity were solely responsible for precession, we would expect the rate of precession to be as constant as their influences. Precession has actually been measured as accelerating by an average of about 0.00035 arc seconds per year since 1900. This means precession appears to be accelerating and decelerating in the same way that it would if the explanation for precession was that the sun were moving in an elliptical orbit typical of binary star systems. This acceleration suggests that the sun has moved past the most distant point in its orbit and is currently accelerating inward toward its companion. The data suggests an elliptical orbit of about 24,000 years in duration, with the sun having passed the most distant point about 1,500 years ago. This is shorter than the current scientific estimate of precession at 25,771 years, because of the acceleration that occurs when the two stars are closest to each other. The standard lunisolar model assumes a steady and unchanging rate of motion. Conventional science attributes this apparent acceleration solely to improvements in the accuracy of the measurement of precession over the last hundred years.

**ESSENTIAL**

Astronomers at the University of Michigan and the University of Arizona have recently discovered that the Kuiper Belt has a very pronounced sheer edge. In a single-sun system this would be very unlikely to happen. It is, however, consistent with the existence of a binary companion, which would tend to sweep objects from the extreme edges of the solar system as it passes.

## Distribution of Angular Motion

In the conventional model, angular momentum in the solar system is inexplicably distributed in a completely uneven way between the planets and the sun. The sun has 99.9 percent of the solar system's mass but only 1 percent of the total angular momentum. This can be accounted for by assuming that the sun's angular momentum is not embodied in the axial spin but in a proposed

24,000-year orbit around its binary twin. The angular momentum-to-mass ratio of all planets and the sun is then consistently distributed.

## The Eccentric Orbits of the Newly Discovered Dwarf Planets

The influence of a binary star would likely create exactly the kind of eccentric orbits found with the newly discovered dwarf planets, Eris and Sedna. "It is logical to assume (the orbit of) Sedna is telling us something about current, albeit unexpected solar system forces, most probably a companion star," Cruttenden concludes. He also points out that Sedna's orbit period of 12,000 years is in neat resonance with the hypothetical solar orbit around our companion star suggested by the BRI, being exactly half its length.

**FACT**

The BRI has calculated that a brown dwarf with a mass 8 percent that of the sun, at a distance of about 800–1,000 astronomical units (the distance from Earth to the sun), would result in a 24,000-year orbit for the sun around the gravitational center of the binary system. A larger companion star further out could produce the same orbital cycle.

# Does Nemesis Cause Precession?

The 24,000-year orbital period suggested by the BRI fits extremely well with the Nemesis hypothesis presented in the last chapter. This is especially true of the model that suggests there may be an undetected brown dwarf–type star located on the far side of the Oort cloud. The mass and location of such a star make it a very credible candidate for the agent of the turning of the ages that accompanies the Great Year.

Where exactly to look in the night sky for this possible binary companion to the sun is still a matter of debate. The BRI's best guess suggests that it may be found in the direction of the galactic center in the constellation Sagittarius. By their estimates, the orbital plane of the companion star is likely to be close to parallel with the plane of the ecliptic. It seems more than a coincidence that the unseen star that is causing the phenomenon of precession should be found in the exact location of the 2012-era galactic alignment.

If we accept Jenkins's theory that the Maya were tracking precession, this raises the interesting possibility that the end date of the Mayan calendar could actually be tied up with the discovery (or possibly rediscovery) of this hidden influence on our solar system. In the next couple of years, a new generation of telescopes that are much more powerful are being launched into space and brought online on the surface of the planet. If the companion star is a brown dwarf, there is a very good possibility it will be discovered before 2012. If it happens to emerge from the mouth of Xibalba, it will certainly fulfill the Mayan prophecy!

## Are You Sirius?

At a distance of 8.6 light years, the Sirius system is one of our solar system's nearest neighbors. Sirius A is about twice as massive as the sun and about twenty-five times as bright. The idea that Sirius could be a companion star to the sun was first proposed by the mathematician and Egyptologist R.A. Schwaller de Lubicz, who made his deductions from studying the ancient Egyptian calendars that used the helical rising of Sirius as their New Year date. In his book *Sacred Science*, he observed, "It is remarkable that owing to the precession of the equinoxes, on the one hand, and the movement of Sirius on the other, the position of the sun with respect to Sirius is displaced in the same direction, almost exactly to the same extent."

**FACT**

Sirius B, the compact companion star to Sirius, is one of the more massive white dwarfs known, almost twice the average size. It has the same mass as the sun but in a volume roughly equal to Earth! The orbit of Sirius B is extremely eccentric, varying from around 750 million to almost 3 billion miles from Sirius A.

Schwaller de Lubicz inspired the father and son research team of Karl-Heinz Homann and Uwe Homann to form the Sirius Research Group, one of the modern pioneers of binary star theory. They believe the sun's binary companion is the dog star, and have compiled a great deal of evidence that supports a close connection between our sun and Sirius.

Conventional astronomical calculations suggest the chance of Sirius being a companion star is remote. Nonetheless, our sun and Sirius are moving toward each other, demonstrated by the distinct blue cast to the appearance of Sirius. This shows a companion relationship is at least possible. One other possibility is that a more complex arrangement exists where the sun and Sirius are both binary systems, yet they also revolve around each other.

## Myths of Precession

In Hamlet's Mill, a comprehensive book about myths associated with precession, Giorgio de Santillana, former professor of the history of science at MIT, and Hertha von Dechend demonstrate that the folklore of more than thirty different ancient cultures contain stories of a long cycle of time alternating between dark and golden ages that move with the precession of the equinoxes.

One precession-related story tells about a huge mythical mill that ground out gold in one age, salt in another, and sand and rock in a third. Two giant maidens, Fenja and Menja, ceaselessly turn the mill, as no human force is able to move it. Cruttenden associates these two mythical giants with our sun and her companion star, whose motion around each other creates the turning of the ages.

## The Yuga Cycle

Another system that has a series of dark and golden ages are the Vedic Yugas from classical Indian culture. These ages have different qualities. The Satya Yuga is a long-lasting golden age, full of peace and spiritual enlightenment. The silver age, or Treta Yuga, follows this and is slightly shorter and not quite as harmonious. This then gives way to the Dwapara Yuga, or Bronze Age, where spiritual practices start to become forgotten and neglected and the world becomes more orientated toward materialism. Then follows the Kali Yuga, an Iron Age or Dark Age, of ignorance, war, suffering, and the collapse of civilization. The cycle then repeats in the reverse order.

## Sri Yukteswar

A relatively modern proponent of the Yuga system was the Sanskrit scholar Swami Sri Yukteswar, author of *The Holy Science,* which was first published in 1894. Yukteswar was also the guru of the famous Paramahansa Yogananda, author of *Autobiography of a Yogi.* His writing radically revised the existing traditions of the Yugas by fundamentally questioning the established dates.

Hindu tradition states that we are now in the darkest age of all; Yukteswar disagreed and challenged both the timing and the very long periods of time that had been ascribed to each of the Vedas. He suggested that the astronomers and astrologers who calculated the almanacs had been misled by wrong annotations of certain Sanskrit scholars about the length of the Kali Yuga. This led them to maintain that it was 432,000 years long, of which only 5,000 years or so had passed. He described this as, "A dark prospect! And fortunately one not true."

## The Ascending Bronze Age

Yukteswar linked the Yuga cycle to a 24,000-year period. He described this great year as moving in an ascending arc for 12,000 years, raising the consciousness of humanity, and then a descending arc of 12,000 years, lowering it. He also specifically attributed the cause of this to the fact that the sun "takes some star for its dual and revolves round it." Yukteswar, in fact, was presenting a complete binary star-based theory of precession more than 100 years ago. He believed we are currently in the ascending Dwapara Yuga and that we had left the Kali Yuga some 300 years before.

The historical precedents for this look promising. This would mean that the height of the Kali Yuga corresponded to the Dark Ages, where European civilization, at least, was at its lowest ebb. Followers of Yukteswar also claim that our current technologically obsessed era is a clear sign that we have entered the Dwapara Yuga, which is characterized by a fascination with mastering the physical world. It also means we have much better times to look forward to, as we are now moving back toward the time of the Golden Age.

**THE ASCENDING YUGAS ACCORDING TO SRI YUKTESWAR**

| Yuga | Dates | Quality |
|------|-------|---------|
| Kali Yuga: The Iron Age | A.D. 500 to A.D. 1700 (1,200 years) | Descent into materialism, ignorance, and forgetfulness |
| Dwapara Yuga: The Bronze Age | A.D. 1700 to A.D. 4100 (2,400 years) | Technological progress, conquest of space |
| Treta Yuga: The Silver Age | A.D. 4100 to A.D. 8900 (3,600 years) | Telepathy, conquest of time |
| Satya Yuga: The Golden Age | A.D. 8900 to A.D. 13,700 (4,800 years) | Harmony with nature, human divinity |

## Changing Consciousness and the Yuga Cycle

Yukteswar even theorized that a binary motion might allow the rise and fall of human consciousness to occur. In *The Holy Science* he states, "When the Sun in its revolution around its dual comes to the place nearest to this grand center . . . dharma, the mental virtue, becomes so much developed that man can easily comprehend all, even the mysteries of the Spirit." This grand center is the shared equilibrium point around which both of the two stars orbit. The Vedic name for this point was Vishnunabhi, and it was considered a magnetic center and seat of the great creative power of the god Brahma.

In the Vedas, one day of Brahma was equivalent to the time taken for 1,000 cycles of all four Yugas. A day of Brahma is followed by the night of Brahma. The Universe is considered to be many days and nights of Brahma old. By this reckoning, one day of Brahma is 24 million years long. This would be very close to the 26 million-year period of the mass extinction cycle proposed by Raup and Sepkoski. If this is the case, a companion star might possibly be the missing link that connects precession, extinction cycles, and the rise and fall of ages.

## Binary Stars and EM Fields

If the solar system is moving in a binary orbit, the electromagnetic (EM) spectrum of the sun's companion star could have a significant impact on our planet. Cruttenden argues this would directly affect our magnetosphere, ionosphere, and indirectly, all life.

Cruttenden suggests that immersion in stellar-generated EM fields might be the mechanism that induces cyclical changes on Earth. It may also be that the binary star orbits have a relationship with the plasma bands that are currently inundating our solar system with greatly increased plasmic energy.

**ESSENTIAL**

Dr. Valerie Hunt, a former professor of physiology at UCLA, has found that changes in the ambient background EM field can dramatically affect human cognition and performance. This shows that consciousness is affected by immersion in EM fields. All stars generate a massive spectrum of EM frequencies.

The Vedic idea of Brahma's magnetism emanating from a grand center and increasing the growth of human consciousness has a close parallel in the work of researcher David Wilcock of *www.divinecosmos.com*. He has suggested that these plasma bands may be organized as a series of ever-tightening phi-based spirals in the space we are moving through. The effect of our passage through these tightening bands would be a progressive and accelerating increase in the growth of human consciousness. This would culminate exponentially as we reach the omega point of winter solstice 2012.

**ALERT**

A possible criticism of the work of the BRI is that their research is based on inspiration from Yukteswar's teachings rather than being an unattached and objective scientific enquiry. This kind of bias may lead the BRI to emphasize some data and exclude others, according to whether or not it fits with the Yukteswar interpretation of the Yugas.

## Critiques of the Binary Star Theory

Probably the greatest barrier to the acceptance of the binary star theory is that no one has yet observed a binary system with the exact orbits and stellar mass ratios that are being suggested by astronomers searching for Nemesis. Critics point out that it would be a more credible theory if we could point to a similar system in the night sky. Mike Brown, who discovered Sedna and Eris, thinks that most binary star systems go through this kind of orbital pattern at some time in their evolution. He concludes that the reason we have not yet found an example of this is because of the difficulty of detecting brown dwarfs so close to another star.

The belief that we are already in the ascending Dwapara Yuga gives a very different outlook than many of the theories that suggest 2012 is the focal point of a major shift. The Yukteswar view would suggest we should be able to expect steady progress toward a more enlightened society that will be provided by advances in technology. Other researchers, including Jenkins, feel that the coming galactic alignment marks the ending or midpoint of the Kali Yuga, as the alignment of the winter solstice sun with the galaxy marks galactic midnight. This viewpoint would suggest that we could expect something quite different and perhaps significantly more dramatic.

# CHAPTER 19

# The Chaos Point
# and the Noosphere

All of the ideas presented in this book point toward some sort of culmination or event happening in or around 2012. A number of philosophers and scientists have been attempting to bring these very different ideas together into a unified theory. Their goal is to explain the rapidly evolving changes happening to both humanity and our planet as we approach the omega point of 2012.

## The Global Tipping Point

The changes in both global society and our physical planet can be studied just as any other large, complex system, whatever its constituent parts. Over the last twenty to thirty years, two branches of science have rapidly developed our ability to understand behavior in interdependent systems with a large number of variables. These are complex systems theory and chaos theory. The laws that these theories articulate work just as well for any large system, from the swarming of locusts to global social trends.

Ervin Laszlo is a former professor of philosophy, systems science, and future studies and has been nominated three times for the Nobel Peace Prize. He is also the founder of the Club of Budapest, an international think-tank dedicated to positive global change, whose members include the Dalai Lama and Mikhail Gorbachev. In his recent book *The Chaos Point*, he has used ideas from both chaos theory and systems theory to propose that in late 2012 we will reach a global tipping point.

**QUESTION**

**What is a tipping point?**
Adding a small amount of weight to a balanced object can cause it to suddenly and completely topple. The tipping point is when change in a complex system becomes unstoppable. This tends to happen quickly and abruptly, rather than gradually and incrementally. This idea is also known as critical mass.

## Chaos Theory

Chaos theory demonstrates that complex systems tend to alternate between steady increments of progressive change or dynamic stability and quite abrupt phases of fundamental and dynamic change or critical instability. When this critical instability becomes irreversible, this is a sign that a bifurcation point is about to be reached. As this happens, the old system appears to collapse.

The values and patterns that have dominated the way things operate within an existing paradigm go into breakdown. From an inside perspective, this looks like a catastrophic failure. From a broader perspective, this can appear as an opportunity for a breakthrough. Historical examples could include the fall of the Berlin Wall or the stock market crash of 1929. The collapse of one thing is often just the beginning of another.

**ESSENTIAL**

The so-called butterfly effect refers to the idea that a butterfly's wings might create tiny changes in the atmosphere that may ultimately alter the path of a storm hundreds of miles away. The work of the mathematician Edward Lorenz showed that very small mathematical changes in climate models could result in dramatically different weather scenarios.

When the old order falters, there is a momentary pause. One set of values no longer applies, but nothing has yet taken its place. This usually brief state can seem to be either chaos or freedom, depending on the way it is viewed. Complex systems theory has shown that when systems reach a sufficient level of organization and complexity they tend to reorganize themselves in a higher level of order after a collapse. This pattern applies whatever the constituent parts of the system are, from atoms to people.

**FACT**

Life has evolved from simple organisms like protozoa, through intermediate stages like invertebrates, and then into much more complex organisms like mammals and primates. New species appear quite distinctly, with few or no in-between stages. Evolution seems to move forward through a process of punctuated equilibrium. This is exactly what would be predicted by complex systems theory.

## Oscillation and Collapse

There are many signs that this sort of process is currently at work in global society. The worldwide banking and financial crisis of 2008 is an example of the sort of oscillation that typically precedes a bifurcation point.

Share and commodity prices rise and fall in a cycle of increasing volatility. Large fluctuations may be followed by periods of relative calm or consolidation, but the underlying trend is irreversibly leading toward a chaos point. At the chaos point, the butterfly effect applies: Small changes in the new initial conditions of a system can create enormously different outcomes. Laszlo suggests that the choices we make around the chaos point of 2012 will have lasting consequences for generations.

# The Civilization of Holos

Laszlo predicts that a series of underlying social and economic trends will force society to confront a very clear choice between a global breakdown and a global breakthrough. In *The Chaos Point*, he concludes, "2012 is indeed likely to be a gateway to a different world, but whether to a better one or to a disastrous one is yet to be decided." The result depends on the new set of initial conditions. These are fundamental changes in structure that will end the increasingly volatile fluctuations inherent in the old order.

## The Origin of Logos in Greco-Roman Society

This change, Laszlo predicts, will be a fundamental shift in the value system of society. Looking back at the past two-and-a-half-thousand years, Laszlo identifies the dominant worldview as being based on Logos. These values are derived from the ideas of rationality and the rational mind first proposed by Greek philosophers. This subsequently became the intellectual template for the classical Greco-Roman civilization. Laszlo believes this mindset has defined our current era, but it reached its logical conclusion in the materialistic-mechanistic philosophy of René Descartes. According to Laszlo, the consequence of Cartesianism, with its division between mind and matter, has been to reduce the natural world to a secondary kind of existence as a mere raw material, or resource to be exploited. Under the culture of Logos, nature has been our captive, leading us into a precipitous ecological crisis.

Laszlo concludes, "Humanity finds itself at the threshold of a sociocultural mutation beyond classical industrial civilization. If the systems do not break down, the next mutation will see the birth of a planetary civilization . . . the civilization of Holos."

## Breakthrough Versus Breakdown

If breakthrough is achieved, the materialistic rationalist civilization of Logos will potentially give way to the holistic culture of Holos. Some of the values Laszlo suggests Holos might initiate include a renewed respect for nature and a sense of custodianship for the natural world:

- The new Holos culture will be truly global but decentralized.
- It will emphasize regional self-governance and celebrate diversity.
- It will be ecologically aware and imitate natural systems in its social design.

If society goes into breakdown, the Logos culture will be reduced to its constituent parts. Rational, technological society then risks going into catabolic collapse. This is where a society temporarily sustains itself by stripping its own infrastructure and consuming it to manufacture resources. This would be succeeded by a return to a nightmarish dark age.

**ESSENTIAL**

The Hopi people have a prophecy that is encoded in a petroglyph carved on Prophecy Rock near Oraibi, Arizona. This depicts two paths that humanity could choose to take at the coming chaos point. Abundantly growing corn represents the path of life. The other, the path of progress, is represented by a set of stairs, which end abruptly.

## The Emergence of a Planetary Culture

All the ideas that attempt to explain the unprecedented social changes in the world seem to share one common theme: Whatever is happening is truly planetary in scale. From the communications revolution to climate change, we are being asked to think on a global level more than ever before. Nationalistic self-interests and the philosophies that served them, including the culture of Logos that prospered during the Age of Empire, now look outdated and inadequate to deal with the challenges humanity faces.

Several ideas first proposed in the twentieth century, including those of the biosphere and the Gaia hypothesis of James Lovelock, are now gaining ascendancy as the search for tools to effectively conceptualize a planetary scale of thinking becomes ever more urgent.

# The Biosphere

Ukranian geochemist Vladimir Vernadsky first articulated the concept that the totality of living systems on the planet could be thought of as a single entity. He coined the term biosphere to describe this. This is the whole of the envelope of life on and around the surface of the planet. The biosphere includes the crust of Earth, the landmasses and oceans, and the parts of the atmosphere that life inhabits.

This idea allows the totality of life to be described as a series of processes transforming energy into different forms. Vernadsky's biosphere could then be studied in the same way as an industrial or chemical process, with inputs, outputs, and by-products. For Vernadsky, the biosphere was "the single greatest geologic force on Earth, moving, processing, and recycling several billion tons of mass a year. It is the central subsystem of a centralized cybernetic system, Earth, which tends towards a dynamic disequilibrium and tremendous internal diversity."

**FACT**

Vernadsky was one of the most important thinkers in Soviet science of the twentieth century. He founded the National Academy of Science of Ukraine and was a pioneer of several new disciplines. He is best known for his 1926 book *The Biosphere*, in which he gave his exposition of the ideas of the biosphere and the noosphere.

# The Gaia Hypothesis

The scientist James Lovelock first formulated the Gaia hypothesis at NASA in the 1960s after studying the atmosphere of Mars for signs of life. Lovelock's idea was that the biosphere and its physical components are closely integrated to form a complex system that homeostatically maintains conditions on Earth in a way that makes life sustainable. In this way, life and its planetary environment are essentially indivisible and work together holistically.

Lovelock came up with the idea of Earth as a single complex feedback system after observing the way that combinations of essential elements for life are maintained in the atmosphere in stable concentrations. From a purely chemical point of view, Earth's atmosphere should be unstable. Traces of methane should not exist, as they are combustible in an oxygen atmosphere. In Lovelock's opinion, the balance of living organisms maintains the creation and removal of methane, allowing the two to coexist.

**ESSENTIAL**

Lovelock originally called his idea the Earth feedback hypothesis. A neighbor, the novelist William Golding, suggested the name Gaia, after the Greek goddess of the earth. Lovelock has subsequently complained that because of this association, his theory has been treated as a quasi New Age pagan religion, rather than as genuine science.

Other observations further support this view, notably the fact that the surface temperature of Earth has remained remarkably constant since the beginning of life, while at the same time the energy reaching our planet from the sun has increased by at least a quarter. The salinity of the oceans is also another long-term constant that defies scientific prediction or explanation. Incoming salts from freshwater sources should have made the oceans much saltier than they are. Lovelock suggests that the processes of life themselves keep these systems in balance. The Gaia hypothesis should now really be called the Gaia theory, as a number of scientific experiments have been carried out that confirm the predictions of the hypothesis.

## Criticisms of the Gaia Theory

Most scientific criticism of the Gaia theory has centered on the fact that Lovelock seems to be suggesting there is an intelligent design that is directing these homeostatic processes. This has been called teleological thinking by some scientists, a belief, usually religious, that the process of life is heading toward some end goal. Lovelock has since refined his concept of Gaia to clarify this. In 1990 he said, "Nowhere in our writings do we express the idea that planetary self-regulation is purposeful, or involves foresight or planning by the biota."

A stronger version of the Gaia theory would be that our planet is both sentient and alive. This has become a popular and widespread interpretation of the original idea. Lovelock does not share this view. He prefers the scientifically more credible version that life and our planet form one single self-regulating mechanism. The Gaia hypothesis is possibly the largest-scale holistic theory ever proposed, and it is one of the fundamental building blocks of Laszlo's emerging Holos culture.

# The Noosphere

Vernadsky also proposed the idea of the noosphere. Derived from the Greek word for mind, *noos*, it means "sphere of thought." Vernadsky theorized that it was the third in a series of fundamental transformations that have happened to Earth. The first was the creation of the geosphere, the inanimate, mineral Earth. The geosphere was then completely transformed by the arrival of life and the creation of the biosphere. The biosphere is in turn being transformed by human thought, or the creation of the noosphere. Vernadsky's theory was that the noosphere truly emerges when humanity masters the science of the physical realm and is able to reorganize the primary sphere of matter. Marked by the beginning of the atomic age, the noosphere is still considered an extremely significant theory in the mainstream of post-Soviet science.

## The Philosophy of Teilhard de Chardin

Vernadsky's original idea of the noosphere was intended to be a material, scientific description of the process of human civilization transforming the environment that gave it life. This was then taken up by the Jesuit philosopher Teilhard de Chardin, who developed it into something much more expansive. Chardin saw the noosphere as the perfect way to describe the emerging collective consciousness of humanity.

Unshackled by the constraints and rigors of science, Chardin was looking for a way to describe what he saw as the process of a self-reflective consciousness emerging in humanity and spreading itself across the planet.

Chardin's philosophy is deeply teleological. He believed evolution was an irreversible process toward more complexity and more consciousness. Rejecting the biblical doctrine of the Genesis creation story, Chardin posited that God was in fact an evolved superconsciousness at the end of time that was drawing us toward its future perfect state.

**FACT**

In honor of his work in the fields of paleontology and geology, the scientific genus of the first true primate, *Teilhardina*, was named after de Chardin. During his lifetime his ideas and philosophies were censured by the Catholic Church and his main work, *The Phenomenon of Man*, was only published posthumously.

## The Law of Complexity/Consciousness

Chardin is, in many ways, the archetypal philosopher of 2012. He has sometimes been called the patron saint of the Internet, because he believed that the social networks created by humans were the stepping stones toward a new order of consciousness. He formulated the fundamental dynamic behind his philosophy into a principle called the law of complexity/consciousness. The law states that there is an inherent compulsion in matter toward complexity. Chardin proposed this as a universal model of evolution, where everything is becoming more complex.

The emergence of humanity takes this process to a higher plane. This is because humans possess self-awareness. This self-reflection creates a new layer of consciousness: the noosphere. With the advent of the noosphere and self-consciousness, the processes of evolution become increasingly voluntary. What had previously been an instinctual drive toward diversity and difference now potentially shifts toward a new goal: reunification. The key at this point is the individual's desire for convergence. As far as Chardin was concerned, "No evolutionary future awaits anyone except in association with everyone else." This new stage of evolution is the final one. It requires a unification of consciousness and is collective.

# The Omega Point

The culmination of the process of evolution ends in what Chardin called the omega point, the point at which the complexity of the universe has reached its maximum function and has become organized in the most optimal way possible. The omega point is nothing less than the purpose of history, the agonies and ecstasies of which are redeemed in a single moment of supreme meaning. Other 2012 theories, like McKenna's vision of a transcendent moment of infinite novelty at the end of time, owe a great deal to Chardin's idea of the omega point.

## Ontology Versus Teleology

The processes of history are normally figured to start with a defined moment, like the big bang of modern physics or the biblical seven days of creation. Cosmologies organized in this way are called ontologies.

In Chardin's cosmology, it is the other way around. The omega point is the strange attractor drawing us toward it. Belief systems that are based on a defined end point rather than a start point are called teleologies. The five attributes of the omega point are:

1. **Already existing.** This attribute explains the power of the omega point to draw us to itself.
2. **Personal.** The omega point must complement and integrate individuality rather than annihilate it. Otherwise, the law of complexity/consciousness is broken.
3. **Transcendent.** It must not be a product of the universe, but a pre-existing condition from which the universe arises.
4. **Autonomous.** The omega point is not subject to the laws of space and time.
5. **Irreversible.** It must be attainable and permanent.

At the omega point, the perfected noosphere becomes synonymous with the "Christosphere," or collective Christ consciousness of humanity. Chardin's philosophy of the noosphere, despite his rejection by the Catholic Church in his lifetime, is a profoundly religious, if unorthodox, vision.

In the perfection of the noosphere, humanity redeems itself and achieves transcendence.

# The Telepathic Human

Chardin's omega point specifically envisages thought-to-thought telepathy between humans becoming the norm as our communication networks evolve toward the omega point. Other 2012 theorists have picked this up. Argüellés has recently written about the emergence of a new species of telepathic human, *Homo noosphericus*. Since Chardin was a paleontologist, he would probably have appreciated this idea.

Argüellés has spoken about the emergence of *Homo noosphericus* as being a permanent physical change that is imminent for humanity. "We are not talking about being the same as we are now," he says in *Cosmic History Chronicles, Volume 3*. "We are talking about a full-on mutational shift, a frequency shift in which our atoms and molecules begin to vibrate at a higher frequency and, thus, genetically self-correct." After this shift, according to Argüellés, the linear third-dimensional perceptions of history will be replaced by a total holographic comprehension of every moment of every day. We will then be able to truly view ourselves as multidimensional beings. From this new perspective, we will be able to create and perfect alignment with our fourth- and fifth-dimensional galactic-celestial bodies.

## The Technosphere

Argüellés has talked about the technosphere as a necessary intermediate stage in the biosphere-noosphere transition described by Chardin. The technosphere could be defined as the sum of all the connecting parts of the global technological society that cover the biosphere like an electronic sheath. In this model, outlined in his book *Time and the Technosphere*, technological society, especially the Internet, is temporary scaffolding that could be used to trigger the genesis of *Homo noosphericus*. Ultimately, Argüellés sees material technology as an alluring trap that must eventually be discarded in order to restore our original connection with nature. The coming telepathy of *Homo noosphericus* represents the real Internet. This is essentially just a development of Chardin's ideas and is in total agreement with his teleological philosophy.

## Entering the Psychozoic Era

Vernadsky believed the next geological era of Earth would be called the Psychozoic Era or the era of mind. The theories of Chardin and Vernadsky both seem to provide valuable intellectual tools to help grasp the end-times zeitgeist of 2012. As the writer Peter Russell wrote it in the book *The Mystery of 2012*: "2012 is a symbol of the times we are passing through. It represents the temporal epi-center of a cultural earthquake, whose reverberations are getting stronger day by day."

If that is the case, the current time may one day be thought of as the Lower Noospheric Era, to reflect the significance of the discovery that humanity is part of one living Earth. The era when humanity collectively acts on that discovery may then be known as the Upper Noospheric Era. It may well be that 2012 indeed represents the epicenter or threshold between the two.

## CHAPTER 20

# The Global Brain
# and the Singularity

The search for meaning in the accelerating times we live in has created a broad range of ideas about the imminence of a possible end point to history as we have known it. The result of this singularity may be a transformation of humanity, the planet, or both. Various theories compete to best describe the possible outcomes.

## The Global Brain

The ideas of Chardin, presented in the last chapter, are further developed in the work of the writer Peter Russell. In his 1983 book *The Global Brain*, Russell puts forward the idea that the true purpose of humanity is to evolve into a massively networked global brain for our planet. In Russell's theory, each individual would perform a function similar to an individual cell in the brain.

By learning to think in this networked way, the global brain would represent a mind of its own with unfathomably large computational power. Humanity would then be able to act in a coordinated and harmonious manner and avoid conflict, greed, and exploitation. Russell's timeline for the emergence of the global brain coincides with 2012, which he views as a white hole in time, his version of Chardin's omega point.

### A Critical Mass

In support of this idea, Russell cites the fact that it takes approximately ten to the power of ten (or ten billion) atoms to form the most basic level of unicellular bacterial life. This number seems to him to be a necessary minimum for the sufficient complexity for the evolution of life. In a parallel to the evolution of life from matter, Russell suggests that a similar number of brain cells (in the region of ten billion) in the neocortex are required to produce the reflective consciousness characteristic of humanity. If this turns out to be a general principle of evolution, Russell suggests that the next evolution could be represented by something in the region of ten billion minds beginning to work together as one global brain.

### The Information Age

Russell formulated these ideas in the early 1980s, and correctly predicted the importance of emerging computer networks in an information revolution. Russell noted that by 1900, more people were employed by industry than the previously dominant activity of agriculture. By the mid 1970s, the number of people engaged in the processing of information (in all of its aspects, from publishing to banking to media to all computer-related occupations) had caught up with those engaged in industry—the processing of energy and matter.

"From that time on," Russell declares, "information processing has been our dominant activity." We had entered the Information Age. The Industrial Revolution took 300 years. The Information Age has been in ascendancy for thirty. Russell predicts that this fits into a pattern of ever-accelerating evolution that stretches back to the dawn of life on Earth:

- The first simple life forms evolved 4 billion years ago.
- Multicellular life appeared about 1 billion years ago.
- Vertebrates with central nervous systems developed several hundred million years ago.
- Mammals appeared tens of millions of years ago.
- The first hominids appeared a couple million years ago.
- *Homo sapiens* appeared a few hundred thousand years ago.
- Language and tool use developed tens of thousands of years ago.
- Civilization, the movement into towns and cities, occurred a few thousand years ago.
- The Industrial Revolution began three centuries ago.
- The Information Revolution is a few decades old.

Similar to the theories of Calleman and McKenna, Russell believes that cultural acceleration is leading toward a culmination at some time in the very near future. Although he is not attached to any specific prediction for what will or won't happen on December 21, 2012, he does embrace the general principle of a major evolutionary breakthrough for humanity somewhere around that time.

## The Dawning of the Wisdom Age

Although for Russell technology is the means by which we have reached our current state of evolution, it is only a means to an end and not an end in itself. Our current computer technology has created the ability to communicate and transfer more information than ever before. In Russell's model, this creates the opportunity for cultures from around the world to share insights about enlightenment and different wisdom traditions. Teachings that otherwise would only have been available to a tiny minority are now effectively available to everyone.

For Russell, the key requirement to making the leap into the Wisdom Age is the ability to dissolve attachment to what the philosopher and writer Alan Watts called the skin-encapsulated ego. This is the idea that the boundary of self starts and ends with the physical body and that the individual is a detached and separate entity from the world. This is replaced with what Russell has called leaky margins, where boundaries are still there but are not solid. In this way, it is possible to function in the world, but also to identify with it and all the other people in it enough to be empathic—and hence, wise.

**FACT**

According to Russell, the exponential growth of the Wisdom Age will be so rapid that it will outstrip the growth of the Information Age in the very near future. "Because each new phase of evolving intelligence takes place in a fraction of the time of the previous phase, we can expect the dawning of a Wisdom Age to take place in years rather than decades. It will be standing on the shoulders of the Information Age."

# The Technological Singularity

Not everyone who is predicting an impending singularity in human development is suggesting that it will be a spiritual Renaissance. Futurists and technologists are predicting that we may be heading toward a technological singularity. This idea was first proposed by the mathematician Vernor Vinge, based on Moore's Law, the observation that the rate of increase in computing power has been consistently exponential for the last fifty years.

Computing power now doubles approximately every eighteen months. If this trend were to continue, Vinge and others argue, computers within a decade of our current era will be more powerful than the human brain. Once this happens, they suggest it is likely that computers themselves will take over the designing of future computers. This could then lead to a runaway train kind of scenario where machines rapidly become much smarter than the humans who initially created them.

In this version of convergence, the technosphere would be the goal, not just the means. The technological singularity would be a convergence of all technologies, until humans became totally embedded and submerged into a virtual world. This singularity is a state in which humans will be components of a cybernetic social network of such complexity that no one person will be able to understand more than a tiny fraction of the whole.

**QUESTION**

**What is Moore's Law?**
Gordon Moore first observed in 1965 that the transistor densities of integrated circuits doubled every two years. This rate of improvement has remained consistent, giving rise to Moore's Law. All technologies ultimately reach the limits of their possible capabilities, but the exponential trend of Moore's Law has been consistent across multiple computer technologies. This suggests it may continue indefinitely.

## Ray Kurzweil

One of the chief proponents of this idea is the futurist Ray Kurzweil, who describes this near-imminent technological omega point in his book *The Singularity Is Near.* His vision of the future is not just a matter of his opinion; it is a template that is being acted upon and implemented by the multinational corporate world.

Kurzweil predicts that not only will computers become more intelligent than humans, but also that computers will become so powerful that it will be possible to download the entire contents of the human brain into one. The result of this would be a sort of digital immortality. Kurzweil does not see a problem with consciousness being transferred along with the information from a brain.

Kurzweil believes that his only responsibility is to stay alive until this technology is in place so that he can live forever. Consequently, he is taking a large number of health supplements and is planning his life to avoid taking any unnecessary risks. Kurzweil's current estimate is that computers will surpass the power of the human brain sometime in the next decade and that the singularity will occur sometime around 2045.

### Critique of the Technological Singularity

Kurzweil's estimates of the computing power required to model the structure of the human brain have taken a major blow from the quantum theory of mind proposed by Dr. Stuart Hammeroff, professor of psychology at the University of Arizona, and Professor Roger Penrose, author of *The Emperor's New Mind*. Their idea is that the human brain doesn't function by electrical impulses being transferred from synapse to synapse. Instead, they propose the brain is a quantum computer that uses coherence states in tiny structures called microtubules to record and store information.

Kurzweil has been forced to admit that if their theory is proven correct, the human brain is many millions of times more powerful than previously estimated. If this is indeed the case, the technological singularity is not quite so close, certainly not anywhere near 2012 and could, in fact, be very distant indeed.

# Transhumanism

Transhumanism is a movement that supports the use of science and technology to radically alter and improve human mental and physical characteristics and capacities. Transhumanists regard mortality as just another technical challenge that will eventually be overcome when scientific advances make immortality possible.

The term "transhumanism" was first coined in 1966 by FM-2030 (formerly known as F.M. Esfandiary), a futurist who taught new concepts of the human at the New School in New York City. The term was aimed at describing the enthusiastic adopters of technology who believe technology and science will eventually have a solution for all humanity's problems. For most transhumanists, the technological singularity is an important goal.

### The Big Crunch

Some of the most extreme examples of the idea of technological convergence can be found in the ideas of Dr. Frank Tipler. Extrapolating from the known laws of physics, he points out that if the universe reaches a finite point of expansion and then begins to contract, it is likely to end in a big crunch. This is an almost exact reverse of the big bang. At this point, all of the matter in the universe will have converged on one point and there will be zero available free energy.

Tipler thinks this situation can be redeemed by the possibility of creating a truly giant computer that will model the entire universe. Even though the length of the universe is finite (and the computer is part of that universe), the computer's ability to process increasing quantities of information is theoretically infinite. According to Tipler, this will result in a transcendent omega point, as the computational capacity of the universe will be accelerating exponentially as time runs out.

**FACT**

Transhumanism is sometimes associated with the term "H+," which stands for "human enhancement." H+ symbolizes the belief that by using technology, humanity can grow capabilities far beyond what is currently possible. The abilities of H+-designated humans may be extended so far in terms of intelligence, longevity, and even strength that they will be considered posthuman.

## The Far Edge of the Eschaton

Kurzweil's vision of the world post singularity is strikingly similar to Tipler's. Kurzweil predicts human-created artificial intelligence will eventually wake up all the matter of the entire universe into sentience. These ideas about the future of humanity are probably only equaled in sheer extremism by those of Terence McKenna, but these are the sorts of concepts that form the far edges of eschatology, the study of the end times. The year 2012 is the archetypal convergence point for all end-times theories. These various ideas are currently now competing for what the philosopher A.N. Whitehead called the formality of actually occurring.

# Which Theory to Choose?

Ample scientific and cultural evidence points to the beginning of a period of unprecedented change, and there are numerous theories that attempt to explain and interpret that data. According to whichever theory is chosen, the resulting predictions for 2012 include an apocalypse, the dawning of a new golden age, the advent of telepathy, or the introduction of posthumanism.

Modern academia has difficulties with 2012 as a subject because it includes pretty much everything. This book has covered subjects as diverse as the Mayan calendar, astronomical discoveries from the edge of the solar system, the ancient Vedas, and the use of psychedelic mushrooms. It would be quite difficult to find a university department or research institute that encouraged or funded the study of all of these elements simultaneously.

## Specialization Versus Generalism

The current paradigm of academia is focused on specialism. This is how individual academics carve out a niche within a specific subject matter and advance their careers. This has encouraged the development of more and more specialization. Some scientific disciplines are so specialized that it is nearly impossible for one person to have a full comprehension of the whole of the field.

Specialization has, for example, limited the debate about the role of carbon dioxide in climate change. This is because atmospheric scientists study only the atmosphere. They can say that both carbon dioxide concentration and global temperatures are increasing, but they can't definitively answer why. If the cause comes from outside the sphere of most scientists' specialized field of study, it remains invisible in their data. It has taken researchers like Dmitriev and Svensmark, who approach their work in a more multidisciplinary way, to question these orthodoxies and suggest other possible outside influences.

The study of 2012 requires holistic generalism. This is an ability to draw from many disciplines and integrate them into a coherent set of explanations. Many of the thinkers whose ideas have been portrayed in this book could be classified as generalist or multidisciplinary in their approaches. For instance, La Violette combines subquantum physics with study of the symbolism of the Tarot and the Zodiac.

# Cosmic Synergism

A multidisciplinary approach allows connectivity to develop between diverse subject matters. For example, plasma is a common factor in a possible explanation for the creation of crop circles and in an interplanetary theory of climate change. By following the links, we are able to create a bigger picture of what is going on. This approach also gives a new criterion for determining the usefulness of a theory: how much information it can integrate.

Theories of everything, based on just one methodology, like Kurzweil's technological singularity or McKenna's psychedelic apocalypse, seem to produce ideas of impending infinities so mindboggling they seem to collapse in on themselves like black holes. While these ideas maintain an inner logic, they refuse to submit to common sense.

More holistic theories that draw from multiple viewpoints or disciplines and integrate diverse data into something comprehensible seem ultimately much more useful. They also produce scenarios that seem more likely. This raises the intriguing possibility that it may be possible to formulate a grand unified theory of 2012 that coherently describes the fundamental underlying forces at work in this convergence, despite all the incredibly diverse data it would have to accommodate.

This grand unified theory of 2012 would have to bring together:

- An explanation of the changing world ages and global climate
- The relationship of our planet to the galaxy and the role of the precession of the equinoxes
- The role of electromagnetism and cosmic radiation in regulating life on Earth
- An explanation of the evolution of consciousness
- An explanation of the apparently accelerating nature of time

Remarkably, a little-known twentieth-century writer and thinker did exactly this. A professor of the philosophy of science at the University of Pittsburgh for more than fifty years, Oliver L. Reiser corresponded and collaborated with Albert Einstein, the poet Rabindranath Tagore, and Sri Aurobindo, the Indian mystic and founder of Auroville.

Reiser's main theory was cosmic humanism, a name Einstein suggested to him. This was an expansive vision that placed the story of human evolution into the broader context of the galaxy. Reiser thought that geomagnetic forces were responsible for both the evolution of consciousness and cyclical changes on our planet.

**ESSENTIAL**

Reiser's ideas have been acknowledged as formative influences on the work of Argüellés, who incorporated ideas from Reiser into *Earth Ascending*, and Jenkins, who devotes a chapter to Reiser in his book *Galactic Alignment*. Yet Reiser's major books, *Cosmic Humanism*, *The World Sensorium*, and *The Intent Of Creation*, are out of print or difficult to find.

## Cosmecology

Reiser also developed a theory of cosmecology, which connected the origin of biological mutation with x-rays to cyclical changes in the sun and the galaxy. This became incorporated into Darwinian evolutionary theory as the idea of punctuated equilibrium, which explains the sudden and distinct appearance of new species. He also connected these evolutionary cycles to the precession of the equinoxes and the geomagnetic reversal of the earth's poles. Reiser correctly predicted that records of these events would be found in magnetically reversed layers in rock samples. In addition, he suggested that the mechanism of cosmic radiation driving evolution might work directly on our DNA through resonance.

## The Psi Bank

Reiser proposed the existence of a psi bank, a kind of magnetic memory field around the planet. The psi bank acts as a depository for thought forms and is held in place by electromagnetic bands around Earth. Reiser favored this idea over the notion that ideas are contained within the brain. He theorized that the brain was an amplification and receiving station for information stored in the psychosphere of the psi bank.

Reiser's work on the magnetic bands of the psi bank prefigured the discovery of the Van Allen radiation belts, which he had accurately predicted the location of. Reiser also thought that the DNA double helix would be a resonant pattern within the psi bank field. Argüellés later resurrected this idea and connected the psi bank with the crossover polarity pattern of galactic activation portals in the Mayan Tzolkin, which he related to DNA.

Mirroring Russell's work on the global brain, Reiser suggested the idea of a global organic brain-mind that individuals can help develop by acting as a voluntary neuroblast, an embryonic cell that can become a part of the emerging planetary nervous system. He envisioned Eastern mysticism and Western science as two complementary hemispheres of this world brain, two halves of the earth's armature whose rotation generates the current to power our evolving planetary society. This is almost identical to Calleman's theory of the World Tree.

Reiser also believed that the processes of evolution are driving toward an approaching singularity that he called the evolutionary spiral. Reiser even suggested that a language of astroglyphs be created to communicate with other intelligences around the galaxy. These are a kind of cosmic universal language based on transforming sounds into pure number. The idea has a resonance with some theories that posit crop circles are a form of extraterrestrial communication.

## The Master Timing Device

Significantly, because of the time he was writing in, Reiser lacked knowledge of two ideas that might have helped him complete his grand theory. These were the winter-solstice galactic alignment identified by Jenkins and knowledge of the Mayan calendar end date in 2012. Reiser knew he still had missing elements, and in his book *The Holyest Earth* he asks:

*"What and where is the master timing device (the sun-planet-galaxy clock) which regulates the interdependent casual sequences to achieve and maintain the astro-geo-bio-homo-social chain of a vast, interlocking, and awesome teleology?"*

That sun-planet-galaxy clock may well be the galactic alignment and the master timing device of the Mayan calendar. Reiser managed to be a 2012 theorist without even knowing about 2012. He did this by thinking synergistically, bringing together many seemingly diverse elements to attempt an explanation of what is driving us toward the event horizon of an impending omega point. It is possible that a similar approach gives us the best possible opportunity to understand the remarkable confluence of circumstances that are leading up to the convergence of 2012.

The best description of what is going on as we reach this possible omega point of 2012 is likely to build on these remarkable foundations. A new science seems to be emerging around the event horizon of 2012 that has expanded vistas from the science of the twentieth century. Our new theory of everything will need to be judged by how holistic and expansive it is, not by how small the pieces of the puzzle can be reduced.

## CHAPTER 21

# What Can We Do?

This book has explored many of the numerous theories and ideas about what may be about to happen in 2012. In this final chapter, the insights and information are integrated into some suggestions about how to prepare for the sort of changes that may be imminent as we approach the global tipping point.

## What Will Happen in 2012?

There are so many different possibilities for any future event that relying on any one set of predictions is always of questionable worth. The prophecies and predictions associated with 2012 are so various that this is even more difficult than usual. What is possible, however, is to prepare for some of the more likely probabilities both practically and psychologically.

### Earth Changes and Survival

Many of the more progressive Earth changes that are forecasted can be prepared for in a way that does not necessarily cause major disruption to normal, everyday life. Even small gradual changes toward self-sufficiency and sustainability are helpful. These can be as various as reducing our consumption of energy and nonrecyclable resources or planting vegetables in an allotment or community garden.

Many schemes that support pathways to lifestyles more integrated with nature already exist. Options include:

- **Transition town:** A network of communities that is planning for the postcarbon economy, including the creation of alternative local currencies.
- **Permaculture:** The creation of integrated urban and rural design solutions for high-yield, low-maintenance organic agriculture.
- **Raw food lifestyles:** Adopting a more organic and closer-to-nature diet can be helpful in staying grounded and healthy through accelerating change.
- **Global Ecovillage Network:** A worldwide alliance of intentional communities for those who are more committed to a fundamental change in lifestyle.

## Low Probability Catastrophic Events

Some of the possible events that have been covered in this book are relatively unlikely to occur in 2012, or even shortly after. A physical pole shift or a major galactic superwave event would likely be calamitous for global humanity. Fortunately, events of this magnitude are by no means any kind of certainty. The search for discovering the real message of 2012 has meant considering these apocalyptic outcomes as possibilities, but even the founder of the galactic superwave theory, La Violette, is relatively optimistic. If there is an event, he believes it is likelier to be a more minor wake-up call type of event, rather than a cataclysm.

That one of these types of major event will happen at some time in our planet's future is actually very likely, but the timescale may be vast. Superwave events of some magnitude may happen once every 13,000 years. Magnetic pole reversals happen, at most, once in 125,000 years. A physical pole shift has probably happened only once in our planet's history, so even a generous guess would put that probability in the order of once every few hundred million years or so.

**ALERT**

It is important not to overestimate the possible likelihood of the very worst-case scenarios. It is true that many of the theories that have been discussed in this book do speculate about a cycle of disaster that accompanies the galactic alignment of 2012, the precession of the equinoxes, or the changing of world ages. However, this may not necessarily be an abrupt, cataclysmic, world-shattering event.

## Cometary Impact

One of the more likely major events with far-reaching global impact would be the possibility that the Oort cloud perturber, whatever that turns out to be, sends more comets into the inner solar system. However, a cometary impact happening in exactly 2012 is very unlikely.

According to the theory pioneered by paleontologists Raup and Sepkoski, a large event happens approximately once every 26 million years. Even if that were timed to coincide with the galactic alignment marking the end of a 26,000-year precessional cycle, the odds would still be 1,000 to one. Raup and Sepkoski calculate that we are not due for another extinction-level event for perhaps another 20 million years.

# Higher Probability Global Crisis Events

The changes in the magnetic poles of our planet combined with the incoming effects of more interstellar plasma may possibly have significant geophysical effects. One scenario that has been suggested is the possibility that the increase in these magnetic changes will lead to increased pressures on Earth's crust that may trigger a supervolcano eruption.

**QUESTION**

**What is a supervolcano?**
Supervolcanoes occur when magma in the earth rises into the crust from a hotspot but is unable to break through. Pressure builds in a large and growing magma pool until the crust eventually gives way. The last major supervolcano to explode was around 75,000 years ago in Lake Toba, Indonesia. It plunged Earth into a volcanic winter, in which it was estimated that more than 60 percent of the human population perished.

The relationship between the magnetic poles and Earth's volcanic activity is not well understood, but there is no clear reason to suggest that a change in the magnetic field causes volcanic eruptions. It is just as possible that volcanic eruptions cause changes in Earth's magnetic field. The most convincing argument for a supervolcano explosion happening in the near future is that the large caldera underneath Yellowstone National Park appears to be overdue for an eruption. This could be soon, but it could also still be many hundreds of years away. In any case, it is more likely than a cometary impact.

## A Major Solar Event

The major disruptive event most likely to occur in 2012 is a major solar flare coinciding with the peak of the sunspot cycle. The changes in the recent behavior of the sun do suggest something major is happening. The steady growth in solar activity that has marked the last hundred or so years seems to be at an end. It may well be that a major solar eruption will precede a period of possibly 100 years or longer when the sun goes into a Maunder minimum–type period, resulting in much less solar activity and a sharp drop in global temperatures.

## The Hole in the Magnetosphere

The recently discovered changes to Earth's magnetosphere by NASA's THEMIS satellite will make our planet more vulnerable to incoming solar radiation. Instead of protecting our planet, the two large cracks in the magnetosphere found by the satellite could potentially accelerate the incoming flare. The discoveries made by THEMIS show that the way the magnetosphere works is exactly the opposite of what scientists had previously believed. This means that in 2012, the magnetic fields of the sun and Earth will be aligned in such a way that as much as twenty times the amount of solar radiation will get through as would if they were antialigned.

If the 2012 solar event were of a similar scale to the Carrington event, likely consequences would include:

- The shutdown of power grids worldwide
- Disruption of all satellite communications
- Computer hard discs and other electronic storage media may be wiped
- The Internet may go offline
- Widespread disruption to industry and commerce

An article in *New Scientist* magazine about exactly this possibility estimates that a global recovery from such an event would take between four and ten years. People who are dependent on intensive health care or who live in high-rise buildings that depend on electrically pumped water would be amongst the most vulnerable. The National Academy of Science estimates that an event like this would cost the global economy more than $3 trillion in just the first year alone. This is still not a probable event, but it is not an unlikely one, either. Therefore, it is worth being aware of and preparing for. Sensible precautions would include:

- Have access to a sufficient supply of water and food for at least a couple of weeks.
- Not being dependent on computer or phone communication is extremely important.
- Solar powered or hand-cranked radios and flashlights are essential items.
- A first aid kit, portable gas stove, and camping supplies are all useful.
- A reasonable reserve of fuel for personal emergency use is important; gas pumps will not work during power outages.
- Important data should be archived on DVD or CD and not just left on hard drives.
- If you live in a high-rise building, have a contingency plan in case of a protracted power failure.
- If you or a relative are dependent on intensive medical care, have a backup plan that doesn't rely on the electricity supply.
- In the case of such an emergency, it is also very helpful to know one's neighbors and have good links to your local community.

## Incremental Changes

What is more likely than any single apocalyptic event in 2012 is that 2012 will mark a major watershed moment in several very important incremental changes. In the year 2012, the fact that climate change, oil consumption, and the human population are all increasingly accelerating may become very much more obvious. That global technological society has gone into overdrive and now needs to change its course seems very likely. Major changes to our lifestyles may be required because of the impact of these incremental changes.

## Survivalism Versus Community

Learning about some of the more extreme possibilities of 2012 makes it tempting to adopt a survivalist mentality and head for the hills. In *How to Survive 2012*, Geryl is convinced that in 2012 a pole shift will result in a mile-high tidal wave. He suggests the only survivable options are to either be more than 4,000 feet high in a mountain range in an underground bunker or to be in a special unsinkable ship. Unfortunately, this kind of preparation only suffices for this very unlikely type of global catastrophe, and even then it is no guarantee of survival. In a broad range of much more likely scenarios, isolated survivalists are actually among the worst placed to survive.

Major urban centers may be undesirable if there is a significant emergency, especially if you do not have a well-established personal network to rely upon. The best options seem to be to go somewhere you have strong community bonds and where, if larger structures do start to break down, there are sufficient local resources to provide for basic needs. Smaller communities and towns, especially ones with enough adjacent land for growing food, are ideal for this.

# Peak Oil and the Deindustrial Revolution

The peak of oil production for our planet will come before 2012. This is a major landmark in the history of global technological civilization, which is still massively dependent on oil as its major resource base. Shortly after this point, reserves of natural gas will also hit their production peak and go into decline. It is impossible to talk about what may happen in 2012 without assessing this as a factor, as it may be a dominant theme. The fundamental problem that global industrial civilization now faces is that it has grown accustomed to the richest source of stored energy ever found.

**QUESTION**

**What is peak oil?**
Peak oil is the point at which the global production of oil is maximized and we have effectively depleted half of all the recoverable oil reserves on the planet. Estimates vary about when this will be reached, but most analysts put it between 2000 and 2010.

## The Energy Gap

Many people believe that oil will be seamlessly replaced by new or alternative technologies, like new nuclear or wind and wave power. Unfortunately, none of these power sources, or even all of them combined, is capable of replacing oil. This is because oil's net energy—the energy cost of harvesting it against the power it generates in its lifetime—is so enormously high. The net energy stored in sweet light crude oil is around 200:1.

By contrast, the best alternative technology is the modern windmill, which is around 6:1. Some estimates of photovoltaic cells estimate their net energy to be just slightly more than 1:1. This means that new technology, unless it improves its net energy value by a factor of at least ten-fold, will not replace the easy, cheap energy we are accustomed to now. Possible consequences of peak oil include:

- As supply dwindles, energy prices inevitably increase substantially.
- Industries that are based on the cheap availability of energy or rely heavily on importing or exporting will be the hardest hit.
- Shortages of consumer products may follow as the economy is forced to retool.
- Economic crisis may be exacerbated by speculation on wildly varying energy prices, making long-term planning extremely difficult for even vital and basic industries.
- Oil-dependent food production will be badly affected and food prices are likely to increase substantially.
- Energy-intensive health care is likely to be very seriously impacted by a global downturn based on escalating energy costs.

Diseases and illnesses that require major resources to treat could be made economically nonviable. Health insurance schemes and health services will risk collapse and bankruptcy.

## The Long Descent

The end of the current form of civilization is not necessarily going to be a rapid affair. In *The Long Descent*, John Micheal Greer estimates that on average, civilizations take around 250 years from the onset of collapse to complete dissolution. Greer observes, "The process of catabolic collapse unfolds, in a stair-step process alternating periods of crisis with breathing spaces at progressively lower levels of economic and political integration."

**QUESTION**

**What is catabolic collapse?**
Greer uses this term to describe what happens to a civilization when it can no longer meet the demands for resources and energy to support itself. It then begins the process of feeding on its own parts. Rather than a sudden apocalypse, Greer believes we should anticipate a long descent toward a different kind of society based on vastly lower energy consumption. He has called this the deindustrial revolution.

The likelihood is that these changes, forced or voluntary, will result in significant political upheaval. In Greer's opinion, "Many of today's political institutions will not survive the end of cheap energy and the changeover to new political arrangements will likely involve violence." Less developed countries that still have substantial subsistence agriculture and less dependence on fossil fuel energy will be better placed to cope. Here are some suggestions from Greer's book for coping with the changes:

**THE FOUR FACETS OF CATABOLIC COLLAPSE**

| Facet | Solution |
|---|---|
| Declining energy availability | Reduce energy use |
| | Plan on reducing energy usage by at least half |
| | Practice dealing with power blackouts and be prepared to do without power at all, if necessary |
| Economic contraction | Choose a viable profession |
| | Choose to learn a craft that requires modest energy inputs and is going to be of use in the local production of essential goods and services |
| Collapsing public health system | Take charge of your own health |
| | Learn about preventative medicine and other alternative forms of treatment |
| | Take an advanced first aid class and have necessary medical supplies on hand |
| Political turmoil | Practice community networking |
| | Get involved in local community groups, such as local farmers markets, community gardening groups, and social forums |

## Life in the Noosphere

These suggestions only cover the physical aspects of what may be about to occur as we approach 2012. The other side of the equation points to an evolution in humanity's consciousness that will lead us toward a different set of social values. These ideas are supported by the research of Dmitriev and the Planetophysical Institute, which suggests that the increase in incoming interstellar plasma reaching our planet may be responsible for changes in human perception, including increasingly common instances of ESP, clairvoyance, and telepathy.

Preparing for what Russell has called the 2012 mindshift has the advantage of being useful whatever the outcome is. There is also a growing body of scientific evidence supporting the idea that human consciousness has a direct and measurable impact upon reality. So, by changing our minds, we may well be able to have a distinct effect on our world.

### The Global Consciousness Project

Research led by Roger Nelson and his team at Princeton University for the Global Consciousness Project (GCP) is exploring the idea that there may be a consciousness field measurable by what they call an electroga-iagram. This effect is measured by utilizing a large worldwide network of random number generators. The hypothesis of the GCP is that human consciousness and emotions create or interact with a global field, which affects the randomness of these electronic devices.

**FACT**

Two space weather satellites monitoring Earth's geomagnetic field registered a significant spike at the time of the 9/11 terror attack and for several days thereafter. This seems to indicate that the stress wave caused by mass-scale human emotion causes modulations in the geomagnetic field of the planet.

The GCP's results have produced some convincing evidence. During the terror attacks of 9/11, there was a large change in the randomness of the numbers generated by these devices. The random number generators were affected some four to five hours before the attack, suggesting a worldwide collective intuition about the impending event.

Global meditations, prayers, and peace events have also demonstrated statistically significant deviations from randomness. There are now more than forty monitoring stations all over the world collating data for the GCP. The GCP results have been consistent for more than a decade; human events, especially ones that generate strong emotions, both negative and positive, have a measurable effect on the apparently random order of things.

# Coherence

Coherence is a measurement of how the body and brain are functioning together as one integrated unit. The fundamental premise of coherence is that it is a real psychophysiological state that can be measured. Coherence registers in the rhythms and waveforms of the heart, which in turn has the effect of bringing the brain, respiratory, and other systems into synchronous alignment. In a state of coherence, very little energy is wasted and the combined systems of the body and mind work together in maximum efficiency.

## The Maharishi Effect

Maharishi Mahesh Yogi, the founder of transcendental meditation, predicted in 1960 that if a critical mass of around 1 percent of a community were to practice this form of meditation, a measurable improvement for the quality of life for the whole community would be recorded. Since then, extensive trials have been conducted to measure the effect that groups of meditators can have on their communities. In 1974, a study showed that, on average, if 1 percent of a community was practicing the transcendental meditation program, the crime rate would fall by around 16 percent. This has now become known as the Maharishi effect.

These studies have been repeated over the following decades on several different continents and with large groups of meditators. The average drop in crime across all these studies was around 11 percent. The probability of this happening by chance is less than one in 1,000. In 1993, a study was conducted in Washington D.C. under scrutiny of an independent review board. The drop in crime was measured as 23.3 percent. The probability of this arising from chance is less than one in 1 billion.

## Community Coherence

The heart generates an electrical field that is many times stronger than the one the brain produces. This field extends out from the body and can be measured up to several feet away. Researchers at the Institute of HeartMath, an international nonprofit education and research organization, have shown that, in a state of heart coherence, a person's electrical field can have the effect of entraining the brain waves of people they come into close proximity with to a more coherent state. This shows a scientifically measurable connection that is not dependent on touch.

**FACT**

When a person is in coherent alignment, it is possible to pass that coherence on to others by sharing activity such as a like-minded project or team sporting activity. If a group of people go into coherence together, it is self-reinforcing, resulting in higher and more stable states of coherence.

## The Global Coherence Monitoring System

The Institute of HeartMath believes it is possible to extend states of coherence out into the world to create profound healing effects and harmonious social change. By consciously developing and maintaining states of personal and community coherence, we are then able to have a positive impact on everyone we meet.

In their attempt to improve global coherence, the Institute of HeartMath is planning an ambitious program to measure coherence around the world, called the Global Coherence Monitoring System (GCMS). The GCMS will use a series of tracking stations around the world to measure how fluctuations and resonances in the ionosphere's magnetic fields affect, or are influenced by, human heart-rhythm patterns, brain activity, stress, and emotions.

## Volcanic Activity and the Ionosphere

Two or three weeks before earthquakes or volcanic eruptions Earth's magnetic field changes. It is possible that the GCMS could act as a global monitoring system to predict earthquakes and volcanic eruptions. Earth's ionosphere produces a range of resonant frequencies between 0.01 Hz to 300 Hz, some of which are also found in the human heart and brain. It seems possible that changes in the ionosphere directly affect human heart and brain operation. When people say they feel an impending earthquake or other events such as weather changes, they may be reacting to actual physical signals occurring in the earth's magnetic field before the event. If the hypothesis of the GCMS is proven correct, it may be that sufficient coherence in human consciousness could stabilize any potential Earth changes.

**ESSENTIAL**

Dr. Elizabeth Rausher, the coordinator of GCMS, and her late husband, Dr. William Van Bise, predicted the volcanic eruption of Mount St. Helens in Washington using sensitive magnetic field detectors. In the eighteen months following the eruption, they were able to predict 84 percent of the seismic activity occurring within a 100 square-mile area around a single detector.

## Introductory Coherence Technique

Developing more coherence can be a quite straightforward practice. The Institute of HeartMath gives a simple outline for an exercise that can be done daily for around five minutes. Personal benefits are claimed to include an increase in focus and effectiveness. According to HeartMath, the exercise is also beneficial for the planet, even if the person practicing is not in total coherence. The following exercise can be practiced while doing ordinary daily activities and does not require a special time to be set aside. Further information is available at *www .heartmath.org*.

Here are some simple daily exercises to build coherence:

1. Breathe and calm yourself in whatever ways you choose.
2. Choose something or someone you appreciate and radiate the feeling of appreciation to them for about two minutes. (This helps open the heart more and increases your effectiveness when you start sending care to the planet or to a situation in need.)
3. Now evoke genuine feelings of compassion and care for the planet.
4. Breathe the feelings of compassion and care going out from your heart.
5. Radiate the genuine feelings of compassion and care to the planet or to a specific area of immediate need.
6. See yourself, along with other caretakers, participating in this process of healing and facilitating peace.

## Coherence and Global Peace Events

Some of the strongest deviations from randomness that have been recorded by the GCP have happened in response to global meditations, prayers, or other intentional events. The deviation of 9/11 was matched by a similar response on the worldwide day of prayer that followed. The stronger the positive focus on subjects like peace and harmony, the stronger the deviations seem to be. Globally networked events like Earthdance, Earth Day, Peace One Day, and similar events score highly on the scale of deviation, making it statistically very unlikely these influences are random.

## The Rainbow Bridge Meditation

The work of Argüellés and the Dreamspell program culminates in a visualization exercise for 2012 where a coherent global telepathic wave of love is sent out on winter solstice 2012. This consists of imagining the planet being surrounded by a rainbow ring, much like one of the rings of Saturn but extended vertically from the north to the south pole instead.

This rainbow bridge is intended to be a visible manifestation of the emerging noosphere. Of particular note is the fact that if a massive solar flare does occur sometime around the calendar end date, widespread auroras are likely to be visible around the world. During the Carrington event of 1859, bright rainbow-colored lights appeared in the sky that were seen as far south as the Caribbean. The rainbow bridge is described by Argüel-lés as being plasmic in nature and as "bipolar rainbow alternators that hold Earth's magnetic fields in place." A more comprehensive version of the rainbow bridge meditation can be found on the planet art network website at *www.tortuga.com.*

# Preparing for 2012

There are many different ways you can prepare for 2012. From meditating to getting involved in your community, you can get ready for whatever is coming.

## The 2012 Mindshift

In *The Global Brain,* Russell has developed a five-part meditation program that is available on double CD. It is designed for coping with the challenges of embracing the shift in values that will occur with the emerging 2012 paradigm. These meditations are intended to help a person stay grounded and remain composed, no matter what the changes bring.

**2012 MINDSHIFT MEDITATIONS**
- **Presence:** Finding peace in the moment
- **Befriending discomfort:** Working with difficult feelings and rigid attitudes
- **Inner wisdom:** Tapping the guidance that waits within you
- **Loving kindness:** Developing greater compassion and community
- **Clarifying purpose:** Strengthen your life's vision

## 2012 Social Forums

Many online forums discuss how best to embrace the changes of 2012. Two very useful points of focus for this community are the multichannel blogging website Reality Sandwich (*www.realitysandwich.com*) and the social network Evolver.Net (*www.evolver.net*).

Daniel Pinchbeck, author of the best-selling book *2012: The Return of Quetzalcoatl,* is one of the founders of both of these sites. His current focus is on promoting integrated political and social thinking to help facilitate the rapid growth of an effective network of people committed to taking on the challenges of preparing for 2012.

## Films about 2012

Getting further educated about the shifting paradigm of 2012 is becoming progressively easier with a number of groundbreaking independent documentary films that have been made on the subject. These include:

- *2012: The Odyssey and Timewave 2013*: Two pioneering documentaries by Sharron Rose and Jay Weidner, author of *The Cross of Hendaye*, that feature interviews with 2012 theorists from around the world (*www.2012theodyssey.com*).
- *2012: Science or Superstition*: A documentary by Disinformation films that features Jenkins, Pinchbeck, and Cruttenden (*www.2012dvd.com*).
- *Time of the Sixth Sun*: Dividing its subject matter into seven chapters for each of the chakras, *Time of The Sixth Sun* combines interviews with scientists and indigenous elders about 2012 (*www.timeofthe sixthsun.com*).
- *2012: Time for Change*: A feature-length documentary by Joao Amorim that combines film and animation and features Pinchbeck interviewing scientists, anthropologists, physicists, and celebrities about 2012 (*www.2012timeforchange.com*).

# Planetization Versus Globalization

If there was one single word that could describe all of the diverse theories competing to define the 2012 mindshift, it would probably be another concept first proposed by Chardin: planetization.

The idea of planetization is that of an expanded frame of reference that places humanity and the biosphere into a new broader context of a symbiotic unity. To become planetized is to adopt new ways of thinking that reflect a holistic viewpoint between humankind and the planet.

A planetized view is one able to conceptually grasp that this planet is just one of many, from one solar system, among billions of star systems, among billions of galaxies. The Mayan calendar and the Vedic Yuga cycle, with their galactic frames of reference, are both planetized calendars. The planetophysical research of Dmitriev and the cosmoclimatology of Svensmark are both planetized sciences.

The new Copernican revolution of planetization shifts the center point of our universe from the sun and our local solar system to the new reference point of the galactic center. This dramatically different sense of scale encourages more holistic global-scale thinking and makes it easier. A rapid shift to a planetized perspective may in fact be the best way to save our planet and ourselves from the blinkers of rampant technological consumerism and its toxic overshoot.

Planetization could be described as almost the polar opposite of globalization. The idea of globalization was to extend a free market around the world to increase international trade. In practice, this has tended to favor large multinational corporations at the expense of local, more sustainable industries. The economic transformation of globalization was only sustainable in a period of unprecedented global economic growth. The dual forces of the current economic crisis and ongoing energy crunch mean that the system of manufacturing parts of a car in China, shipping them to Europe to be assembled, and then sending them to Australia or Argentina to be sold no longer makes sense.

If globalization was the *de facto* economic religion of the expansionist late twentieth and early twenty-first centuries, planetization is the balancing force of the emerging holistic paradigm of 2012. Dramatic choices await humanity as we approach 2012. As in the Chinese proverb, "We are born in interesting times." It will be up to us collectively to decide whether this is a curse or a blessing.

# A Glossary of Mayan Words

**Ahau**—Yucatec Mayan name of the twentieth Tzolkin day sign, the Sun.

**Ajq'ij**—Quiché Mayan name for a calendar day keeper.

**Akbal**—Yucatec Mayan name of the third Tzolkin day sign, the House.

**Bacab**—The gods of the four directions.

**Baktun**—A calendar period of just under 400 years.

**Ben**—Yucatec Mayan name of the thirteenth Tzolkin day sign, the Reed.

**Bolontiku**—The nine lords of the underworld.

**Buk Xok**—A permutational table of the Tzolkin.

**Caban**—Yucatec Mayan name of the seventeenth Tzolkin day sign, Earth.

**Cahib xalcat be**—The four junction roads of Maya mythology.

**Cauac**—Yucatec Mayan name of the nineteenth Tzolkin day sign, the Storm.

**Chicchan**—Yucatec Mayan name of the fifth Tzolkin day sign, the Serpent.

**Chichén Itzá**—Important postclassic city in the Yucatán.

**Chik'in**—The black western bacab.

**Chilam Balam**—The order of jaguar priests responsible for prophecy.

**Chol'qij**—Quiché Mayan word for the 260-day Tzolkin count.

**Chuen**—Yucatec Mayan name of the eleventh Tzolkin day sign, the Monkey.

**Cib**—Yucatec Mayan name of the sixteenth Tzolkin day sign, the Vulture.

**Cimi**—Yucatec Mayan name of the sixth Tzolkin day sign, Death.

**Eb**—Yucatec Mayan name of the twelfth Tzolkin day sign, the Road.

**Etznab**—Yucatec Mayan name of the eighteenth Tzolkin day sign, the Mirror.

**Haab**—The yearly 365-day calendar.

**Hablatun**—The largest named period of the calendar. A period of 1.26 billion years.

**Hun Yecil**—The flood that destroyed the last world.

**Hunab Ku**—"One god," or "the giver of movement and measure."

**Ik**—Yucatec Mayan name of the second Tzolkin day sign, the Wind.

**Imix**—Yucatec Mayan name of the first Tzolkin day sign, the Alligator.

**Inlakech**—Mayan greeting meaning, "I am another yourself."

**Itzá**—The postclassic-period invaders of the Yucatán peninsula.

**Ix**—Yucatec Mayan name of the fourteenth Tzolkin day sign, the Jaguar.

**Izapa**—Pre-Mayan site in the south of Mexico considered the possible birthplace of the Long Count.

**Kan**—Yucatec Mayan name of the fourth Tzolkin day sign, the Seed.

**Katun**—A calendar period of just under 400 years.

**Kin**—A day; also used as a mantra.

**Kulkulkan**—Mayan name for the feathered serpent.

**Lamat**—Yucatec Mayan name of the eighth Tzolkin day sign, the Rabbit.

**Likin**—The red eastern bacab.

**Manik**—Yucatec Mayan name of the seventh Tzolkin day sign, the Deer.

**Mayapan**—Important postclassic city in the Yucatán.

**Men**—Yucatec Mayan name of the fifteenth Tzolkin day sign, the Eagle.

**Muluc**—Yucatec Mayan name of the ninth Tzolkin day sign, the Moon.

**Nohol**—The southern yellow bacab.

**Oc**—Yucatec Mayan name of the tenth Tzolkin day sign, the Dog.

**Olmec**—Mayan civilization in Mexico famed for their giant sculpted heads.

**One Hunahpu**—The first father; representative of the birth of a world age.

**Pacal**—Ruler of Palenque whose sarcophagus was found buried in the Temple of Inscriptions.

**Popol Vuh**—Quiché Mayan creation story featuring the hero twins.

**Quetzalcoatl**—The Aztec name for the feathered serpent.

**Quiché**—Strongly traditional Mayan tribe living in Guatemala.

**Tun**—A calendar period of just 360 days.

**Tzab**—The Pleaides star cluster or Rattlesnake's tail.

**Tzolkin**—The Yucatec Mayan word for the 260-day count.

**Uayeb**—The five days of purification at the end of the yearly Haab calendar; considered unlucky.

**Uinal**—A twenty-day period of the Haab or Tun calendar.

**Wajshikib Batz'**—Traditional Quiché day keepers hold one of their most important ceremonies on the day Eight Batz to mark the beginning of a new 260-day cycle.

**Xaman**—The white northern bacab; also a Yucatec word for Shaman.

**Xibalba**—The underworld whose mouth is in the dark rift near the center of the galaxy.

**Xochipilli**—The Aztec prince of flowers, a god of intoxicating and hallucinatory plants.

# A Glossary of Scientific Terms

**Big bang**—The idea that the universe has explosively expanded from a condensed state at some time in the past and continues to expand to this day.

**Big crunch**—A possible scenario for the ultimate fate of the universe, in which the expansion of space eventually reverses and the universe collapses, ultimately ending as a black-hole singularity.

**Biosphere**—The global sum of all ecosystems. It can also be called the zone of life on Earth.

**Black dwarf**—A hypothetical stellar remnant, created when a white dwarf becomes sufficiently cool and no longer emits significant heat or light.

**Black hole**—A region of space where the gravitational field is so powerful that nothing, including light, can escape its pull.

**Carrington event**—The biggest solar flare in the 160-year recorded history of geomagnetic storms.

**Chandler's wobble**—A small motion in Earth's axis of rotation, relative to Earth's surface, which occurs because Earth is not a perfect sphere.

**Chaos theory**—The behavior of certain dynamic systems whose states evolve with time. Usually highly sensitive to initial conditions (popularly referred to as the butterfly effect).

**Colony collapse disorder (CCD)**—A phenomenon in which worker bees from a beehive or European honeybee colony abruptly disappear.

**Concrescence**—An assemblage or a drawing together of a plurality; the production of novel togetherness.

**Coriolis effect**—An apparent deflection of moving objects when they are viewed from a rotating reference frame. The effect explains why water rotates clockwise in the northern hemisphere and anticlockwise in the southern.

**Cosmic rays**—Energetic particles originating from outer space that impact Earth's atmosphere. Almost 90% are protons, 9% are helium nuclei, and about 1% are electrons.

**Cosmoclimatology**—A term coined to describe research that involves a range of disciplines from space physics to atmospheric science and cloud microphysics.

**DNA**—Deoxyribonucleic acid, a nucleic acid that contains the genetic instructions used in the development and functioning of all known living organisms.

**Eschaton**—The end of everything, especially time; the final destiny of the world.

**Extremely low frequency (ELF) waves**—A band of radio frequencies from three to thirty Hz, used for submarine communication.

**Galactic alignment**—The alignment of the winter solstice sunrise with the galactic equator. This alignment occurs as a result of the precession of the equinoxes.

**Gamma rays**—High energy electromagnetic radiation that is produced by subatomic particle interactions, such as radioactive decay.

**Geosphere**—The densest parts of Earth's strata, mostly consisting of rock and regolith.

**Gothenburg magnetic flip**—A 180-degree flip in the geomagnetic pole of Earth that happened between 12,000 and 13,000 years ago.

**HAARP**—The High-Frequency Active Auroral Research Program, designed to conduct experiments on ionospheric phenomena.

**Heliocentrism**—The theory that the sun is at the center of the universe.

**Heliosphere**—An elongated bubble in space blown into the interstellar medium by the solar wind.

**Ionosphere**—The uppermost part of the atmosphere, distinguished because it is ionized by solar radiation.

**Kepler's Third Law**—The square of the orbital period of a planet is directly proportional to the cube of the semi-major axis of its orbit.

**Kuiper Belt**—A region of the solar system extending from the orbit of Neptune to twice that distance. Similar to the asteroid belt, although twenty times larger.

**Local interstellar space medium**—The relative density of the gas and dust that pervades interstellar space.

**Magnetosphere**—A highly magnetized region around Earth that protects the planet from incoming cosmic radiation.

**Maunder minimum**—The name given to the period roughly from 1645 to 1715, when sunspots became exceedingly rare and temperatures were unusually low. Also known as the Mini Ice Age.

**Moore's Law**—A description of the long-term trend in the history of computing hardware toward exponential growth in cost performance.

**Neutron stars**—A remnant that can result from the gravitational collapse of a massive star during a supernova event. Such stars are composed almost entirely of neutrons.

**Noosphere**—A mental envelope or thinking layer that surrounds the atmosphere of the planet containing the totality of all thought forms.

**Novelty**—The quality of being new. Novelty Theory claims this quality can be objectively measured.

**Ontology**—The philosophical study of the nature of existence or reality in general.

**Oort cloud**—A spherical cloud of comets nearly a light year from the sun.

**Orbital eccentricity**—A measure of how much an orbit deviates from a circle.

**Plasma**—Partially ionized gas in which a certain proportion of electrons are free rather than being bound to an atom or molecule. Responds strongly to electromagnetic fields.

**Plasmoids**—A coherent structure of plasma and magnetic fields. Occur in natural phenomena such as ball lightning.

**Precession of the equinoxes**—A gradual shift in the orientation of Earth's axis of rotation that traces out a conical shape in a cycle of approximately 25,771 years.

**Schumann resonance**—A set of spectrum peaks in the extremely low frequency (ELF) portion of Earth's electromagnetic field spectrum.

**Seyfert galaxies**—A subclass of galaxies with active galactic nuclei that appear to be in the process of exploding.

**Strange attractor**—The result of a series of bifurcations in fluid chaotic systems. An organizing principle of many fractals.

**Sunspot cycles**—Sunspots are magnetic storms on the face of the sun that form areas of reduced surface temperature. Sunspot activity follows a cycle that quickly rises and more slowly falls over about eleven years. Significant variations of the eleven-year period are known over longer spans of time.

**T-Tauri stars**—A class of variable stars found near interstellar dust clouds.

**Transient luminous event**—A short-lived, fluorescent, electrical phenomenon that occurs above storm clouds; less commonly called upper-atmospheric lightning.

**Van Allen radiation belts**—Bands of plasma around Earth held in place by Earth's magnetic field. There are two main belts: The inner one is mostly composed of protons; the outer one is composed mostly of electrons.

**White dwarf**—A small star composed mostly of electron-degenerate matter. The faint luminosity of a white dwarf comes from the emission of stored heat.

**Younger dryas**—A brief cold climate period approximately 12,800–11,500 years ago, also known as the big freeze.

# Online Resources

**2012: Dire Gnosis**
One of the most comprehensive 2012 websites online
*www.diagnosis2012.co.uk*

**2012 Supplies**
Survivalist supplies store and discussion forum with lots of 2012 stories
*2012supplies.com*

**Alignment2012**
John Major Jenkins's website
*alignment2012.com*

**Authentic Maya**
Lots of information about the history and culture of the Mayan people
*www.authenticmaya.com*

**Binary Research Institute**
Home website for Walter Cruttenden's Conference on Precession and Ancient Knowledge
*www.binaryresearchinstitute.org*

**BLT Research**
Website of the BLT crop-circle research team
*www.bltresearch.com*

**Crop Circle Connector**
The world's foremost crop circle website with news and pictures of all the latest formations
*www.cropcircleconnector.com*

**Crop Circle Science**
The website of crop circle artist and researcher Andreas Mueller
*www.cropcirclescience.org*

**Daily Galaxy**
A great source of space discovery stories and cutting edge astronomy
*www.dailygalaxy.com*

**Divine Cosmos**
David Wilcock's site, an excellent web resource with many in-depth articles on the emerging science of 2012
*www.divinecosmos.com*

**Earth Changes**
Michael Mandeville's site tracking the incidence of earthquakes and other earth changes
*www.earthchanges-bulletin.com*

**Enterprise Mission**
Richard Hoagland's site includes hyperdimensional and torsion physics information relevant to 2012
*www.enterprisemission.com*

**Evolver**
A social network site for conscious collaboration that also hosts offline 2012 events
*www.evolver.net*

**Foundation for the Law of Time**
Jose Argüellés's official website
*www.lawoftime.org*

**Global Coherence Initiative**
A science-based initiative to shift global consciousness from instability and discord to balance and cooperation
*www.glcoherence.org*

**Global Consciousness Project**
Multidisciplinary collaboration at Princeton University to study the effects of consciousness on the planet
*noosphere.princeton.edu*

**Institute of HeartMath**
Research institute dedicated to studying the effects of human coherence and heart-based living
*www.heartmath.org*

**Maharishi University of Management**
Research into the Maharishi effect of transcendental meditation
*www.mum.edu/m_effect/*

**Mayan Majix**
Information on the Carl Calleman interpretation of the Mayan calendar on a site founded by Ian Xel Lungold
*mayanmajix.com*

**Peter Russell**
Lots of interesting visualization tools relating to Russell's global brain theory including a life expectancy calculator and world clock
*www.peterrussell.com*

**Planet Art Network**
Global web portal for the Thirteen-Moon Calendar Change Movement
*www.tortuga.com*

**Project Condign**
Download site for the declassified UK Ministry of Defence UFO reports
*www.mod.uk/DefenceInternet/FreedomOfInformation/PublicationScheme/SearchPublicationScheme/UnidentifiedAerialPhenomenauapInTheUkAirDefenceRegion.htm*

**Reality Sandwich**
Web magazine and multichannel blog site with lots of 2012 content
*www.realitysandwich.com*

**The Sirius Research Group**
Binary star theorists who believe our sun is twinned with Sirius
*www.siriusresearchgroup.com*

**Space Weather**
News and information about the current sun-earth environment, including sunspot cycles, near-miss asteroids, and more
*www.spaceweather.com*

**Sphinx Stargate**
Website of Paul La Violette, includes lots of information on a broad range of subjects from archaeo-astronomy to subquantum kinetics
*www.etheric.com*

**S.P.I.R.I.T.**
Scientific Paranormal Investigative Research Information and Technology is David M. Rountree's organization dedicated to the collection, documentation, and analysis of paranormal phenomena
*www.spinvestigations.org*

**Thirteen-moon calendar**
Natural time calendars based on *Dreamspell*
*www.13moon.com*

**Time Surfer**
Excellent free program for following the traditional, Long Count, and *Dreamspell* versions of the Mayan calendar for Mac OS X
*www.gaianmysteryschool.com/timesurfer/*

**Tribe.Net 2012 discussion group**
One of the best and longest-running discussion boards about 2012
*2012.tribe.net*

# Text Resources

Argüellés, Jose and Stephanie South. *Cosmic History Chronicles Vol. 1–4.* (Ashland, OR: Law of Time Press, 2004–2008)
*A seven-part series, released one each year until 2012, giving an in-depth view of Argüellés's ideas.*

Argüellés, Jose. *Earth Ascending.* (Boulder, CO: Shambhala, 1984)
*A treatise of the whole Earth that synthesises the Tzolkin, I Ching, and the philosophies of Teilhard and Reiser.*

Argüellés, Jose. *The Mayan Factor.* (Santa Fe, New Mexico: Bear & Co., 1987)
*The book that brought the Mayan calendar to popular awareness.*

Argüellés, Jose. *Time & The Technosphere.* (Rochester, VT: Bear & Co., 2002)
*A treatise on the ecological crisis caused by global industrial society and the need to change the world's calendar.*

Calder, Nigel and Henrik Svensmark. *The Chilling Stars.* (Cambridge, MA: Icon Books, 2007)
*A guide to the idea that cosmic radiation plays a major part in climate change on Earth.*

Calleman, Carl. *The Mayan Calendar and the Transformation of Consciousness.* (Rochester, VT: Bear & Co., 2004)
*Callemans's theories about the parallels between Mayan pyramids and their calendar.*

Craine, Eugene R. and Reginald C. Reindorp. *Codex Perez and the Book of Chilam Balam of Mani.* (Oklahoma: University of Oklahoma, 1979)
*A compilation of Mayan prophecies and writings from after the European invasion.*

Cruttenden, Walter. *Lost Star of Myth and Time.* (Los Angeles: St. Lynn's Press, 2005)
*A complete guide to the binary star theory and its relationship to Yukteswar's interpretation of the Vedic Yuga cycle.*

de Chardin, Teilhard. *The Phenomenon of Man*. (New York: Harper Perennial, 1975)
The most important exposition of the philosophy of Teilhard de Chardin.

de Santillana, Giorgio and Hertha von Dechend. *Hamlet's Mill*. (Boston: David R. Godine, 1992)
A compilation of myths about precession from around the world.

Duncan, David Ewing. *The Calendar*. (London: Fourth Estate, 1998)
The story of the development of the Gregorian calendar and the modern concept of time.

Geryl, Patrick. *How to Survive 2012*. (Kempton: Adventures Unlimited Press, 2007)
A theory that a global cataclysm is imminent in 2012 and what to do in order to survive it.

Greer, John Michael. *The Long Descent*. (Gabroila Island: New Society Publishers, 2008)
A study of the overshoot and collapse of previous civilizations in the light of the current peak oil energy crisis.

Jenkins, John Major. *Galactic Alignment*. (Rochester, VT: Bear & Co., 2002)
Jenkins explores the galactic alignment in other cultures and philosophical traditions.

Jenkins, John Major. *Maya Cosmogenesis 2012*. (Rochester, VT: Bear & Co., 1998)
The definitive guide to the theory of galactic alignment.

Jenkins, John Major. *The Story of 2012*. (New York: Tarcher Penguin 2009)
Jenkins chronicles the history and development of the 2012 movement in his new book.

Johnson, Kenneth. *Jaguar Wisdom*. (St. Paul: Llewellyn Publications, 1997)
A guide to working with the traditional Mayan calendar with much information about Mayan folklore.

Joseph, Lawrence E. *Apocalypse 2012: A Scientific Investigation into Civilization's End*. (New York: Morgan Road Books, 2008)
A personal journey through theories about 2012 that includes a rare interview with Alexey Dmitriev.

Kurzweil, Ray. *The Singularity Is Near.* (London: Viking, 2005)
A futurist's view of what life might be like as we approach the
technological singularity.

Laszlo, Ervin. *The Chaos Point.* (London: Piatkus Books, 2006)
An analysis of global society at the tipping point of 2012.

LaViolette, Paul. *Earth Under Fire.* (Portland: Starlane Publications, 2000)
The galactic superwave theory and its relationship to cycles of
catastrophe on Earth.

Lovelock, James. *Gaia: A New Look at Life on Earth.* (Oxford: Oxford
University Press, 1982)
Lovelock's guide to the hypothesis that Earth should be considered as a
single living system.

Makemson, Maud Worcester. *The Book Of The Jaguar Priest: a translation
of the Book of Chilam Balam of Tizimin.* (New York: Henry Schuman,
1951)
A translation of an important book of Mayan prophesies.

McKenna, Terence. *The Invisible Landscape: Mind, Hallucinogens, and the
I Ching.* (San Francisco: Harper San Francisco, 1994)
The story of the timewave-zero hypothesis.

McKenna, Terence. *True Hallucinations.* (San Francisco: HarperOne, 1994)
The travelogue of the McKenna brothers as they journey into the
Amazon in search of hallucinogenic plants.

Pinchbeck, Daniel. *2012: The Return Of Quetzalcoatl.* (New York: Jeremy
Tarcher/Penguin, 2006)
A personal travelogue through psychedelic awakening into a journey of
synchronicity and discovery of 2012.

Pretchel, Martin. *Secrets of the Talking Jaguar.* (New York: Tarcher, 1999)
An account of life as an initiated Mayan day keeper in a traditional
Mayan community.

Pringle, Lucy. *Crop Circles: The Greatest Mystery of Modern Times.* (New
York: Thorsons Publishers, 2000)
A good introduction to the phenomenon of crop circles and the mystery
that surrounds them.

Reiser, Oliver L. *Cosmic Humanism*. (Rochester: Schenkman Books, 1966)
*An overview of Reiser's work, including the psi bank and concepts of the role of magnetism in evolution.*

Rennison, Susan Joy. *Tuning The Diamonds*. (Burton-upon-Trent: Joyfire Publishing, 2006)
*An in-depth look at the relationship between emerging science and subtle energies.*

Russell, Peter. *The Global Brain Awakens*. (Shaftesbury: Element Books, 2000)
*The theory that humanity's true purpose is to create a telepathic brain for planet Earth.*

Shearer, Tony. *Beneath The Moon and Under The Sun*. (Texas: Sun Publishing Company, 1975)
*The original source for the harmonic convergence and the first modern reinterpretation of the Tzolkin calendar.*

Spilsbury, Ariel and Michael Bryner. *The Mayan Oracle: Return Path To The Stars*. (Rochester: Bear & Co., 1992)
*A card set and accompanying book that gives many correspondences for working with the day signs of the Tzolkin.*

Stray, Geoff. *2012 in Your Pocket*. (Virginia Beach: A.R.E Press USA, 2009)
*A summary in miniature of Stray's Beyond 2012.*

Stray, Geoff. *Beyond 2012: Catastrophe or Awakening*. (Rochester, VT: Bear & Co., 2009)
*A comprehensive compendium of theories and ideas regarding 2012, as well as the conclusions of the author.*

Stray, Geoff. *The Mayan and Other Ancient Calendars*. (Glastonbury: Wooden Books, 2007)
*A simple introduction to how the Mayan calendar works and its relationship to other ancient calendars.*

Tedlock, Barbara. *Time and the Highland Maya*. (Santa Fe: University of New Mexico Press, 1992)
*An account of life with the traditional indigenous Maya.*

Tedlock, Dennis. Popol Vuh: *The Mayan Book of the Dawn of Life*. (New York: Simon & Schuster, 1996)
*A translation of the Quiché Mayan classic of Mayan mythology.*

Thompson, J. Eric S. *The Rise and Fall of Maya Civilization*. (Norman: University of Oklahoma Press, 1954)
*A good introduction to the history and culture of the Mayan people.*

Various authors. *The Mystery of 2012: Predictions, Prophecies and Possibilities*. (Louisville: Sounds True Inc., 2008)
*A series of essays from a number of contemporary authors about 2012.*

Vernadsky, Vladimir. *The Biosphere*. (New York: Springer, 1998)
*Vernadsky's ideas about the biosphere and noosphere.*

Yaxkin, Aluna Joy. *Mayan Pleadian Cosmology*. (Mt. Shasta: Hauk'in, 1995)
*An intuitive guide to working with the energies of the twenty day signs of the Tzolkin.*

Yukteswar, Sri Swami. *The Holy Science*. (Self-Realization Fellowship, 1894)
*The original source of Yukteswar's reinterpretation of the Vedic Yuga cycle.*

# Index

# THE EVERYTHING SERIES!

## BUSINESS & PERSONAL FINANCE

Everything® Accounting Book
Everything® Budgeting Book, 2nd Ed.
Everything® Business Planning Book
Everything® Coaching and Mentoring Book, 2nd Ed.
Everything® Fundraising Book
Everything® Get Out of Debt Book
Everything® Grant Writing Book, 2nd Ed.
Everything® Guide to Buying Foreclosures
**Everything® Guide to Fundraising, $15.95**
Everything® Guide to Mortgages
Everything® Guide to Personal Finance for Single Mothers
Everything® Home-Based Business Book, 2nd Ed.
**Everything® Homebuying Book, 3rd Ed., $15.95**
Everything® Homeselling Book, 2nd Ed.
Everything® Human Resource Management Book
Everything® Improve Your Credit Book
Everything® Investing Book, 2nd Ed.
Everything® Landlording Book
Everything® Leadership Book, 2nd Ed.
Everything® Managing People Book, 2nd Ed.
Everything® Negotiating Book
Everything® Online Auctions Book
Everything® Online Business Book
Everything® Personal Finance Book
Everything® Personal Finance in Your 20s & 30s Book, 2nd Ed.
**Everything® Personal Finance in Your 40s & 50s Book, $15.95**
Everything® Project Management Book, 2nd Ed.
Everything® Real Estate Investing Book
Everything® Retirement Planning Book
Everything® Robert's Rules Book, $7.95
Everything® Selling Book
Everything® Start Your Own Business Book, 2nd Ed.
Everything® Wills & Estate Planning Book

## COOKING

Everything® Barbecue Cookbook
Everything® Bartender's Book, 2nd Ed., $9.95
Everything® Calorie Counting Cookbook
Everything® Cheese Book
Everything® Chinese Cookbook
Everything® Classic Recipes Book
Everything® Cocktail Parties & Drinks Book
Everything® College Cookbook
Everything® Cooking for Baby and Toddler Book
Everything® Diabetes Cookbook
Everything® Easy Gourmet Cookbook
Everything® Fondue Cookbook
**Everything® Food Allergy Cookbook, $15.95**
Everything® Fondue Party Book
Everything® Gluten-Free Cookbook
Everything® Glycemic Index Cookbook
Everything® Grilling Cookbook
**Everything® Healthy Cooking for Parties Book, $15.95**
Everything® Holiday Cookbook
Everything® Indian Cookbook
Everything® Lactose-Free Cookbook
Everything® Low-Cholesterol Cookbook

**Everything® Low-Fat High-Flavor Cookbook, 2nd Ed., $15.95**
Everything® Low-Salt Cookbook
Everything® Meals for a Month Cookbook
Everything® Meals on a Budget Cookbook
Everything® Mediterranean Cookbook
Everything® Mexican Cookbook
Everything® No Trans Fat Cookbook
**Everything® One-Pot Cookbook, 2nd Ed., $15.95**
**Everything® Organic Cooking for Baby & Toddler Book, $15.95**
Everything® Pizza Cookbook
**Everything® Quick Meals Cookbook, 2nd Ed., $15.95**
Everything® Slow Cooker Cookbook
Everything® Slow Cooking for a Crowd Cookbook
Everything® Soup Cookbook
Everything® Stir-Fry Cookbook
Everything® Sugar-Free Cookbook
Everything® Tapas and Small Plates Cookbook
Everything® Tex-Mex Cookbook
Everything® Thai Cookbook
Everything® Vegetarian Cookbook
Everything® Whole-Grain, High-Fiber Cookbook
Everything® Wild Game Cookbook
Everything® Wine Book, 2nd Ed.

## GAMES

Everything® 15-Minute Sudoku Book, $9.95
Everything® 30-Minute Sudoku Book, $9.95
Everything® Bible Crosswords Book, $9.95
Everything® Blackjack Strategy Book
Everything® Brain Strain Book, $9.95
Everything® Bridge Book
Everything® Card Games Book
Everything® Card Tricks Book, $9.95
Everything® Casino Gambling Book, 2nd Ed.
Everything® Chess Basics Book
**Everything® Christmas Crosswords Book, $9.95**
Everything® Craps Strategy Book
Everything® Crossword and Puzzle Book
**Everything® Crosswords and Puzzles for Quote Lovers Book, $9.95**
Everything® Crossword Challenge Book
Everything® Crosswords for the Beach Book, $9.95
Everything® Cryptic Crosswords Book, $9.95
Everything® Cryptograms Book, $9.95
Everything® Easy Crosswords Book
Everything® Easy Kakuro Book, $9.95
Everything® Easy Large-Print Crosswords Book
Everything® Games Book, 2nd Ed.
**Everything® Giant Book of Crosswords**
Everything® Giant Sudoku Book, $9.95
Everything® Giant Word Search Book
Everything® Kakuro Challenge Book, $9.95
Everything® Large-Print Crossword Challenge Book
Everything® Large-Print Crosswords Book
**Everything® Large-Print Travel Crosswords Book**
Everything® Lateral Thinking Puzzles Book, $9.95
Everything® Literary Crosswords Book, $9.95
Everything® Mazes Book
Everything® Memory Booster Puzzles Book, $9.95

Everything® Movie Crosswords Book, $9.95
Everything® Music Crosswords Book, $9.95
Everything® Online Poker Book
Everything® Pencil Puzzles Book, $9.95
Everything® Poker Strategy Book
Everything® Pool & Billiards Book
Everything® Puzzles for Commuters Book, $9.95
Everything® Puzzles for Dog Lovers Book, $9.95
Everything® Sports Crosswords Book, $9.95
Everything® Test Your IQ Book, $9.95
Everything® Texas Hold 'Em Book, $9.95
Everything® Travel Crosswords Book, $9.95
**Everything® Travel Mazes Book, $9.95**
**Everything® Travel Word Search Book, $9.95**
Everything® TV Crosswords Book, $9.95
Everything® Word Games Challenge Book
Everything® Word Scramble Book
Everything® Word Search Book

## HEALTH

Everything® Alzheimer's Book
Everything® Diabetes Book
Everything® First Aid Book, $9.95
**Everything® Green Living Book**
**Everything® Health Guide to Addiction and Recovery**
Everything® Health Guide to Adult Bipolar Disorder
Everything® Health Guide to Arthritis
Everything® Health Guide to Controlling Anxiety
Everything® Health Guide to Depression
**Everything® Health Guide to Diabetes, 2nd Ed.**
Everything® Health Guide to Fibromyalgia
Everything® Health Guide to Menopause, 2nd Ed.
Everything® Health Guide to Migraines
**Everything® Health Guide to Multiple Sclerosis**
Everything® Health Guide to OCD
Everything® Health Guide to PMS
Everything® Health Guide to Postpartum Care
Everything® Health Guide to Thyroid Disease
Everything® Hypnosis Book
Everything® Low Cholesterol Book
Everything® Menopause Book
Everything® Nutrition Book
Everything® Reflexology Book
Everything® Stress Management Book
**Everything® Superfoods Book, $15.95**

## HISTORY

Everything® American Government Book
Everything® American History Book, 2nd Ed.
**Everything® American Revolution Book, $15.95**
Everything® Civil War Book
Everything® Freemasons Book
Everything® Irish History & Heritage Book
Everything® World War II Book, 2nd Ed.

## HOBBIES

Everything® Candlemaking Book
Everything® Cartooning Book
Everything® Coin Collecting Book
Everything® Digital Photography Book, 2nd Ed.

Everything® Drawing Book
Everything® Family Tree Book, 2nd Ed.
**Everything® Guide to Online Genealogy, $15.95**
Everything® Knitting Book
Everything® Knots Book
Everything® Photography Book
Everything® Quilting Book
Everything® Sewing Book
Everything® Soapmaking Book, 2nd Ed.
Everything® Woodworking Book

## HOME IMPROVEMENT

Everything® Feng Shui Book
Everything® Feng Shui Decluttering Book, $9.95
Everything® Fix-It Book
Everything® Green Living Book
Everything® Home Decorating Book
Everything® Home Storage Solutions Book
Everything® Homebuilding Book
Everything® Organize Your Home Book, 2nd Ed.

## KIDS' BOOKS

All titles are $7.95
Everything® Fairy Tales Book, $14.95
Everything® Kids' Animal Puzzle & Activity Book
Everything® Kids' Astronomy Book
Everything® Kids' Baseball Book, 5th Ed.
Everything® Kids' Bible Trivia Book
Everything® Kids' Bugs Book
Everything® Kids' Cars and Trucks Puzzle and Activity Book
Everything® Kids' Christmas Puzzle & Activity Book
Everything® Kids' Connect the Dots
  Puzzle and Activity Book
**Everything® Kids' Cookbook, 2nd Ed.**
Everything® Kids' Crazy Puzzles Book
Everything® Kids' Dinosaurs Book
**Everything® Kids' Dragons Puzzle and Activity Book**
Everything® Kids' Environment Book $7.95
Everything® Kids' Fairies Puzzle and Activity Book
Everything® Kids' First Spanish Puzzle and Activity Book
Everything® Kids' Football Book
**Everything® Kids' Geography Book**
Everything® Kids' Gross Cookbook
Everything® Kids' Gross Hidden Pictures Book
Everything® Kids' Gross Jokes Book
Everything® Kids' Gross Mazes Book
Everything® Kids' Gross Puzzle & Activity Book
Everything® Kids' Halloween Puzzle & Activity Book
**Everything® Kids' Hanukkah Puzzle and Activity Book**
Everything® Kids' Hidden Pictures Book
Everything® Kids' Horses Book
Everything® Kids' Joke Book
Everything® Kids' Knock Knock Book
Everything® Kids' Learning French Book
Everything® Kids' Learning Spanish Book
Everything® Kids' Magical Science Experiments Book
Everything® Kids' Math Puzzles Book
Everything® Kids' Mazes Book
**Everything® Kids' Money Book, 2nd Ed.**
**Everything® Kids' Mummies, Pharaoh's, and Pyramids
  Puzzle and Activity Book**
Everything® Kids' Nature Book
Everything® Kids' Pirates Puzzle and Activity Book
Everything® Kids' Presidents Book
Everything® Kids' Princess Puzzle and Activity Book
Everything® Kids' Puzzle Book

Everything® Kids' Racecars Puzzle and Activity Book
Everything® Kids' Riddles & Brain Teasers Book
Everything® Kids' Science Experiments Book
Everything® Kids' Sharks Book
Everything® Kids' Soccer Book
**Everything® Kids' Spelling Book**
Everything® Kids' Spies Puzzle and Activity Book
Everything® Kids' States Book
Everything® Kids' Travel Activity Book
Everything® Kids' Word Search Puzzle and Activity Book

## LANGUAGE

Everything® Conversational Japanese Book with CD, $19.95
Everything® French Grammar Book
Everything® French Phrase Book, $9.95
Everything® French Verb Book, $9.95
**Everything® German Phrase Book, $9.95**
Everything® German Practice Book with CD, $19.95
Everything® Inglés Book
Everything® Intermediate Spanish Book with CD, $19.95
**Everything® Italian Phrase Book, $9.95**
Everything® Italian Practice Book with CD, $19.95
Everything® Learning Brazilian Portuguese Book with CD, $19.95
Everything® Learning French Book with CD, 2nd Ed., $19.95
Everything® Learning German Book
Everything® Learning Italian Book
Everything® Learning Latin Book
Everything® Learning Russian Book with CD, $19.95
Everything® Learning Spanish Book
Everything® Learning Spanish Book with CD, 2nd Ed., $19.95
Everything® Russian Practice Book with CD, $19.95
**Everything® Sign Language Book, $15.95**
Everything® Spanish Grammar Book
Everything® Spanish Phrase Book, $9.95
Everything® Spanish Practice Book with CD, $19.95
Everything® Spanish Verb Book, $9.95
Everything® Speaking Mandarin Chinese Book with CD, $19.95

## MUSIC

Everything® Bass Guitar Book with CD, $19.95
Everything® Drums Book with CD, $19.95
Everything® Guitar Book with CD, 2nd Ed., $19.95
Everything® Guitar Chords Book with CD, $19.95
**Everything® Guitar Scales Book with CD, $19.95**
Everything® Harmonica Book with CD, $15.95
Everything® Home Recording Book
Everything® Music Theory Book with CD, $19.95
Everything® Reading Music Book with CD, $19.95
Everything® Rock & Blues Guitar Book with CD, $19.95
Everything® Rock & Blues Piano Book with CD, $19.95
**Everything® Rock Drums Book with CD, $19.95**
**Everything® Singing Book with CD, $19.95**
Everything® Songwriting Book

## NEW AGE

Everything® Astrology Book, 2nd Ed.
Everything® Birthday Personology Book
**Everything® Celtic Wisdom Book, $15.95**
Everything® Dreams Book, 2nd Ed.
**Everything® Law of Attraction Book, $15.95**
Everything® Love Signs Book, $9.95
Everything® Love Spells Book, $9.95
Everything® Palmistry Book
Everything® Psychic Book
Everything® Reiki Book

Everything® Sex Signs Book, $9.95
Everything® Spells & Charms Book, 2nd Ed.
Everything® Tarot Book, 2nd Ed.
Everything® Toltec Wisdom Book
Everything® Wicca & Witchcraft Book, 2nd Ed.

## PARENTING

Everything® Baby Names Book, 2nd Ed.
Everything® Baby Shower Book, 2nd Ed.
Everything® Baby Sign Language Book with DVD
Everything® Baby's First Year Book
Everything® Birthing Book
Everything® Breastfeeding Book
Everything® Father-to-Be Book
Everything® Father's First Year Book
Everything® Get Ready for Baby Book, 2nd Ed.
Everything® Get Your Baby to Sleep Book, $9.95
Everything® Getting Pregnant Book
Everything® Guide to Pregnancy Over 35
Everything® Guide to Raising a One-Year-Old
Everything® Guide to Raising a Two-Year-Old
Everything® Guide to Raising Adolescent Boys
Everything® Guide to Raising Adolescent Girls
Everything® Mother's First Year Book
Everything® Parent's Guide to Childhood Illnesses
Everything® Parent's Guide to Children and Divorce
Everything® Parent's Guide to Children with ADD/ADHD
Everything® Parent's Guide to Children with Asperger's
  Syndrome
**Everything® Parent's Guide to Children with Anxiety**
Everything® Parent's Guide to Children with Asthma
Everything® Parent's Guide to Children with Autism
Everything® Parent's Guide to Children with Bipolar Disorder
Everything® Parent's Guide to Children with Depression
Everything® Parent's Guide to Children with Dyslexia
Everything® Parent's Guide to Children with Juvenile Diabetes
**Everything® Parent's Guide to Children with OCD**
Everything® Parent's Guide to Positive Discipline
Everything® Parent's Guide to Raising Boys
Everything® Parent's Guide to Raising Girls
Everything® Parent's Guide to Raising Siblings
**Everything® Parent's Guide to Raising Your
  Adopted Child**
Everything® Parent's Guide to Sensory Integration Disorder
Everything® Parent's Guide to Tantrums
Everything® Parent's Guide to the Strong-Willed Child
Everything® Parenting a Teenager Book
Everything® Potty Training Book, $9.95
Everything® Pregnancy Book, 3rd Ed.
Everything® Pregnancy Fitness Book
Everything® Pregnancy Nutrition Book
Everything® Pregnancy Organizer, 2nd Ed., $16.95
Everything® Toddler Activities Book
Everything® Toddler Book
Everything® Tween Book
Everything® Twins, Triplets, and More Book

## PETS

Everything® Aquarium Book
Everything® Boxer Book
Everything® Cat Book, 2nd Ed.
Everything® Chihuahua Book
Everything® Cooking for Dogs Book
Everything® Dachshund Book
Everything® Dog Book, 2nd Ed.
Everything® Dog Grooming Book

Everything® Dog Obedience Book
Everything® Dog Owner's Organizer, $16.95
Everything® Dog Training and Tricks Book
Everything® German Shepherd Book
Everything® Golden Retriever Book
**Everything® Horse Book, 2nd Ed., $15.95**
Everything® Horse Care Book
Everything® Horseback Riding Book
Everything® Labrador Retriever Book
Everything® Poodle Book
Everything® Pug Book
Everything® Puppy Book
Everything® Small Dogs Book
Everything® Tropical Fish Book
Everything® Yorkshire Terrier Book

## REFERENCE

Everything® American Presidents Book
Everything® Blogging Book
Everything® Build Your Vocabulary Book, $9.95
Everything® Car Care Book
Everything® Classical Mythology Book
Everything® Da Vinci Book
Everything® Einstein Book
Everything® Enneagram Book
Everything® Etiquette Book, 2nd Ed.
**Everything® Family Christmas Book, $15.95**
Everything® Guide to C. S. Lewis & Narnia
**Everything® Guide to Divorce, 2nd Ed., $15.95**
Everything® Guide to Edgar Allan Poe
Everything® Guide to Understanding Philosophy
Everything® Inventions and Patents Book
Everything® Jacqueline Kennedy Onassis Book
Everything® John F. Kennedy Book
Everything® Mafia Book
Everything® Martin Luther King Jr. Book
Everything® Pirates Book
Everything® Private Investigation Book
Everything® Psychology Book
Everything® Public Speaking Book, $9.95
Everything® Shakespeare Book, 2nd Ed.

## RELIGION

Everything® Angels Book
Everything® Bible Book
Everything® Bible Study Book with CD, $19.95
Everything® Buddhism Book
Everything® Catholicism Book
Everything® Christianity Book
Everything® Gnostic Gospels Book
**Everything® Hinduism Book, $15.95**
Everything® History of the Bible Book
Everything® Jesus Book
Everything® Jewish History & Heritage Book
Everything® Judaism Book
Everything® Kabbalah Book
Everything® Koran Book
Everything® Mary Book
Everything® Mary Magdalene Book
Everything® Prayer Book

Everything® Saints Book, 2nd Ed.
Everything® Torah Book
Everything® Understanding Islam Book
Everything® Women of the Bible Book
Everything® World's Religions Book

## SCHOOL & CAREERS

Everything® Career Tests Book
Everything® College Major Test Book
Everything® College Survival Book, 2nd Ed.
Everything® Cover Letter Book, 2nd Ed.
Everything® Filmmaking Book
Everything® Get-a-Job Book, 2nd Ed.
Everything® Guide to Being a Paralegal
Everything® Guide to Being a Personal Trainer
Everything® Guide to Being a Real Estate Agent
Everything® Guide to Being a Sales Rep
Everything® Guide to Being an Event Planner
Everything® Guide to Careers in Health Care
Everything® Guide to Careers in Law Enforcement
Everything® Guide to Government Jobs
Everything® Guide to Starting and Running a Catering
    Business
Everything® Guide to Starting and Running a Restaurant
**Everything® Guide to Starting and Running
    a Retail Store**
Everything® Job Interview Book, 2nd Ed.
Everything® New Nurse Book
Everything® New Teacher Book
Everything® Paying for College Book
Everything® Practice Interview Book
Everything® Resume Book, 3rd Ed.
Everything® Study Book

## SELF-HELP

Everything® Body Language Book
Everything® Dating Book, 2nd Ed.
Everything® Great Sex Book
**Everything® Guide to Caring for Aging Parents,
    $15.95**
Everything® Self-Esteem Book
**Everything® Self-Hypnosis Book, $9.95**
Everything® Tantric Sex Book

## SPORTS & FITNESS

Everything® Easy Fitness Book
Everything® Fishing Book
**Everything® Guide to Weight Training, $15.95**
Everything® Krav Maga for Fitness Book
Everything® Running Book, 2nd Ed.
**Everything® Triathlon Training Book, $15.95**

## TRAVEL

Everything® Family Guide to Coastal Florida
Everything® Family Guide to Cruise Vacations
Everything® Family Guide to Hawaii
Everything® Family Guide to Las Vegas, 2nd Ed.
Everything® Family Guide to Mexico
Everything® Family Guide to New England, 2nd Ed.

Everything® Family Guide to New York City, 3rd Ed.
**Everything® Family Guide to Northern California
    and Lake Tahoe**
Everything® Family Guide to RV Travel & Campgrounds
Everything® Family Guide to the Caribbean
Everything® Family Guide to the Disneyland® Resort, California
    Adventure®, Universal Studios®, and the Anaheim
    Area, 2nd Ed.
Everything® Family Guide to the Walt Disney World Resort®,
    Universal Studios®, and Greater Orlando, 5th Ed.
Everything® Family Guide to Timeshares
Everything® Family Guide to Washington D.C., 2nd Ed.

## WEDDINGS

Everything® Bachelorette Party Book, $9.95
Everything® Bridesmaid Book, $9.95
Everything® Destination Wedding Book
Everything® Father of the Bride Book, $9.95
**Everything® Green Wedding Book, $15.95**
Everything® Groom Book, $9.95
**Everything® Jewish Wedding Book, 2nd Ed., $15.95**
Everything® Mother of the Bride Book, $9.95
Everything® Outdoor Wedding Book
Everything® Wedding Book, 3rd Ed.
Everything® Wedding Checklist, $9.95
Everything® Wedding Etiquette Book, $9.95
Everything® Wedding Organizer, 2nd Ed., $16.95
Everything® Wedding Shower Book, $9.95
**Everything® Wedding Vows Book, 3rd Ed., $9.95**
Everything® Wedding Workout Book
Everything® Weddings on a Budget Book, 2nd Ed., $9.95

## WRITING

Everything® Creative Writing Book
Everything® Get Published Book, 2nd Ed.
Everything® Grammar and Style Book, 2nd Ed.
Everything® Guide to Magazine Writing
Everything® Guide to Writing a Book Proposal
Everything® Guide to Writing a Novel
Everything® Guide to Writing Children's Books
Everything® Guide to Writing Copy
Everything® Guide to Writing Graphic Novels
Everything® Guide to Writing Research Papers
**Everything® Guide to Writing a Romance Novel, $15.95**
Everything® Improve Your Writing Book, 2nd Ed.
Everything® Writing Poetry Book